The Films of James Bridges

The Films of James Bridges

Peter Tonguette

McFarland & Company, Inc., Publishers
Jefferson, North Carolina, and London

Frontispiece: Gordon Willis (left) and James Bridges during the making of *The Paper Chase* (1973).

LIBRARY OF CONGRESS CATALOGUING-IN-PUBLICATION DATA

Tonguette, Peter Prescott, 1983–
    The films of James Bridges / Peter Tonguette.
        p.   cm.
    Includes bibliographical references and index.
    Includes directoral filmography.

    ISBN 978-0-7864-3949-2
    softcover : 50# alkaline paper ∞

    1. Bridges, James.   2. Motion picture producers and directors — United States — Biography.   I. Title.
PN1998.3.B7557T77   2011
791.4302'33092 — dc22   2011011669
[B]

BRITISH LIBRARY CATALOGUING DATA ARE AVAILABLE

© 2011 Peter Tonguette. All rights reserved

No part of this book may be reproduced or transmitted in any form or by any means, electronic or mechanical, including photocopying or recording, or by any information storage and retrieval system, without permission in writing from the publisher.

Front cover, from the top: Michael Douglas, Jane Fonda and David Valdez in *The China Syndrome* (1979; Columbia Pictures/Photofest); Debra Winger and John Travolta in *Urban Cowboy* (1980; Photofest/Paramount Pictures)

Front cover by TG Design

Manufactured in the United States of America

McFarland & Company, Inc., Publishers
   Box 611, Jefferson, North Carolina 28640
     www.mcfarlandpub.com

To the memory of my father

Contents

Acknowledgments	ix
Preface	1
One. An Arkansan	5
Two. Making Babies ... and Movies	17
Three. Hart and Kingsfield, Bridges and Houseman: *The Paper Chase*	39
Four. Going Home: *September 30, 1955*	62
Five. Going Nuclear (and Commercial): *The China Syndrome* and *Urban Cowboy*	104
Six. What Became of Jimmy J.: *Mike's Murder*	126
Seven. Perfecting *Perfect*	144
Eight. *Bright Lights, Big City*, Big Legacy	156
Directorial Filmography	173
Notes	177
Bibliography	191
Index	197

Acknowledgments

In the researching and writing of *The Films of James Bridges*, I am indebted to many people, and I must emphasize my gratitude to several in particular.

My task would have been impossible without the assistance and support of Jack Larson, who was James Bridges's partner and collaborator for more than thirty years. Jack was exceedingly generous with his time, memories, and insights. He also directed me to a number of Bridges's friends and colleagues. Jack's dedication to Bridges's legacy is untiring. I hope that he will see this book as an attempt to further that legacy.

I am grateful to Joseph McBride for his many years of friendship, advice, and support. My friend David Baron provided several key pieces of assistance. My friend Alexandra Asher Sears was extremely supportive and helpful. David Ehrenstein was kind enough to put me in touch with Jack Larson. For alerting me to notable critical essays on Bridges's films, I thank Margaret Barton-Fumo, Adrian Martin, and Dan Sallitt. Jared Gardner, associate professor at the Ohio State University, was extremely obliging in tracking down two much-needed articles as time was running short.

Jimmy Bryant, Director of Archives and Special Collections at the University of Central Arkansas, was helpful in making available photos and other materials from UCA's extensive James Bridges Collection. In his efforts, Jimmy truly went above and beyond the call of duty. Also at UCA, I thank Christina McDougal and Heidi Reutter for their help. And at the University of Colorado at Boulder's Howard B. Waltz Music Library-American Music Research Center, I appreciate the courteous assistance of Eric Harbeson.

For their friendship, I thank Peter Bogdanovich, Dann and Judy Cahn, Bilge Ebiri, Keith Gordon, Bob Rafelson, and Jonathan Rosenbaum.

I also must thank: Greg Carr at Industry Entertainment, Nick Dawson, Patty Harris, Dave Kehr, Bill Krohn, Aaron Latham, Vincent LoBrutto, Tim Lucas, Mark Martucci, Sonya Masinovsky, Patrick McGilligan, Antony Merkel at Brookside Artist Management, Scott Paxton and the late Collin Wilcox Paxton, Marion Rosenberg, Emily Saex at SMS Talent, Randolph P. Shaffner at the Highlands Historical Society, Ken Storer, Tom Weaver, and Rebecca Yerkovich at Impression Entertainment.

I am profoundly grateful to those whom I interviewed for this book: Brooke Alderson, Graham Beckel, Jack Bender, Deborah Benson, John Bloom, Lisa Blount, Tom Bonner, Mary Kai Clark, Francesca Emerson, Marty Ewing, Debbie Getlin, Jeff Gourson, Edward Herrmann, Barbara Hershey, Swoosie Kurtz, the late Kim Kurumada, Jack Larson, Norman Lloyd, Laurence Luckinbill, Chris Newman, John Jay Osborn, Jr., the late Collin Wilcox Paxton, Michael Preece, David Rawlins, Charles Rosher, Jr., Marshall Schlom, Richard Thomas, Reynaldo Villalobos, Sam Waterston, Gordon Willis, Jane Wilson, and Debra Winger.

Finally, I thank my brother, Patrick Tonguette, for his help and especially for his insights into *The Paper Chase*, and my parents, Del R. and Diane Tonguette, for their incredible and unwavering support. I dedicate this book to the memory of my father.

Preface

"The gifted young director James Bridges" was how Tennessee Williams described him.[1]

Bridges was selected by Williams personally to direct the twenty-fifth anniversary production of *A Streetcar Named Desire* at the Ahmanson Theatre in Los Angeles in 1973. Jon Voight was Stanley. Faye Dunaway was Blanche. Many of the reviews were lukewarm. "Respectful, cautious, traditional and straightforward, James Bridges's production has no excitement, no inventiveness, and — apart from Faye Dunaway's performance — very little genuine artistry," critic Stephen Farber wrote in *The New York Times*.[2] For his part, Bridges considered working with his two stars to be "positively the worst experience I've ever had in my life. Looking back, I think I was very weak with them, and they were at each other's throats all the time. It was my first experience with name performers and it didn't make me anxious to repeat it."[3]

Even so, it is difficult to talk down the good fortune of having been chosen by the greatest American playwright to direct an anniversary production of one of his greatest plays. Bridges surely must have viewed it (at least before rehearsals began) as one of the highlights of his career. But his was a career of highlights. Interviewed several years later, upon the release of his third film as a writer-director, *September 30, 1955*, Bridges recalled, "I've been a very lucky boy. I've done exactly what I wanted to do."[4]

Just how lucky was he? His first play, *The Days of the Dancing*, was staged at the Beverly Hills Playhouse in 1961, when Bridges was all of twenty-five years old. The young scribe received considerably better reviews than he later would for *A Streetcar Named Desire*. In the *Los Angeles Times*, critic Frank Mulcahy wrote that the play was "an entertaining and slightly offbeat variation of a theme that has captivated playwrights for a long time. Essentially it sums up the old truism that the past is of no real consequence. Today is all that matters."[5]

The Days of the Dancing also caught the attention of another prominent member of the audience: actor-producer-director Norman Lloyd, who felt that the play "was not successful" but that "the writing revealed a considerable talent."[6] Bridges remembered, "He was very enthusiastic about my writing and some months later when I was stage managing a play for John Houseman at the UCLA Theatre Group, I got a call from Norman who asked me if I would be interested in writing an episode of *The Alfred Hitchcock Hour* which he was producing. I was and I did."[7] Fifteen more episodes (and an Emmy nomination) were to follow. "He was our best writer," Lloyd proclaimed.[8]

Hitchcock's "best writer" had also been a bit part actor, appearing in both the final film of Ethel Barrymore *(Johnny Trouble)* and one of the first films of Andy Warhol *(Tarzan and Jane Regained ... Sort Of)*. About the latter, he said, "I chased the older Jane down the beach with a palm frond."[9] He was a protégé of Montgomery Clift, John Houseman, Norman Lloyd, Salka Viertel, and others. He was a friend to John Cassavetes, Christopher Isherwood, Virgil Thomson, and many others. He was a mentor to Jack Bender, Aaron Latham, Lisa Blount, Debra Winger, and countless others. He was, every bit as much as Orson Welles (the subject of my previous book, the oral history *Orson Welles Remembered*, and in so many superficial ways so different), a renaissance man.

In the three years I have been at work on this book, I have been struck again and again by the charmed nature of Bridges's career. Examples abound. When he directed his first film, *The Baby Maker*, less than a decade after *The Days of the Dancing* had its premiere, Robert Wise—the editor of *Citizen Kane*, later the Academy Award–winning director of *West Side Story* and *The Sound of Music*—produced it. This was far from an everyday occurrence. "In addition to the films that he both produced and directed," Sergio Leemann noted in his book on the filmmaker, "Wise produced two films by first-time directors."[10] Only two! And one of those two was by Bridges. No less remarkable is his fifteen-year collaboration with the legendary cinematographer Gordon Willis, who first worked with Bridges on *The Paper Chase* and went on to photograph three more films for him. In the end, Willis photographed a higher percentage of films by Bridges than he did films by any other director; four out of Bridges's eight features were shot by Willis.

In this light, Tennessee Williams's description of him, generous though it is, hardly does Bridges justice. And his accomplishments can't be accounted for by mere "luck" either, as Bridges himself would have it. Norman Lloyd called him "charming, laidback," yet also noted that "he was strong. In this charm and laidback thing, you couldn't push him over. He was very strong in that regard. On *Urban Cowboy*, I know they didn't want Debra Winger. He wanted her. His strength on that proved beneficial to the picture."[11] Winger recalled, "Jim was a very unsuspecting hard-ass. He could get in there and fight with the best of them. Although I fear he suffered later, because he really was not that kind of a person."[12]

What kind of a person was James Bridges? In the course of my research, I have interviewed thirty-two of his colleagues and friends, among them Gordon Willis, who said that collaborating with him was "the better part of my working experience. A lovely man who somehow remained on the edge of the Hollywood experience.... He was a nice person."[13] Impressive as Bridges's professional accomplishments are, they pale next to his qualities as a person, according to the accounts given to me by those who knew him best. Bridges was, quite plainly, beloved. "Once you met him," said Kim Kurumada, who worked on five of his films, including as the executive producer of *Mike's Murder* and *Perfect*, "you never forgot him."[14]

* * *

I will not attempt to examine in these pages every facet of James Bridges's exceptional career. While I will detail some of his most notable forays into theatre and television, a thorough study of his work in those arenas will be left for another day. (Bridges's plays deserve a book all to themselves.) It is his films — and one in particular — that brought me to Bridges, and it is those films that I have sought to scrutinize and honor here.

The film that made such an impression on me was *September 30, 1955*, which is the subject of this book's longest chapter. When I first saw it, I was glancingly familiar with Bridges's other work. I had seen and admired *The Paper Chase*. I knew already that he had collaborated frequently with Gordon Willis. I was aware that Pauline Kael had championed *Mike's Murder* in *The New Yorker* two years after its theatrical release. I remembered that Norman Lloyd made a point to mention Bridges to me when he and I were discussing *The Alfred Hitchcock Hour* during an interview about a completely unrelated subject.[15]

But *September 30, 1955* was the film that did it. The plot, the tone, and the setting of this film was so specific that I assumed it was based on its maker's own life. And I wanted to find out more about that life. I quickly discovered that *September 30, 1955* isn't uncommon in the Bridges oeuvre in its basis in truth.

At the beginning of Truman Capote's novella *Breakfast at Tiffany's*, the narrator says, "I am always drawn back to places where I have lived, the houses and their neighborhoods."[16] So, too, was James Bridges, who in his films would return again and again not just to the places where he had lived, but to places he had visited and people he had known. "Write what you know" is a cliché often attributed to Hemingway. A cliché it may be, but it was certainly a maxim to which Bridges was faithful.

The most personal of his films, such as *The Baby Maker*, *September 30, 1955*, and *Mike's Murder*, were drawn explicitly from events in his life or in the lives of friends and acquaintances. But my contention is that even those films of his conceived by others, such as *Perfect* (based on articles by Aaron Latham), or those drawn from books, such as *Bright Lights, Big City* (based on a novel by Jay McInerney), bear Bridges's imprint.

Because of the way in which Bridges's life was reproduced in his films, when I set out to write about them, I knew that I would be embarking on more than just a critical study. I would also have to understand, to some extent, Bridges's biography. To that end, I sought to interview as many people as I could, as I had for *Orson Welles Remembered*. But since Bridges was born twenty-one years after Welles, I was able to speak with many who knew him at the beginning, including friends from childhood and college, as well as those who worked with him in his early plays and films.

Maybe one of the things that piqued my curiosity about Bridges was the fact that what I did know about him was mostly pieced together on my own. No critic ever took up his cause. Many liked individual films, but none argued on behalf of his work on a consistent basis. Even Pauline Kael's rave review of *Mike's Murder* was an anomaly; she was unenthusiastic about most of his other films. Bridges receives no mention in Peter Biskind's popular study of 1970s filmmaking, *Easy Riders, Raging Bulls*. He has no entry in the most recent (2010) edition of David Thomson's *The New Biographical Dictionary of Film*.

My fondest hope is that this book — the first ever written on the subject — will bring attention to, and awaken memories of, the extraordinary films of James Bridges.

One

An Arkansan

James Bridges was an Arkansan. He was born in the city of Paris in that state, on February 3, 1936, to Doy Bridges and the former Celestine McKeen. His mother's surname inspired the nickname he would always be known by: "Jim Mac." "I think he was an Arkansas boy deep down inside," said Debra Winger.[1]

Of Orson Welles's midwestern background (he was born in Kenosha, Wisconsin), his biographer Simon Callow observed, "A part of all that remained with Orson Welles, however far he wandered."[2] The same was true of Bridges and his relationship to Arkansas. His best film, *September 30, 1955*, was set in Arkansas; his biggest commercial success, *Urban Cowboy*, was set but one state over, in Texas.

In truth, however, Bridges never "wandered" very far at all. His friend since high school, Jane Wilson, recalled how he kept in touch with her family, especially her parents, Bush and Katherine Satterfield, for decades. "Even after he left school and went to Hollywood, he came home every year to visit his family in Paris," Wilson said. "He always came to visit us." He would return to California with Katherine Satterfield's homemade chili sauce. "He only would part with one jar to Katharine Hepburn," Wilson remembered.[3]

"Anybody who grew up in Arkansas has a sweetness about them and they have a sense of the sweet earth," observed actor and fellow Arkansan Laurence Luckinbill, who starred with Sam Waterston in a play Bridges directed in 1972. "I would call it a pure friendliness and Jim Bridges just had that. I think that's why he succeeded in Hollywood as well as he did. He didn't carry around a lot of malice; although you'd think that would be a part of the job description of being a Hollywood person, it's not, really."[4] Debra Winger said, "He had a community spirit, ethics that I identify as more Midwest, he had a sense of humor that was definitively Southern, and he was an incredible gentleman."[5]

But, even as a young man, he had more than just "sweetness" about him. He had focus, determination, and confidence — the same single-minded grit that Winger and Norman Lloyd would identify in him decades later. Jane Wilson recalled, "He told me, sitting in our backyard on a summer night, that he was going to be a famous director."[6]

Childhood friend Martha Reid Scott remembered, "When I was in the ninth grade and Jimmy Mac was in the, oh, the sixth grade, I think, our mutual interest in the theatre caused us to become friends. He stopped by my house one day and asked me to read a play he had written. And this was a sixth-grader, but it was a very good play. Then it became a regular occurrence. He would stop by, oh, maybe once a week or so and we would talk about movies we had both seen or plays we had read. Now he subscribed to *Theater Arts* magazine and in those days, *Theater Arts* included a full-length play in each edition. And we would read those plays and discuss them."[7] By the time Reid Scott knew Bridges, "his parents were divorced, and he and his mother lived with his grandparents a few blocks from where I lived. He was a happy, handsome child, usually had a big smile."[8] Eventually, his mother married Melvin Wiggins.

Like Reid Scott, Wilson's bond with Bridges originated in their shared interest in theatre: "He and his good friend, Barbara Banks, who was also a friend of mine, were kind of running buddies. They were in the drama department and very interested in all sorts of theatre. Conway High School did a lot of remarkably good theatre for a small town high school because we had a good drama teacher. Her name was Gussie Scales. This is so silly, but I'll never forget Jim Mac for it. "I won the beauty pageant at the high school and he and Barbara came to that and they came to our house afterwards. He walked in the kitchen and I still had my crown on. He gave me a big hug and he said, 'Every girl should be a queen once in her life!'"[9]

He probably didn't know it when he enrolled there, as a freshman in 1954, but Arkansas State Teachers College, in Conway, Arkansas, would have a lifelong effect on Bridges's life and career. When he made *September 30, 1955*—which was largely set in and around the campus of his alma mater— he returned to ASTC (by then known as the University of Central Arkansas) to make the movie. He could have easily filmed it at another college campus; he could have even substituted another, better-known school in Arkansas to stand-in for ASTC. But he didn't. In an interview he gave to ASTC's paper, *The Echo*, when filming was about to begin, he spoke of the university in glowing terms: "I love this school."[10]

Bridges acknowledged two professors who made an impression on him: "Those two men, Ralph Behrens and Dr. Eugene Nolte, were so important in my career. I went to California, after coming to this school and being taught by the people that I was taught by. I felt myself absolutely equipped to deal on the professional level with the people of California."[11]

One. An Arkansan 7

Bridges with Mary Ann Rickey in an ASTC production of Arthur Miller's *Death of a Salesman*. (Courtesy of the University of Central Arkansas Archives.)

"Ralph Behrens was one of the most literate, educated humans I have ever known," Tom Bonner, Bridges's friend and classmate at ASTC, recalled. "I regret to this day that I did not take, for instance, his Greek mythology course, which was legendary on that campus.

"Bridges was so intelligent; he was one of the most intelligent humans I have ever known, ever. He and Behrens would be on the same level, and the same with Nolte. They were the literati. They could have sat down at the roundtable at the Algonquin Hotel and held their own with anybody who walked in. And Jim Bridges loved talking with them because they imparted that knowledge. He picked it up immediately.

"What you could say about those friendships is that cream rises to the surface and he was gravitating to the people who were on his level of thinking and his level of intelligence and knowledge. And bear in mind, he was only nineteen years old."[12]

Bonner was a year behind Bridges at ASTC. When they met in the fall of 1955, Bridges was a sophomore. Bonner, Bridges, and Barbara Banks formed "a rat pack of three who ran around together," he explained. "There were a few mothers who joined us from time to time, but it was the three of us who were inseparable."[13]

In *September 30, 1955*, Bridges's alter ego, Jimmy J., played by Richard Thomas, is depicted as being obsessed with James Dean after seeing the actor in Elia Kazan's *East of Eden*. As Bonner remembered it, this depiction was accurate so far as it goes, but, if anything, Bridges was even *more* passionate than his cinematic counterpart: "I'm telling you, he was obsessed. Now there were others he was absolutely crazy about, too. I remember when Anna Magnani's movie, *The Rose Tattoo*, started showing in Little Rock, which was an hour drive away at that time. I was the one with the car. He said, 'Come on, come on, we've got to go to Little Rock Saturday afternoon. The movie opens with Anna Magnani.' As he and Banks and I drove down there, he was saying, 'Hurry up! Anna Magnani is burning the screen up and I'm out here in this car!' It was just a funny way he had of showing his enthusiasm.

"Well, the James Dean movies were even just a cut above that," Bonner continued. "He was just a kid who was enthralled with acting and making movies and Hollywood, and here was the biggest star in the world. He really wanted to know James Dean. He would just have died to have met him."[14]

Years later, Bridges recounted, "I got jolted by *East of Eden* when I went to Memphis on a band trip from Arkansas State Teachers College.... I had never heard of James Dean. But seeing that picture changed my life. I wanted to go to California and meet people who knew him. I met Dennis Hopper. I was, like, nuts."[15]

As "nuts" as Bridges was about Dean and *East of Eden*, Magnani and *The Rose Tattoo*, and many other movies and movie stars, it was a twirling scholarship, of all things, that brought him to ASTC. According to *The Echo*, he "held the title as State Twirling Champion."[16] He never lost the knack, as friends and co-workers attest. His assistant on *September 30, 1955*, *The China Syndrome*, *Urban Cowboy*, and *Mike's Murder*, Debbie Getlin, remembered, "Jim had a ton of energy and he needed to keep moving. I remember he couldn't sit in one place for very long, so he had to keep distracting himself.

He kept a baton in his office and he always had it with him. He would walk through the offices and he would just be flipping the baton. He would just be twirling it and twirling it and twirling it with two hands going back and forth. He would walk down the hallway, go to one office, come back. It felt like there was a fan constantly going in the office! And then, just on the spur of the moment, he would walk out the front door, throw the baton up in the air, turn around, catch it behind his back, and then walk back in the door!"¹⁷

Bridges as drum major (with batons) at ASTC. (Courtesy of the University of Central Arkansas Archives.)

* * *

Many of us who have seen *September 30, 1955* are compelled to wonder: Why *East of Eden*? The presence of James Dean notwithstanding, what was it about that particular film that struck such a chord in Jimmy J.— and in Bridges? "I went to see *East of Eden* over and over and over. A lot of us in the South did. Maybe it was the rural and religious aspects of it," he explained to the *Los Angeles Times*. "We were the Silent Generation, comfortable kids in the Eisenhower years. It was the proper political and social climate for a James Dean. He was the first non-hero and we all identified greatly. Part of the mystique was his great, unfulfilled potential."¹⁸

The power of Dean's persona held sway even with a director as cynically minded as Robert Altman. Speaking about his early documentary *The James Dean Story*, Altman told David Thompson, "I really wanted to deflate Dean, but it didn't turn out that way. I began to realize how basically he was a good actor and brought a whole new personality that kids responded to at that time."¹⁹

In *September 30, 1955*, the story propels Jimmy J. to leave Arkansas State

Teachers College for Hollywood during homecoming week, less than a month following Dean's death. In actuality, Bridges left the following summer, after school was out. Tom Bonner recalled, "He had begun to get a little quiet toward the end of the school year, more quiet about what was going on in his mind. Then in his own dramatic way — and he was a drama guy from the word go, he would do things unexpectedly for shock value sometimes — I looked around on the last day of school and I couldn't find him anywhere.... I don't know who it was, some person who just knew us both, not a member of our rat pack, I said to him, 'Have you seen Jim Mac?' 'Oh, he got in the car with so-and-so and left. He's gone.'"[20]

Bonner discovered that Bridges had gotten "as far as Paris, Arkansas, which is where he lived with his mother and stepfather. His plan was to spend the night in Paris and then drive out the next morning early with a relative of his who was going to California or who lived in California. The plan was to leave the next morning. This was early evening, already after dark, the last day of school. I thought, 'Well, I'm not going to let him get out of here'.... I went over and yelled up to the dorm window where Banks was. There were some girls around who could hear me and I said, 'Hey, is Banks up around there somewhere?' 'Yeah, just a minute, we'll get her.' She hung her head out the window and I said, 'I'm going to Paris this evening. Do you want to go?' She said, 'Yes.' She came bounding down the stairs and we jumped in the car and we headed for Paris, Arkansas, that night.

"We caught him and I was just mad and irritated at him. He said, 'I hate goodbyes and I'd rather just break it off. Now I'll be there and you'll be here.' We had a nice visit that evening. Barbara and I drove back to Conway, and he went on to California the next morning....

"The next year, Banks and I hung out together all year. You wouldn't say we were dating necessarily, but we might as well have been. We went to everything together, just the two of us. She was Miss Arkansas by the next year. So we would be at a dance that he would know about, like the spring dance, and somebody would come running in and say, 'Jim Mac is on the phone for you.' There was a phone out in the hallway or out at the desk in the place where we had the dance, and we'd go out there and talk. He kept in touch. He wasn't isolated from us at all."[21]

* * *

"I wanted to be an actor," Bridges remembered. "I went out to the Pasadena Playhouse, then known as the 'star finder session.'"[22] According to the presskit of his film *The Baby Maker*, Bridges subsequently "appeared in more than 50 television shows and five feature films. It was, he recalls wryly, at the height of the cycle of juvenile delinquency films 'and I was typed.'"[23]

"I got small roles. Then I got larger roles," Bridges said.²⁴ One of his larger roles was in *Johnny Trouble*, directed by John H. Auer. The film starred Ethel Barrymore, Cecil Kellaway, Stuart Whitman, and Jack Larson. Larson, who played Jimmy Olsen on the hit television show *The Adventures of Superman*, would become Bridges's partner, both personally and professionally. "That's where we met," Larson recalled, "We met actually at the first reading of that film. It was a great thrill to go to work with Ethel Barrymore. Stuart Whitman was playing the lead and I was playing his best friend and roommate. Jim and I became friends on that. We became friends, and then always stayed friends."²⁵

"Larson and Bridges became fast friends," Anthony Tommasini recounted in his essential biography of Virgil Thomson (with whom Larson, later a celebrated playwright and librettist, would collaborate on the opera *Lord Byron*). "Within a year they were lovers. Their lifelong relationship would become one of the most admired domestic partnerships in Hollywood."²⁶ The star of *The Baby Maker*, Barbara Hershey, observed, "They had a very profound relationship with each other, a deep, deep, long-lasting love for each other, which is an unusual thing for anyone."²⁷

Bridges's friends in Arkansas accepted him without hesitation. Tom Bonner remembered, "It was not until a short time after he arrived in L.A. that Jim broke the news to me by phone that he was gay, and that he had been struggling with that for some time and had finally accepted it. I remember being totally shocked at the time, but it was really a non-issue. And of course our friendship didn't change a bit on the news. It was as though my older brother had told me that, and I supported him a hundred percent."²⁸

The world might have been deprived of James Bridges, the writer-director, were it not for the counsel he received from Montgomery Clift, for whom he worked briefly during his salad days in Hollywood. "Clift was letting me read scripts for him and advise him on parts," Bridges said.²⁹ Clift's suggestion to his young disciple was blunt: "Jim, you're not going to be a star. If you can't be a star as a movie actor, get out. You don't want to be playing bit parts until you're 50."³⁰

Bridges (who, as Martha Reid Scott made clear, had always written) now began to devote himself to the craft. He was the beneficiary of encouragement from the screenwriter Salka Viertel, whom he knew through his friendship with Larson. "Jim was writing kind of bizarre poetry about erotic nuns," Larson remembered. "I read a lot of it and it was always very gifted. He didn't ever have any trouble writing; it just flowed quickly from him to the typewriter. But it was Salka who adored him. She certainly adored him more than she did me, though she loved me and I loved her. But she just loved Jim. He showed her some of his writing. She encouraged him to write a script and then a play. She encouraged him and he wrote *The Days of the Dancing*, this play which is very of the oeuvre of Tennessee Williams."[31]

The Days of the Dancing would change Bridges's life. As with so many of Bridges's creations, its roots were to be found in his own experiences. It was inspired by people he knew at "a wild bar called the Carousel," as Larson explained.[32] The play premiered at the Beverly Hills Playhouse in May 1961 and was directed by Denis Deegan. It starred, among others, Jan Sterling, Stephen Joyce, and Romney Tree. But, for its significance in the direction of Bridges's career, the most important performer on the stage was, without question, Joan Houseman, who played "a genteel barfly," as her husband, producer-director John Houseman, described it.[33] It was only because of Joan Houseman's appearance in *The Days of the Dancing* that Norman Lloyd, a friend of the couple, came to see the show.

Lloyd had been a member of Orson Welles's Mercury Theatre, where he played Cinna the Poet in the Mercury's groundbreaking production of *Julius Caesar* in 1937. As an actor on screen, he had roles in major films by Hitchcock (*Saboteur*) and Chaplin (*Limelight*). By the time he and Bridges crossed paths, Lloyd was the producer of the half-hour *Alfred Hitchcock Presents* on television. A year later, in 1962, he would become the producer of the program's 60-minute successor *The Alfred Hitchcock Hour*, and, eventually, its executive producer.

"I was impressed with the play. I thought there was a real writer here," Lloyd said of *The Days of the Dancing*. "I was then producing with Joan Harrison the *Hitchcock* show. I was always looking for writers and I thought this fellow would be a good writer for our show. As a consequence, I asked to meet him and the rest is history."[34] What Lloyd found most appealing about the play was the "very nice, relaxed style in the writing."[35]

The first *Alfred Hitchcock Hour* episode Bridges wrote was "A Tangled Web," directed by Alf Kjellin and starring Robert Redford and Zohra Lampert, broadcast on January 25, 1963. "It was Jim Bridges's first writing for the screen, large or small," Lloyd said.[36] Bridges's teleplay was based on a novel by Nicholas Blake, which, as Lloyd recalled, "was the *nom de plume* of C. Day-Lewis, who was the father of Daniel Day-Lewis. When I years later acted with Daniel Day-Lewis in *The Age of Innocence,* we had a wonderful rapport because of my doing his father's work."[37] Soon Lloyd began consciously "pairing" particular stories with Bridges, playing to what he felt were Bridges's strengths. "In the case of Jim," he said, "I would quickly recognize this was a story for Jim in that it had an almost folksy quality, a very human, relaxed, easygoing quality."[38]

Perhaps nowhere are these qualities more in evidence than in the classic episode Bridges wrote more than a year into his association with *The Alfred*

Hitchcock Hour: "The Jar," adapted by Bridges from a short story by Ray Bradbury and directed by Lloyd himself. The plot concerns the eponymous jar (purchased by a gullible country bumpkin named Charlie [Pat Buttram] at a sideshow for twelve dollars); its mysterious contents beguile the residents of a small Louisiana town. It makes the hapless Charlie feel like an "emperor."[39] Of Bridges being chosen to adapt the piece, Lloyd remembered, "That assignment to Jim did not sit too well with Ray Bradbury, who always thought he should do his own stories. I adore Ray. He's a dear friend and we've done wonderful work together on many things, but when I read that story, I knew it was Jim. I could not conceive of getting that folksy quality which worked so well in a horror story from Ray, who is a very high style writer. He's written wonderful horror stories, but it's another style. The style I wanted in 'The Jar' was Jim."[40]

In addition to those by Day-Lewis and Bradbury, Bridges adapted stories and novels by such writers as Davis Grubb ("The Return of Verge Likens," "Where the Woodbine Twineth") and Margaret Millar ("Beast in View") during his tenure on *The Alfred Hitchcock Hour*. It was here, perhaps, where he learned how to successfully translate another writer's work to the screen. As a feature filmmaker, he later adapted novels by John Jay Osborn, Jr., and Jay McInerney, and in some respects the most notable aspect of those films are their faithfulness to the novels upon which they are based. (Bridges's unproduced screenplays include adaptations of John Updike's *Of the Farm*, Dashiell Hammett's *Red Harvest*, and John Irving's *The World According to Garp*.)

"The Jar" was a turning point for Bridges in so many different ways. He was nominated for an Emmy for his teleplay. But every bit as important in the long run was the relationship he formed with the actress who co-starred in the episode, Collin Wilcox. She was only two years removed from her performance as Mayella Ewell in Robert Mulligan's film of Harper Lee's *To Kill a Mockingbird*. Appearing opposite Pat Buttram, the native North Carolinian shines as his restless wife Thedy, about whom Charlie complains, "I work the bottom land to the butt-bone every year, and she grabs the money and runs off down home visitin' her folks nine weeks at a stretch. I can't keep hold of her."[41] Lloyd explained how he decided to cast Wilcox: "I wanted someone very Southern, whom I would obviously admire as an actress. And Collin just came to mind, particularly being very Southern. I'd seen her work and I thought she was dynamite."[42]

Bridges and Wilcox first met on the set of "The Jar," two Southerners "far from the South," as she put it. "I just remember him standing there [on the set] in his own sweet self, smiling and grinning and so forth."[43] Subsequently, Wilcox appeared in one Bridges play (*Bachelor Furnished*) and two Bridges films (*The Baby Maker* and *September 30, 1955*). It wasn't a rarity for

Bridges to work again and again with someone whose company he enjoyed. "He worked only with people who he liked enormously," Jack Larson said.[44]

Wilcox eventually left Hollywood and returned to her home in Highlands, North Carolina, a fact much bemoaned by Norman Lloyd: "I think that Collin's sort of retirement from the profession was a great loss to American theatre and pictures. She could have gone as far as anyone.[45] She may be most famous for *To Kill a Mockingbird*, and justifiably so, but her best performances were in films by James Bridges.

Wilcox remembered the making of "The Jar" with fondness. "It was adapted from a Ray Bradbury story and he came on the set with all of his daughters. He was lovely. Everybody was lovely. It was a *wonderful* experience," she said. Of being directed by Lloyd, she added, "He was very precise. He was quick and his movements were quick. Because he was also an actor, he was very aware of actors and how to talk to them. He wasn't warm and fuzzy like Jim, but he was perfectly pleasant. Very on schedule, very in command of what was happening, and really loving what he was doing. I remember that—but, then, we all were."[46]

In his short story, Bradbury described the jar as "[o]ne of those pale things drifting in alcohol plasma, forever dreaming and circling, with its peeled, dead eyes staring out at you and never seeing you,"[47] though he had Thedy later reveal what it was truly made of.

But the question remains: What *was* in the jar—the actual jar used during the filming of the episode?

Collin Wilcox: "As I remember, it had some coils of wire in it. And Thedy Sue says, 'It's just junk.' Sometimes I think in the dialogue it says what it is. I'm pretty sure there was a marble or a glass eye and there seems to me to be some wadded-up material like stiff cotton."[48]

Norman Lloyd: "A lot of sponge rubber. It was like very spongy white rubber or something. I think there were a couple of springs in it or something. Then we had a kind of glass eye in it. And, of course, a lot of liquid, which would be water."[49]

"The Jar" was a triumph; Bridges would later proclaim that his time on *The Alfred Hitchcock Hour* was "easily my happiest years as a writer."[50] Although he never personally met the Master of Suspense, "the word filtered down that he was pleased."[51] Lloyd's discovery was panning out. And it wasn't only Bridges's talent that pleased his mentor, it was his human qualities, too, and what he was like to work with as a colleague. "He was very easy, had a ready ear, he listened," Lloyd recalled. "One of the great things of working with Jim was that he might bring in a first draft and you could sit down with him and say, 'Now, Jim, this doesn't work for the following reasons.' And he would come back in three or four days and it worked perfectly. He was a most wonderful person to cooperate with, to collaborate with, in that sense of producer and writer. I never wrote anything with him, but in talking out the script with him, you found a ready ear and no resistance. He worked towards a common end. You didn't feel the resistance of a writer saying, 'I put it down, it's imperishable.'"[52]

Another great *Hitchcock* episode was "An Unlocked Window," adapted from a story by Ethel Lina White, directed by Joseph Newman, and starring Dana Wynter, John Kerr, and T.C. Jones. It aired on February 15, 1965. Lloyd summarized the main plot points of "An Unlocked Window," which concerns a serial killer on the loose: "There's a sick man in the house, John Kerr, and there are two nurses who are tending to him. These killings go on and there's the rain. They have locked the house. The whole neighborhood is locked up. But they have neglected to lock a window in the basement. They've forgotten about it and it's swinging open periodically. There is some kind of mad fellow wandering in the neighborhood.

"Well, to get to the end of the story, he is not the killer. He is just a decoy," Lloyd revealed. "One of the nurses was Dana Wynter. The other was one of the most famous female impersonators at the time. It is revealed at the very end, as he starts to kill, that this woman is really a man. What I remember most about it is talking to Hitchcock about the script. Hitchcock said you had to, at that moment, not only rip off his wig. A shaved head will not indicate it's a man. But you have to rip the garment and bare his breasts and show that they are not a woman's breasts to reveal that it's a man who is the killer. So that's what I remember most about that. I remember also that it had an enormous suspenseful effect on an audience. They were properly frightened by it."[53]

In his own films, Bridges didn't often seek to frighten his audiences in such a manner, but when he did, he undoubtedly relied on the wealth of experience he gained on *The Alfred Hitchcock Hour*. *Mike's Murder*, in particular, has a number of Hitchcockian touches.

Previously nominated for an Emmy for "The Jar," Bridges won an Edgar Award for Best Television Play from the Mystery Writers of America for "An Unlocked Window."[54]

* * *

It is a good thing that Bridges took Montgomery Clift's advice to quit acting, and a good thing that Salka Viertel was so enthusiastic about his promise as a budding writer. By the time *The Alfred Hitchcock Hour* was cancelled, Bridges had left acting behind almost entirely. His final screen appearance was a cameo in John Cassavetes's masterpiece *Faces*, in which he played a film executive. Jack Larson recalled, "John at that point, after *Shadows*, always had young filmmakers in tow, acolytes in tow. We were up there at the house once, helping out, because he was shooting at his own house. Then he asked Jim if he would be in this scene with executives. Jim has a couple of lines, but he was a little bit overweight, from his point of view, at that time. He said that he has one of the fatter faces in *Faces*."[55]

In fact, Bridges makes quite an impression in his few minutes of screen time (and his face does not appear unduly full). In the film's opening scene, he introduces himself as Jim Mortensen. Dressed in a dark suit and tie, sitting in the front row of the screening room with the other executives, he says, "We were trying to capture several approaches," after one of his colleagues describes the film they are about to view as the "*Dolce Vita* of the commercial field." He says lines like, "We were talking about facts and figures until we practically went out of our minds. Losses, gains, ratings, schmatings. You can lose your mind if you keep analyzing things like that," with great aplomb, and with nary a hint of an Arkansas accent.

You watch the scene and think, James Bridges would have made a fine character actor. But you're also grateful that he found other lines of work.

Two

Making Babies ... and Movies

"Behind locked doors of the Leo S. Bing Center Theater in the County Museum of Art, director James Bridges, 19 [sic], was rehearsing a professional cast for the premiere of a new play the other day," Margaret Harford reported in the *Los Angeles Times* on February 10, 1966. "Not just another prose theater piece, but a play in rhymed verse.... The play is Jack Larson's *The Candied House*, a modern mystery play based on the fairy tale *Hansel and Gretel*."[1]

Less than a year after *The Alfred Hitchcock Hour* ended, Bridges made his official directorial debut with *The Candied House*. Two days later, in a rave review in the *Times*, Harford wrote that the production was "an enchanting discovery for young and old, one of the happiest, most imaginative evenings any theatrical company has provided theatergoers in Los Angeles in a long time."[2]

Larson's unique rhymed verse style would continue to attract considerable attention many decades after *The Candied House* premiered. In a 1998 *New York Times* profile of the writer-actor, Anthony Tommasini quoted from a scene in which a witch "tells the captive Hansel of her plan to fatten him up:

> But with care you will be a digestible joy,
> A meaty, well-nourished muscular boy.
> When your skin swells sweet with muscle and meat,
> When your veins seem to flood with rich red blood,
> When you're fed till you're an Adonis of food,
> Then dear, you'll be most delicious to eat.[3]

Larson's play, Harford judged at the time, was "far removed from the Albee-cum Pinter school," and of its rhymed verse, she noted, "In a day when the ugliest words in the English language are perpetrated on a stage in the guise of realistic drama, it's a joy to hear from a man who loves and respects words and does not see language as the enemy of images."[4]

A year earlier, Bridges directed a tryout of his own play, *Bachelor Furnished*, at the Highlands Community Theatre in Collin Wilcox's hometown.

"My parents had started the Highlands Community Theatre in 1939. It was a logical place to try it out because there was the theatre and here we were," Wilcox remembered. "He wanted me to be in it and he wanted my then-husband, Geoffrey Horne, to be in it. He wanted our good friend, Ralph Williams, to be in it."[5] "They are great people to work with, and I feel extremely fortunate to have Collin, Geoffrey, and Ralph doing my play," Bridges said appreciatively.[6]

For Bridges, directing was often a family affair. Wilcox and Horne had been married for two years when he cast them in *Bachelor Furnished*. Already an accomplished actor, Horne was well known for his supporting roles in David Lean's *The Bridge on the River Kwai* and Otto Preminger's *Bonjour Tristesse*. In the latter film, he played Phillipe, the French boyfriend of Jean Seberg's Celeste. A few years after *Bachelor Furnished*, he reteamed with Bridges and his wife on their film *The Baby Maker*, but not as an actor; he received the credit "Dialogue Supervisor" on the production.

Bachelor Furnished consisted of three one-act plays, all set in the same apartment: *"K" Like in Karma*, *A Question Every Thursday*, and *The Rehearsal of Sterling Underhill*. The last is, without doubt, among Bridges's finest pieces of writing. "It is a very peculiar play about an ex-female impersonator and his daughter, and a Marine, who he brings home for his spinster daughter," Larson said.[7] Ironically, when Margaret Harford reviewed a subsequent Los Angeles production of *Bachelor Furnished* (also directed by Bridges), she compared *A Question Every Thursday* in favorable terms to the work of Edward Albee and Harold Pinter, the very writers whom she seemed to commend Larson for *not* emulating in *The Candied House*. In any case, Harford labeled Bridges "an emerging playwright worth listening to, an inventive, shrewdly perceptive Jacob wrestling with dark angels of soul searching, pessimism, and alienation."[8] To be sure, *Bachelor Furnished* is no *Who's Afraid of Virginia Woolf?* or *The Birthday Party*, but it's an accomplished work that deserves to be far better known than it is.

"Oh, I love that play," Wilcox said. While *Bachelor Furnished* represented the first time the newly minted friends had worked together as actor and director (as opposed to actor and writer), she said the experience was easy and natural: "Everything about working with Jim was lovely. There was no such thing as any kind of argument, cross words. It was all smooth. He was always supportive. He gave gentle suggestions. He left lots of room for the actor to be creative. Rather than imposing his will, he would wait to see what you were going to bring to the table. That's the main quality a director has to have: the real ability to cast and then, once he/she has cast, to trust their actors to do what they were cast to do. And Jim did that."[9]

"I just hope this is the beginning," Bridges told Harford as *The Candied*

House was about to open, and it was.[10] His Hollywood odyssey had taken him from actor to writer and now to director. But he still wasn't directing *movies*, despite the fact that, as a writer, he had graduated from episodic television to feature films. In 1966, his adaptation of Robert MacLeod's novel *The Appaloosa*, co-written with Roland Kibbee, was directed by Sidney J. Furie, while in 1970, his adaptation of D.F. Jones's novel *Colossus* was directed by Joseph Sargent (as *Colossus—The Forbin Project*). Bridges disliked both films. His assistant in the 1970s and '80s, Debbie Getlin, recalled of the latter project, "That film was very frustrating for him, to see his work be translated differently by another producer and director. That was the beginning of his goal to always direct his own projects."[11]

Collin Wilcox in James Bridges's *Bachelor Furnished*. (Courtesy of Collin Wilcox Paxton via Highlands Historical Society, Inc.)

"It was totally satisfying to him, all of the *Hitchcock* things," Jack Larson remembered. "But when he went into film, with those two films ... Marlon Brando made [*The Appaloosa*] an absolute impossibility and admired Jim for walking off of it. Jim was hesitant to ever give interviews about it, but he did walk off of it and he decided that the next film that he wrote, he would direct.

"Houseman tried to help through Robert Wise. Bob Wise had a production unit to produce independent films. So Jim wrote *The Baby Maker*. But then everybody said—this was National General Pictures, this was Bob Wise, but not John Houseman—'But he's not a director. You have to have a director direct it.' And I had this play that Jim had directed Off-Broadway called *Cherry, Larry, Sandy, Doris, Jean, Paul*. I previously had some success Off-Broadway with a play called *Chuck*. It was an evening called *Collision Course*, and *The New York Times* had several times liked my work. And now this play [*Cherry, Larry*] was going to be done on Bleecker Street and Jim directed it. It's about young Americans in England.

"Initially, it had a different title but everybody didn't like the title. The fellow that directed my things here, Ed Parone, who directed *Chuck* and several plays, thought it was an awful title that I'd given it—*Angel's Flight*. I had a series of titles. I said, 'Well, what's a good title?' And he said, 'Names are good titles. *King Lear. Romeo and Juliet. Macbeth.* Those are good titles.' So I called it every name in the play out of perversity! Everybody thought it was chic. Everybody said that it was the play that no one can remember its title."[12] Like *The Candied House* before it, *Cherry, Larry, Sandy, Doris, Jean, Paul* was written in rhymed verse.

In the summer of 1969, John Blankenchip, a professor at the USC School of Theatre, expressed interest in presenting the play at the Edinburgh International Festival as part of his Festival Theatre USC-USA company. Larson jumped at the chance, as did Bridges, who was again slated to direct. He saw it as an opportunity to persuade National General and Robert Wise that he was, in fact, a director. The reception of *Cherry, Larry, Sandy, Doris, Jean, Paul* would make or break his chance to direct *The Baby Maker*.

In the words of the critic for *The Stage and Television Today*, the play "examines the relationship between a gay affair, Larry and Sandy, and their girl friend, Cherry."[13] The cast was comprised entirely of USC students. Gayla Kalp was Cherry, described by critic Walter Reid in *The Scotsman* as "the powerful mother figure who has tied her Larry and Sandy to her with doses of natural laxative."[14] As Larry and Sandy, Bridges cast John Ritter and Jack Bender, respectively.

"My best friend — becoming my best friend — John Ritter auditioned. I remember, as fate would have it, I read," Bender said. "Jim had originally cast this other guy in the role of the friend of John's. Then it was described to me by Jim and Jack that Jim, after putting up the cast list, had an instinctive freak-out, pulled the car over, called Blankenchip, who was the guy who ran our European acting company, and didn't get him, and was up all night, freaking out that he had made a horrible mistake and should have cast me, his gut was telling him. I learned in later years that Jim's casting gut was kind of remarkable. In my case, I'm not so sure, although for my life it sure meant a lot. Actually, truthfully, I was the better actor than this other guy....

"Jim and Jack loved us as actors because we weren't techniquey. We were very natural and much more movie-acting."[15] Bender credited this primarily to the influence of Blankenchip, who, "whether you were a dental student or a drama student, was a genius at letting people just get on stage and sink or swim and be who they were. There was no drama department really that taught any classes of any value, like voice or any of that stuff. When I was first at USC, I was learning Restoration bows and bullshit like that that would never matter because some teacher thought he had to teach the Moliere school of acting or something."[16]

Bender remembered that Bridges encouraged his young troupe to perform *Cherry, Larry, Sandy, Doris, Jean, Paul* naturalistically, despite the fact that the lines they were speaking were written in rhymed verse: "The musicality of verse was not something I ever paid a lot of attention to. In a similar way, aside from the normal direction and orchestration and rhythms of a play, I don't seem to remember there was a lot of specific direction about how to deal with the rhymed verse. My memory is that it was pretty naturalistic. But I don't remember Jim directing us a lot to pay attention — like sometimes you do with Shakespeare, when they're really into rhythm and hitting certain things....

"I think part of the beauty of it was that the juxtaposition was naturalistic and it wasn't putting a gilded frame around language that was a little heightened to begin with. I think that Jim's approach, with Jack's encouragement, was probably to keep it as real as possible, otherwise the whole thing could be too elevated."[17]

"It went first to London and we played at the Jeanetta Cochrane Theatre," Larson recalled.[18] Opening night was something less than a total success, as Bender recounted: "John [Ritter] and I made an entrance. We were smoking cigars and we were supposed to have been out drinking. We go to make our entrance and I hear dialogue that we don't recognize. We think, 'Fuck, we've screwed up our cue.' And it was an open set so you saw us coming down a hall into the apartment flat. We turned around and walked off-stage because we felt we were going to enter at the wrong time, when in fact somebody either went up on lines or ... the play was in iambic pentameter. So, like Shakespeare, you can't ad-lib this. Well, Gayla and Vickie Rue [as Rosella] were ad-libbing because they went up on lines and we were late. It was just a disaster. They ad-libbed all this dialogue, pages of dialogue they were making up, which wasn't rhyming at all. Then we realized, 'Holy shit, we've got to get on stage,' and we carried on with the play. Jack was ready to jump off the balcony of the Jeanetta Cochrane Theatre."[19]

Nevertheless, the reviews, first in London and then in Edinburgh, were superb. "It is written in rhymed verse, which the company says is the language of innocence," Walter Reid wrote. "Bridge['s] direction does nothing to weigh it down, and the odd snatch of recorded music adds to the holiday atmosphere."[20]

Larson said, "The best reviewer in England at that time was B.A. Young of the *Financial Times* and he went bonkers over the performances. He liked everything. He compared me to Christopher Marlowe. It was just a hats-in-the-air kind of thing. He actually gave a little cocktail thing. He came up to London for Jack and the kids in the play, who were all wonderful.

"We had a success. We got wonderful reviews, which Jim sent back to John Houseman, with whom he was in touch at all times.... Houseman showed them to Robert Wise who showed them to National General and the people who were financiers for what would be the film *The Baby Maker*. While they'd all said before that Jim wasn't a director, with these terrific reviews out of London and Edinburgh, everybody said, 'Well, he's a director!' So, while still in Edinburgh, the film was set up, greenlighted, and Jim flew back to direct *The Baby Maker*.

"We had about a week at the Jeanetta Cochrane in London, which is a tiny theatre in the West End, and a terrific Hollywood agent came and saw John Ritter, who was spectacular in it. He signed John Ritter. The two things that happened were Jim came back and directed *The Baby Maker* and John Ritter came back and began his career as an actor."[21]

For Jack Bender, however, it wasn't about the reviews. "It was an extraordinary experience to go to London and to perform for a European international audience and to do these plays," he conceded. "But I have to say that Jim Bridges and Jack Larson coming into our lives was the real gift of that. Most of us were these Southern California, protected, naïve kids who, as fate would have it, were lucky enough to have this extraordinary injection in our lives of these guys who had such history and connections, through John Houseman back to Virgil Thomson back to Gertrude Stein. I remember at one of our plays, Christopher Isherwood showed up. We met this nice Englishman named Christopher Isherwood. It was like, 'Christopher Isherwood wrote *The Berlin Stories*. What are *The Berlin Stories*? *Cabaret*? Oh, yeah, I know *Cabaret*.' But that's as far as I went. I was like a TV kid and that was my culture, growing up in Southern California, so meeting Jim and Jack just connected us to worlds that we would have never known about, aside from their lifelong friendship."[22]

The circle of friends that Bridges and Larson had at this time was indeed formidable. As Collin Wilcox remembered, "Jim introduced us to their friends Christopher Isherwood and Don Bachardy and then their friend Gavin Lambert. We just were a little group. We had supper at each other's house at least once a week. We just had a wonderful time together."[23] While Larson was responsible for Bridges making some of these connections, he admitted, "I was always lucky in life with friendships. And in all my friendships — the people like John Houseman, Monty Clift, Leslie Caron — everybody who were my close friends always liked Jim better than they liked me! Definitely. I wasn't the least bit queasy or envious of it. Everybody loved Jim. They just loved him."[24]

To Bender, just as significant as the friendship of Bridges and Larson, and the friends *they* had, was the inspiration Bridges provided Bender, then a nascent actor who was vaguely dissatisfied with the direction of his career. In Bridges, he found that rare thing: a role model. He explained, "When Jim first came into our lives, I wanted to be an actor. I just watched Jim in rehearsals and I kept thinking to myself, 'I want to be that guy. I want to be that guy standing out there with his hands in his pockets and his blue jeans directing. I don't think I want to be this guy on stage.' As time went on, I started to focus more on that. But a glimpse at Jim Bridges and how he operated as a director and how he allowed magic to happen around him without being either dictatorial in any way or dogmatic but very inclusive and creating an environment like a nest for birds to fly, that was part of his mastery, and I emulated it and wanted to be it. He was the first guy I felt that way about."[25]

Bender continued to act throughout the 1970s — even appearing in another play Bridges directed, *A Meeting by the River*, in 1972 — and eventually carved out a career that included stints on such television shows as *The Mod Squad*, *All in the Family*, and *The Mary Tyler Moore Show*. When he was ready to direct, however, Bridges would again provide him with a crucial opportunity.

* * *

In actuality, *The Baby Maker* was not Bridges's first film — it was only his first *completed* film. While in London, Bridges began shooting exteriors for an independent film version of *Cherry, Larry, Sandy, Doris, Jean, Paul*. Bender, who reprised his role as Sandy, recalled, "[Bridges and Larson] both admired and were friendly with Andy Warhol and all those guys who were making movies at the Factory. In fact, I remember Jim pointing to the film *Chelsea Girls*, saying it was a masterpiece, and that *Midnight Cowboy* wasn't as good as *Chelsea Girls*, or that *Chelsea Girls* was the real *Midnight Cowboy*. And Cassavetes was a friend of theirs. Jim very much admired that independent filmmaking. I think that as much as he wanted to make his version of big Hollywood movies that were always personal, they were looking to make *Cherry, Larry* this funky little independent film on 16mm black-and-white and they figured, 'Since we're in London, let's shoot the exteriors. If we shoot the exteriors in London, then we can go back and rent a flat in Los Angeles and shoot it there.'" So that was the plan with all of us. He shot a lot of John and me walking around Hyde Park and these various places. We shot for a couple of days and then I remember that we all watched the dailies and he said, 'Oh, my God, you're like Monty Clift!' He was referring, I think, to my presence on screen, which he and Jack were very positive about."[26]

But the film was never finished. "Jim went on to *The Baby Maker*," Bender explained. "I think we occasionally talked about *Cherry, Larry* and then other things took precedence."[27] It's fascinating to consider what kind of film Bridges would have made had he seen *Cherry, Larry* through to completion. But when Bridges began to direct films in earnest, as Bender astutely observed, he made *Hollywood* films. Robert Wise produced his first film; Sydney Pollack produced his last. Despite his encounters with the avant-garde, this fan of *Chelsea Girls*, who had bit parts in *Tarzan and Jane Regained ... Sort Of* and *Faces*, would nevertheless always be a maker of commercial cinema.

Author John Jay Osborn, Jr., whose novel *The Paper Chase* was adapted by Bridges for his second film, reflected, "You've got to also remember that Jim loved Hollywood. He told me the story about how he was petrified that Jane Fonda was going to back out of *The China Syndrome* or choose a new director. He *loved* Jane Fonda. He was just star-struck with Jane Fonda, so this would have been the worst thing in his life. He loved all of that stuff."[28]

* * *

Critics sometimes strained to identify what themes (if any) united James Bridges's eight feature films. In his entry on Bridges in *The Film Encyclopedia*, Ephraim Katz claimed that "nearly all" of his films "effectively examined contemporary problems of young adults."[29] Nathan Rabin, reviewing *Bright Lights, Big City* on the occasion of the release of the twentieth anniversary DVD, proffered, not implausibly, "Bridges had a distinctly sociological and journalistic bent. His films delved into hot-button political issues (the 1979 nuclear meltdown thriller *The China Syndrome*), brought articles about lifestyle trends to the big screen (1980's *Urban Cowboy*, 1985's *Perfect*) and adapted autobiographical novels about narrow cultural milieus, like the classic 1973 law-school drama *The Paper Chase* and 1988's yuppie-tastic *Bright Lights, Big City*."[30]

This is all persuasive. But somehow the deeper connections between his films are being missed, including the most notable connection: More often than not, the kernels of Bridges's stories were inspired by real life. In the case of *The Baby Maker*, Jack Larson said that Bridges's imagination was stirred by "a girl that we both knew who worked in a bar in Venice [California]. She enjoyed being a surrogate mother. It was the first time I had ever heard of such a thing. She did it a couple of times. Jim wrote the script based essentially on that idea."[31]

That girl came to life on screen in the form of Barbara Hershey, whose relatively modest feature film work to this point included *With Six You Get Eggroll*, starring Doris Day in her final film appearance, and, rather more memorably, Frank Perry's *Last Summer*, for which she was nominated for an Academy Award. In *The Baby Maker*, Hershey played Tish Gray, who has a baby for an upper middle-class couple, Jay and Suzanne Wilcox (Sam Groom and Collin Wilcox, billed here as Collin Wilcox-Horne), unable to have their own.

"As far as I remember, it was just through the normal route of an agent setting up the meeting," Hershey recalled of being cast in the role. "I don't remember in any way auditioning or anything like that. It was just a meeting and I got the part. In my career, I've worked with a lot of first-time filmmakers and I had no prejudice or hesitation about that. All I ever judge someone by is what I feel from them and what they emanate. He and Jack are two of the kindest people I've ever met. That's what emanated from him: this kindness and appreciation and enthusiasm. So I knew it would be a beautiful thing to work with him. Honestly, I count ninety percent of the decision on the script. If it's a bad script and you have a good director, it's still going to be a bad script! But if it's a good script, which I thought this was — certainly an unusual one — that counted for a lot. So I had confidence going in that he was going to be fine."[32]

Even so, Bridges surrounded himself with collaborators who would enable him to make the sometimes painful transition from theatrical director to film director easier. Michael Preece, a script supervisor since 1955, was hired to work on *The Baby Maker*. During their first meeting, Bridges said to him, "I know nothing about screen direction or matching or any of those things, so I'm relying on the cameraman and the script supervisor."[33] Preece recalled, "He was smart enough to know that he would do what he was supposed to do and let everybody else do their job."[34] The assistant director was the formidable Howard Koch, Jr., who had recently served in the same capacity on Roman Polanski's *Rosemary's Baby*.

Later, perhaps a bit too modestly, Bridges would reflect, "I still don't know that much about the camera. I hire the best people, and I work with them and tell them what I want."[35] So on *The Baby Maker*, Bridges relied not just on Preece and Koch, but on cinematographer Charles Rosher, Jr., who brought with him a wealth of experience, despite the fact that this was only his second film as DP (following *Adam at Six A.M.*) Rosher remembered, "That was a time period where cameramen were hired because they were commercial cameramen. I was shooting commercials. I had a contract with a commercial company. I had a commercial reel and that's how I got a movie. If you did television, you couldn't get a movie; you were a television cameraman. I was raised in the movie business because I was Conrad Hall's operator and worked on movies in that way."[36] Rosher was indeed "raised in the movie business": His father and namesake was the legendary Hollywood cinematographer whose many credits included the F.W. Murnau classic *Sunrise*. In film scholar Kevin Brownlow's estimation, Rosher, *pere*, along with "a small group of top-flight cameramen, changed the look of American films" in the silent era.[37]

Nothing so grand can be claimed for *The Baby Maker*, of course, but Bridges and Rosher are to be admired for their visual restraint in a period of film history in which simplicity wasn't considered a virtue. The film opens with a zoom-in to a tree at the front of the unassuming house Tish shares with her boyfriend Tad (Scott Glenn). But zooming is relatively atypical of the film's style. "I've never been a big fan of the zoom lens at all," Rosher admitted. "I've learned how to do it in commercials, from being an operator, how you can move a camera and zoom and nobody knows you're zooming. You're dollying with a camera on a dolly track and zooming at the same time, going cross screen, and no one knows you're doing it, but you're using that lens to your advantage instead of just sitting there and zooming for the sake of zooming....

"The only director I know that uses a zoom and really doesn't care if it's known is Bob Altman. And that's his own style."[38] Rosher would know; several years after *The Baby Maker*, he photographed two Altman masterpieces back to back, *3 Women* and *A Wedding*.

Even though there are some trendy rack focuses and handheld shots in *The Baby Maker* (and one wide-angle shot of Tad cruising on his motorcycle), the overwhelming impression we get is that Bridges and Rosher are holding back, letting the story unfold sans elaborate camerawork. Maybe Barbara Hershey put it best in summarizing the film's style: "It wasn't self-conscious in any way. It was pure storytelling."[39]

Rosher explained how he and Bridges worked together: "He gave me freedom. He was a very gentle person. He knew the locations. He had a good eye. He had that nice Frank Lloyd Wright house, you know? I lived about a block and a half from him, so we were neighbors and we got to know each other quite well. I found that he had good taste. When we went out on a scout, he knew how to pick the locations. That's usually what the director says to me: 'I want to shoot my scene here because I like the way this looks here.' He knew how to do all of that. He had a good sense of that. When it comes down to the lighting or the compositions of shots, he allowed me to do that. It was a good collaboration. We shared it all together, too. I wasn't trying to take over on him or anything. He was so likable. You just can't help but like Jim Bridges."[40]

Rosher mentioned the locations, which Bridges preferred to sets.[41] So did his star. "There's something about the big soundstage that makes you feel like you're making a movie," Hershey said. "It gives you shivers. That I always kind of like. The smell of it and walking out into that bright sunlight after you've been inside. But in terms of reality and not having to imagine and the stimulation of change — different environments — there's nothing like real locations. I always find them really great. As an actor, you never know where you're going or what you're walking into, and it can be very stimulating."[42]

Rosher recalled, "When we location scouted on the film, he knew exactly what he wanted and where he wanted to shoot the stuff. He had a great feel for all of that. That was just a natural thing for him to do. He knew exactly the right places to shoot. He didn't have to be taken by the hand and told, 'Here, this is where you're going to shoot it.' He knew exactly what he wanted and if he didn't like it, he would say so and we'd find another location to shoot."[43]

The Baby Maker offers the first instance of a moment of critical importance in a James Bridges film being played over the phone. In the opening scene, Tish receives a call from Mrs. Culnick (Lili Valenty). Bridges stays on Tish during the entire conversation, as she munches on a mayonnaise sandwich, but her casualness doesn't obscure the gravity of the reason for Mrs. Culnick's call. She informs Tish, "I have someone I want you to meet, someone I want to meet you. You are still interested in meeting someone, aren't you? You haven't changed your mind?" It is through this disembodied, Eastern European-accented voice (Valenty was from Poland), speaking in ambiguities, that we receive our first clue as to what Tish does. Tish answers, "No," to Mrs. Culnick's question about not having changed her mind. Until that moment, Bridges has framed Tish loosely, as she walks around her kitchen and living room, listening to Mrs. Culnick talk. But when Tish hears Mrs. Culnick's pointed question, and then gives her answer, Bridges slowly pushes in on Tish's face with an almost imperceptible zoom, the kind favored by Rosher.

At Mrs. Culnick's house, Tish meets Suzanne Wilcox. (Jay is at work.) Mrs. Culnick introduces the two with a peculiar formality considering the purpose of their meeting, which is still unclear: "This is Tish, Patricia Gray, and this is Suzanne, Suzanne Wilcox, Mrs. Jay Wilcox." As the two shake hands and greet each other, Bridges introduces *us* to Suzanne in a manner that keeps our identification, for now, with Tish. In a medium shot, Tish is fully visible on screen right, while Suzanne is at an angle on screen left, facing Tish and Mrs. Culnick, who is positioned behind and between them. We cannot get a clear view of Suzanne's face in this shot. When the camera pans and the two "sit down and get acquainted"—as Mrs. Culnick orders them to do—Tish is again positioned in such a way so that she faces us, while Suzanne, sitting opposite her on a couch, wearing sunglasses, has her back to the camera.

If this staging initially promotes our continued identification with Tish—the character whom we have gotten to know first, the character played by the radiant, appealing Barbara Hershey, whose "natural beauty just jumps right out at you," as Rosher put it[44]—it isn't long before Bridges removes the icy mystique from Suzanne. The film begins to cut to a series of shot/reverse shots of Suzanne and Tish as they talk. They learn their mutual backgrounds as they feel each other out. When we learn why Suzanne is here, it makes her that much more sympathetic. She and her husband are happily married, she says, but they cannot have children. She has ruled out adoption, she explains to Tish later, because "I want his child. I want a Jay, Jr. Even if it isn't mine, it's a Jay, Jr."

Already Bridges is poking mild fun at Tish and her milieu, as when she tells Suzanne that she previously was employed at "a sort of teenybopper topless joint until the boss found out my ID was faked. Mrs. Culnick didn't mention that, did she?" Suzanne answers brightly, and with a polite smile, "No. No, she didn't!"

Like Tish Gray, the character of Suzanne Wilcox was inspired by somebody Bridges knew. In this case, it was the actress who would end up playing the role in the film. The presskit informs us, "Bridges says he had the talented blonde actress and her family in mind when he first conceived the basic idea for *The Baby Maker*."[45] He didn't try to conceal this fact. "I believe he named the character 'Wilcox,'" Collin Wilcox pointed out. "I was the right age and the right look, I suppose, for that role."[46] Both true. The review in *The Hollywood Reporter* noted that Wilcox was "physically perfect as the wife who is willing to go to almost any length to guarantee her husband an heir."[47]

It is a tribute both to Bridges's fairness as a scenarist and to Wilcox's seemingly limitless gifts as an actress that Tish's perspective is not allowed to dominate the film, that Suzanne's humanity is always apparent to us. For critic David Shipman, *The Baby Maker* was "exploitative" in its desire "to appeal to preppies and hippies alike,"[48] but it is this very even-handedness that accounts for why the film holds up as well as it does. As Hershey observed, "There's not a bad person in the film. Even the girl who's having the affair with my boyfriend isn't a bad person. Nobody's bad! We're just people and that's kind of refreshing."[49]

Bridges insisted to an interviewer, a few years after the release of *The Baby Maker*, that he wasn't a hippie,[50] but that much is obvious from the film itself: Bridges is every bit as fond of his upper-middle class couple as he is of his flower child. At the same time, he would probably share the warm feeling about hippies that prompted Orson Welles to once compare them to Shakespeare's Falstaff: "He's good in the sense that the hippies are good."[51]

At the same time, Bridges isn't hesitant to gently mock Jay and Suzanne, too. Consider the moment when Suzanne tells Tish that she wants her to meet her husband "right now." After she says this line, we immediately cut to a shot of an anonymous-looking, monolithic skyscraper in downtown Los Angeles—a nice bit of droll editing. When Suzanne explains Jay's job to Tish, it's hard to decipher what, exactly, he does for a living out of her mumbo-jumbo about "efficiency experts" and "management engineers."

The film is a series of rhymes in these early scenes, as the Wilcoxes and Tish become acquainted. When Tish asks Suzanne which one of the businessmen exiting the aforementioned skyscraper is Jay, she replies, "The handsome one, of course." Later, after Jay has met Suzanne for the first time when she comes to dinner at their fine house, he tells Suzanne privately that he thinks Tish is "very attractive." These two moments complement each other perfectly, as neither Tish nor Jay — the two who will be making the baby, after all — are unable to set aside entirely the other's physical attractiveness as they contemplate the task at hand. Suzanne is a kind of matchmaker here, but not too crassly or obviously. Bridges's touch is always light.

Jay finds himself alone with Tish for the first time as he prepares dinner on the backyard patio. They stand on opposite sides of the grill, all the while Jay "grilling" *her* about her boyfriend. Then, in a particularly elegant camera move, the shot shifts to include the bay window at the back of the house in the composition. Suzanne is visible inside, setting the table, briefly positioned between Jay and Tish in the frame. She even pauses for a moment to surreptitiously observe them. But Jay, self-conscious, sees her and looks back at her. (The shot purposefully recalls the earlier shot showing Jay and Tish being introduced to each other, with Suzanne standing between them.)

By the time Tish impulsively strips nude and jumps into the swimming pool, Suzanne has joined Jay outside. They look to each other and Suzanne smiles first, her gentility mollifying the sheer awkwardness of the situation. But, we mustn't forget, it is Suzanne who has *engineered* the situation. We never have the sense that Jay desires a "Jay, Jr.," more than he does an adopted child.

Tish's carefree skinny-dipping, meanwhile, anticipates a comparably impetuous moment later in Hershey's career. In James Ivory's *A Soldier's Daughter Never Cries* (one of the high points in American film in the 1990s), she played a character inspired by the wife of expatriate novelist James Jones. In an exhilarating scene, upon learning that her young son has been unfairly disciplined by a French elementary school teacher, she confronts the teacher in the playground and chucks a fistful of sand in her face.

For her part, it's never clear if Tish is fully cognizant of the situation's absurdity or even its delicacy. Sometimes her character is very hard to like. At dinner, Suzanne explains in fuller, more somber detail why she is unable to have children, after which Tish asks if she can have a doggy bag to take home what's left of her meal. This isn't funny or cute — it's cruel — but Suzanne laughs it off once again.

* * *

In those days, Jack Larson did not take a screen credit on James Bridges's films, as he would beginning on *Mike's Murder*. But he very much had a role to play and, even on this first film, his role was well defined: "My role was very precise on the films, starting with the first film, *The Baby Maker*. I was his sounding board on script. He wrote; I did *not* write things, but he trusted me."[52]

Apart from that, Larson explained, "My work in relationship with Jim was to see dailies and to stay off the set. Actors always have problems. Having been an actor, they do these things and they convince you and they can even convince a director on the set. But if you know the script ... and I knew Jim's scripts in and out, I knew everything, I knew always what Jim was working for, I knew how he felt the script would work if it worked, I knew the colors that he had in mind of the various characters and how they were to work. So I would see dailies and I would tell Jim, 'This isn't working. This character is becoming too lovable and it's going to get a bit icky here.' Anyway, it was that kind of thing. That's all I did and that was through all of the films. I definitely was his sounding board on script. He was interested in my criticisms or whatever and we would disagree, sometimes violently. I had him throw the script at me on *Perfect*! We had a huge disagreement on that, but he apologized the next day and he said, 'I only get furious at you when I know you're right!' So that was Jim."[53]

On *The Baby Maker*, Larson also made several key casting suggestions, recommending Sam Groom and Scott Glenn to Bridges. They had both appeared in *Collision Course*, the omnibus of short plays which was performed Off-Broadway (Groom was in Larson's own play, *Chuck*). In its cast of players, the film is made up of a striking mix of the old and the new. While Wilcox was an old hand by then, and Hershey had already been nominated for an Oscar, the film came along early in the careers of Groom and Glenn, among others. Playing Charlotte, a friend of Tish's, was Elaine May's daughter Jeannie Berlin, who herself would be Oscar-nominated two years later for her performance in *The Heartbreak Kid*, directed by her mother. *The Hollywood Reporter* called her brief appearance in *The Baby Maker* "a smashing debut."[54] It's not quite that, but Berlin is undeniably memorable.

Helena Kallianiotes had a supporting role as a belly dancer with whom Tad starts an affair during Tish's pregnancy. The same year that *The Baby Maker* came out, Kallianiotes had a role in Bob Rafelson's masterpiece *Five Easy Pieces*. In fact, the two films premiered less than a month apart—*Five Easy Pieces* in September 1970, *The Baby Maker* in October—a potent reminder of the rich cinematic climate that surrounded Bridges's first film. "Helena was a friend," Larson said. "She was living with and then married a great friend of mine, Billy Gray from *Father Knows Best*."[55]

But while the film's cinematographer was young, and so was much of the cast, in other departments Bridges could count on the expertise of veteran Hollywood moviemakers. He was in no way averse to "the old days of Hollywood," as he explained in an interview: "Despite the big studio system, there were great craftsmen, great directors, great stars."[56] (George Cukor once expressed a similar thought in a different way: "People say, 'Oh, how could you work under that terrible system?' Well, the pictures you see from the 1930s and 1940s were done under that system. So they were smart, they were clever people."[57])

As often as Bridges would work with people at the beginning of their careers—such as Rosher on *The Baby Maker* or cinematographer Reynaldo Villalobos on *Urban Cowboy*—he would just as often choose to work with those whose filmographies reached back to the "the old days." For example, his production designer on *Urban Cowboy* was Stephen B. Grimes, who began as an assistant art director on John Huston's *Moby Dick* in 1956. Over the next three decades, he would work as an art director or production designer on numerous other Huston films, including *Heaven Knows, Mr. Allison*, *The Misfits*, and *The Night of the Iguana*, as well as on Sydney Pollack's *This Property Is Condemned* and David Lean's *Ryan's Daughter*. An impressive résumé, to say the least—and Bridges had the good sense to hire him.

The editor of *The Baby Maker* had a résumé that was every bit as imposing as Grimes's. "I've been very fortunate," Bridges said in the mid-seventies. "I work with one cutter all the time, by the name of Walter Thompson.... He cut Renoir's first film in America. He cut for John Ford *Wee Willie Winkie* and *Young Mr. Lincoln*. He's a terrific, wonderful cutter."[58] In addition to the classics by Renoir and Ford, Thompson's other films included Robert Stevenson's *Jane Eyre*, Abraham Polonsky's *Force of Evil*, and Fred Zinnemann's *The Nun's Story*. *The Baby Maker* was the first of two films he made with Bridges in the final decade of his life.

But, really, how *did* the editor of *Wee Willie Winkie* wind up cutting *The Baby Maker*? Thompson's involvement was thanks to another figure of "the old days," the film's producer, Robert Wise (and more about him in a moment). "Bob brought the wonderful editor Walter Thompson. He got Walter, who Jim absolutely adored," Larson recalled. "Walter was married to a hot woman by the name of Verita, who had a little Mexican bar-restaurant. Vera was her name, she called herself Verita. He was tons of fun and a wonderful man. He was one of the great editors. He came aboard and they had a kind of father-son relationship, which Jim often had, like he had with John Houseman. Walter taught Jim a lot."[59]

Script supervisor Michael Preece gave credit to Thompson for his role in the development of the film's subtle aesthetic: "He also had an editor who was an older man and very straight-laced, Walter Thompson. It was an era when lots of fancy shots were made. People were trying to experiment. For an editor that worked with John Ford, the picture was shot very straightforward with Chuck Rosher. The lighting was very nice, but you could see everybody."[60]

One of the best examples of Thompson's skill and sensitivity as an editor comes in the scene in which Mrs. Culnick finalizes the arrangement between Tish and the Wilcoxes. She itemizes what Tish will receive for her services ($500 down, all expenses, rent, food, etc., $500 upon affirmation of pregnancy, maternity ward, doctor and hospital bills, and so on). The scene opens with a medium shot of Mrs. Culnick at her typewriter, reading what the Wilcoxes will pay Tish. Tish is standing directly behind Mrs. Culnick, looking out a window; her lower torso is visible in the medium shot of Mrs. Culnick. Cut to a close-up of Tish, who turns from the window. Cut back to Mrs. Culnick, as she continues to read. Cut to a close-up of Suzanne, who is standing to the left of Mrs. Culnick; Jay is opposite her, to the right of Mrs. Culnick. Suzanne is taking all of this in, her eyes meeting Jay's. Cut to a close-up of Jay, who listens and smiles slightly at his wife. Cut back to Mrs. Culnick, who finally says, "And at birth, two thousand dollars in cash." Cut to Tish, who suddenly interjects, "An extra hundred if it's a boy." (A "Jay, Jr.," presumably.) Everyone is speechless at first. Cut to Suzanne, who shoots an oddly worried look to Tish and then turns to Jay. Cut to Jay, who is looking at Tish and then looks to Suzanne. Cut to Suzanne, who breaks a tiny smile. Cut to Jay, who does the same before laughing and saying, "Okay." He takes a sip of his drink. Cut to Tish, who is turned toward Jay and smiles at him. She then looks toward Suzanne, as if she is measuring *both* of their reactions to her surprise request. What is remarkable about the editorial choices so far is how much of the scene is played off of the reaction shots of Suzanne and Jay, even though Tish is in many ways who we are most interested in, and Mrs. Culnick is doing almost all of the talking.

Mrs. Culnick adds the provision to the document and moves on. We see her in the same medium shot as before. Cut to Tish, who tosses her hair back, appearing to grow restless with all of this business. She tries to make eye contact with Jay again. Cut to Jay, who is looking down at Mrs. Culnick. Cut to Suzanne, who is looking at Jay. Cut to Tish, who is now studying a list of "rules" prepared by Suzanne which Mrs. Culnick has just handed to her. Cut to a wide shot, the first time in the scene all four characters can be viewed in the same frame. Mrs. Culnick says, "Voila!" as she pulls the sheet of paper from her typewriter.

Thompson's editing focuses our attention to the various emotional states of the characters, particularly Suzanne's fragility and Jay's anxiousness. And it is the editing, and the selection of shots, that makes the scene; the dialogue itself—consisting mostly of Mrs. Culnick reading—is uninspiring.

Thompson's editorial brilliance is on display in another key scene later in the film. We have already seen Suzanne observing the developing affection between Jay and Tish (when she looks at them through the kitchen window). This occurs again when the three of them, in what Bridges presents as essentially a tragicomic situation, drive to the cabin (in Big Bear Lake, California) where Jay and Tish are to conceive their child. They enter the cabin together. Suzanne sets down a bag of groceries on the kitchen countertop. Facing the stove as she unpacks, her back to the camera, she begins talking about making "snow ice cream" with the ingredients she has purchased at the store. As she is speaking, there is a cut to Jay, who shoots a look to Tish, standing in another part of the cabin. Cut to Tish, with a broad, slightly lascivious smile on her face. Before Suzanne finishes speaking, she innocently turns to Jay and catches him. Caught, Jay says nothing.

With characteristic tact, Suzanne hastily asks Tish to go outside and sprinkle rock salt on the steps, thereby giving Jay and Suzanne an all-too-rare moment to themselves. He approaches her as she finishes unpacking the groceries and she promptly buries her head in his chest, a gesture that reminds us of the fundamental sadness of their predicament. We then see Tish, spreading the salt outside as directed, who glimpses Jay and Suzanne's embrace looking through a window. For the first time, perhaps, Tish is made aware of the obvious love Jay and Suzanne have for each other.

Suzanne soon departs from the cabin, leaving Jay and Tish, but not before asking Tish to wear her wedding ring. This could be a terribly portentous moment, but Bridges neutralizes it with his dialogue. "Look, this is absolutely ridiculous," Suzanne tells Tish, admitting the obvious. "You don't have to wear it if you don't want to, Tish, but it would mean a great deal to me." By conceding the "ridiculousness" of her request, Bridges renders it that much more poignant. There is then an almost Bressonian close-up of Tish's hand, extended in front of her body, as Suzanne places the ring on her finger. The camera pans up as Tish brings her hand to her face and looks at the ring. Suzanne says, "Thank you," and leaves. Wilcox is breathtakingly good here. As Barbara Hershey noted, "She had a very difficult part, I thought. It's a tough thing to pull off."[61] But she *does* pull it off. In his sympathetic review of *The Baby Maker* in *Time* magazine, critic Mark Goodman wrote of how Suzanne "awaits, with as much dignity as possible, the qualified glories of stepmotherhood."[62] As Wilcox plays her, there isn't a single instant in the film in which Suzanne lacks dignity.

Tish has intuited that Jay and Suzanne have something she does not. During the night of their assignation, as Jay and Tish drink wine and talk, she tells him that she doesn't think he has ever been unfaithful to Suzanne. He asks her, "Does that make me square? Does being faithful to my wife make me square?" She replies, maybe a little unexpectedly, though the earlier scene has prepared us for it, "I think it's beautiful. I don't understand it, but I don't understand a lot of beautiful things." The domestic bliss of the Wilcoxes is totally appealing to her and to us, especially when contrasted with Tish and Tad's world. In the final scene of *The Baby Maker*, when she and Jay say their goodbyes, she refuses to see him again — her way of doing her part to preserve Jay's faithfulness to Suzanne.

Critic Roger Greenspun didn't find "the dry-eyed pathos of Suzanne's Night Alone" moving when he reviewed the film in *The New York Times*, but it is just that.[63] Shots of Tish and Jay in the cabin are masterfully intercut with shots of Suzanne, walking by herself on the grounds of the motel she is staying at in the hours leading up to what Tish calls "our relation." Later she is seen reading alone in bed and looking to Jay's side, which is undisturbed on this particular evening. The next morning, Suzanne shows up at the cabin to cook breakfast for the trio. The embarrassment of Jay and Tish walking in from their bedroom to find Suzanne preparing eggs is not lessened when Tish casually deposits Suzanne's wedding ring on her plate as Suzanne is pouring the coffee. Such behavior is not charming.

"[A]s a companion of the way we now live," Greenspun regarded the film as being "complete to the point of lunacy." As an example, he cited the scene in which Jay tells Tish, "Norman Mailer says booze is the active man's pot," to which she replies, "Oh, yeah? Who's Norman Mailer?"[64] But surely this exchange is paid off later, when Tish unexpectedly quotes George Bernard Shaw ("Marriage and motherhood are the greatest slavery invented by man") and Jay kiddingly retorts, "Who's George Bernard Shaw?" Roger Ebert understood better than Greenspun the spirit in which such dialogue was intended, arguing in his three-star review in the *Chicago Sun-Times* that "[t]he movie has to be taken, I think, as a comedy of manners.... The girl notes that the couple has all the Frank Sinatra albums. 'Yes,' the husband says, 'but we have all the Beatles albums, too.' Well of course the Beatles are maybe two years beyond being contemporary, but the movie knows that and that's why the dialog works with a sort of sly understatement."[65]

On the other hand, Greenspun did find "Suzanne's helplessly selfish supervision of Tish's pregnancy" to be moving,[66] and indeed it is. Her readings from books for expectant mothers are periodically heard in voiceover during montages depicting Tish going about her daily life during her pregnancy. At one point, Suzanne is horrified when she finds Tish roughhousing with Tad on a slide near a beach, contrary to the advice she has read which counsels against "riding on roller coasters or any similar amusement rides." But she will later admit, "Sometimes I do forget who's having the baby."

In the end, much of Bridges's achievement in *The Baby Maker* is to avoid the various predictable outcomes his story might have had in the hands of another director. As Mark Goodman noted in *Time,* "*The Baby Maker*'s saving grace is that Bridges never resorts to cheap, boudoir-farce gimcracks where fundamental relationships are concerned. Jay does not run off with Tish, nor is Tish transformed into a Supermother who demands the baby at birth."[67] Indeed, there is never any suggestion in the slightest that Jay feels the same for Tish as he does for Suzanne; the film is bracing in its depiction of a happy and committed marriage. What's more, Jay and Suzanne do not, as we cringingly half-expect, fall irretrievably under the spell of Tish and her ways. For example, there is no indication that they will take Tish's advice to raise their child "on a farm." Maybe she is right and they should, but Bridges resists including the scene of the hippie teaching the "square" upper middle-class couple how to lead their lives.

Bridges does, however, permit Tish to grow over the course of the film. When her friend Charlotte cruelly calls the Wilcoxes "the enemy," Tish stands up for them, saying, "Jay is not the enemy." (I'm sure she means Suzanne, too.) Bridges paints many of Tish's friends, with their talk of "false values" and of "changing the world," in far broader strokes, and far more critically, than he does Jay and Suzanne. This thread of the film reaches a climax of sorts when Jay and Suzanne witness a hippie-led protest of war toys outside of a local toy store, and a fake "killing" is staged by the demonstrators to make their point. Such scenes ultimately feel extraneous to the central drama; surely this scene and others like it are what *Variety* was referring to in noting that "some sidebar events simply halt the story."[68] But they also serve to "[say] farewell to hippiedom's illusions," as critic Armond White once wrote of Arthur Penn's contemporaneous *Alice's Restaurant.*[69]

Beyond developing an ability to appreciate the Wilcoxes for who they are, Tish's views evolve in other, more important ways, too. Early in the film, she says she gave her other baby up for adoption because she was "too young" and "didn't want to be trapped." Her character comes to conclude that to have kept her child wouldn't have resulted in her being "trapped." So while Goodman is correct in stating that Tish isn't "transformed into a Supermother" when she gives up the baby she has with Jay (which turns out to be a boy), it seems obvious she has mixed emotions about it.

In the final scene, checks are given out (including that extra $100) and looks are again exchanged among our three protagonists, as they hover over the baby on the floor of Mrs. Culnick's house. Tish picks him up and hands him to Suzanne in a two-shot that the entire film has been leading up to. "You have a very beautiful son, Mrs. Wilcox," she says. Suzanne exits first, leaving Jay and Tish, who embrace in a wide shot. There *is* something between them — how could there not? — but it isn't meant to be.

Mrs. Culnick tells Jay and Suzanne not to worry about Tish. "I'll take very good care of her until she's all well," she promises them. But we know from the look on Tish's face that it will be a very long time before she is well. We see Jay and Suzanne depart from Mrs. Culnick's house through the eyes of Tish. She sprints around the property to find vantage points from which she can see their station wagon drive off. She watches them and we watch her, in a medium close-up in profile that lingers, as she looks off into the distance until the car is out of sight. She really *is* "trapped" now, standing alone. She isn't in tears, but she is clearly inconsolable. And who is there to console her? Mrs. Culnick? Charlotte? Tad?

James Bridges usually ended his films with a wide shot. Such is the case in *The Paper Chase, September 30, 1955, Urban Cowboy, Perfect,* and *Bright Lights, Big City.* But in *The Baby Maker*, as in *Mike's Murder*, he ends with a close-up of the face of a woman lost in her thoughts — a suggestive and enigmatic image to leave an audience with.

"It's a strange film in that it's not like any film before or after it, I think in its subject matter," Hershey reflected. "But it was so misunderstood as a film. I remember that it was released third bill to sex films and things. The title disturbed people who thought it was something that it wasn't. It's a quite innocent film. It's kind of, to me, almost clinical at times. It's not sexual. It's kind of wholesome and ultimately, I found, very touching when she gives up the baby. She didn't know what she was getting into. When she hands it over at the end, it's very touching, I think."[70]

* * *

The Baby Maker seems to have been a happy set. Charles Rosher, Jr., remembered, "It was your regular, perfect Hollywood shoot. Forty days. Twelve-hour shoot days. It's absolutely heaven on earth how the film industry was then.... You were human. You worked from 7:30 to 7:30, and that's it. It was civilized.

"I would sum it up as a very pleasurable experience. It was my second movie. I was excited to death myself, just as excited as I was when I did the first movie. I would sum it up as a fabulous experience, a fabulous time, everything about it was perfect. There was nothing wrong with it."[71]

Hershey noted, "I remember Collin was very sweet. The whole cast was very sweet. The atmosphere was sweet on the set. There were no negatives. I just remember everyone loving each other and getting on."[72]

Rosher felt that Bridges had an advantage in being the film's writer *and* director: "I think it's terrific, in fact, because he has total control of any changes that have to be made. He knows the feeling and when to change them and where, if something is going wrong. I think that's a real plus.

I noticed that working with Robert Benton, too [on *The Late Show*]. He's always writing when we're shooting. When we're lighting, he's sitting there re-writing or adjusting and working on the script constantly. I think that's a real plus to have the director be the writer."[73]

In Hershey's experience, however, "sometimes that can be good and sometimes that can be bad. And the only reason I say that sometimes it's bad is, they have this saying that the writer has to give the film to the director and the director has to give the film to the actor. If it's the writer directing, sometimes the writer won't give up a line or something that needs to change because of what's happening in that moment. Sometimes there's a rigidity in that translation to director — not always, but sometimes. And with Jim, it wasn't at all. He was totally open to use ourselves and whatever would stimulate us."[74]

While Collin Wilcox did not recall the actors doing too much in the way of improvisation, as such, "I do remember him saying, 'Let me see what you want to do.'"[75] As Hershey remembered it, Bridges was receptive to his actors' ideas. "Not that every idea I had worked or ended up being in the film, but he was open to it," she said. "I think a secret for any director is that kind of openness. That's probably the biggest quality of Scorsese is his openness. It stimulates you, it gets your juices flowing creatively, because you know that ideas you come up with will actually be considered! Jim definitely did that."[76]

"He was, I felt, an actor's director," observed Michael Preece. "He would talk to the actors. For instance, we rehearsed for a week or two before we started filming and everyone would sit at a big table."[77]

Rosher concurred, saying, "He was fantastic with actors. He knew his script so well, and he was such a personable, charming man, and such a nice guy. Actors loved him, they just loved him. He was just so warm to them and friendly and helpful if they needed help of any form. He handled actors just absolutely beautifully."[78]

The presence of Robert Wise helped to protect Bridges and his collaborators from external pressures. By the time of *The Baby Maker*, Wise's clout was enormous. He was twice the recipient of Academy Awards for Best Director (for *West Side Story* and *The Sound of Music*), and his films included classics ranging from *The Set-Up* and *I Want to Live!* to *Odds Against Tomorrow* and *The Haunting*. He was a good man to have on your side if trouble sprang up.

Rosher said, "Robert Wise was wonderful. At a certain point on our film, we were running a little bit behind. [National General] wanted to take out pages, which would mean days. Jimmy didn't want that, of course, and he told Robert Wise that. I'll never forget it: It was like a movie within a movie. We were shooting at National General Studios and Robert Wise came in his old Rolls-Royce. We were sitting outside the stage door like little kids, knowing he was going to go upstairs and defend us. He went upstairs and defended us and we were trying to hear anything we could. We naturally couldn't hear anything, but we heard a lot of voices being raised. We watched him leave and we stayed there. Whatever Robert Wise did to the executive at National General, they agreed to keep it the way it was, shoot the schedule we were shooting, even though we were two days behind or whatever. We just said, 'Oh, thank God for our great father here!'

"I crossed his path many times afterwards. Maybe twenty years later, at Musso Franks for lunch, I came up to him when he was sitting with a group of people. I kneeled down and told him, 'I just want to thank you. I don't know if you remember what you did for us on that movie by telling them to leave us alone.' He was big enough of a person at that time to be able to say things like that. I thanked him and he was so nice. He said, 'I remember doing that now!'"[79]

Hershey recalled, "It was a very free set. It was a very different atmosphere to sets now. There was no feeling of the studio breathing down your neck and people looking at their watches, though I'm sure that was going on. But it was probably a credit to Jim that you just never felt it on the set."[80]

* * *

"*The Baby Maker* was a successful film," Jack Larson said. "Not a triumphantly successful film, but Barbara Hershey was wonderful in it, Scott was wonderful in it."[81]

The reviews were positive, even if many of them expressed astonishment at the film's quality, a viewpoint best represented by Roger Ebert's candid assessment: "It could have been awful, but it's actually pretty good."[82] Mark Goodman's recommendation in *Time* was qualified in a similar way. He wrote that "the viewer who can wade through an implausible situation, a clutch of cardboard dropouts and painful patches of dialogue will discover a film that is curiously sensitive and affecting."[83] "Curiously"!

There is no need to apologize for liking a film as good as *The Baby Maker*. It is a long way from being Bridges's best film, but that speaks more to his rapid evolution as a director than it does to the inherent qualities of his debut effort. In the end, perhaps Barbara Hershey offered the fairest judgment of *The Baby Maker* when she contended that it is "a time capsule film versus a classic film. It's very much of its time. It's a window into me at that time in my life, definitely, even though I wasn't that character or doing what that character was doing, but that's very much me there, and probably all of us. And the environment that existed at that time — the houses — it's almost documentary-like that way."[84]

Three

Hart and Kingsfield, Bridges and Houseman: The Paper Chase

He was now a film director, but James Bridges wasn't done with the theatre — not just yet.

In 1972, Bridges directed an adaptation of Christopher Isherwood's novel, *A Meeting by the River*, at the Mark Taper Forum in Los Angeles. The novel, first published in 1967, took the form of letters between two English brothers, Oliver and Patrick. The younger brother, Oliver, is in India, studying to become a Hindu monk. "I was the older brother, Patrick, who was a totally worldly fellow," recalled Laurence Luckinbill. "He was the counterpart. He was the ying, or the yang, or whichever one is which. It was kind of a dialectical between matters of the spirit and matters of the flesh."[1] Isherwood wrote the adaptation with his partner, the painter Don Bachardy.

"I would never have thought we could dramatize [the novel]," Isherwood confessed to *The Paris Review*. "It was largely James Bridges, who's an old friend, who insisted that we could. Then we asked ourselves: *Is* it possible?"[2]

It turned out that it *was* possible, though the backstory of how the play came to be was more complicated than Isherwood let on. Jack Larson remembered,

> Chris, as with John Houseman, was a mentor. He was an extraordinarily great man, whatever his reputation is now. I think posthumously his reputation will eventually go to the heights it deserves again....
>
> Chris wanted very much ... for Jim to do a film of his novel, *A Meeting by the River*. I could have told Chris, but I just didn't say a word about it: Jim was never going to go on location to India. Jim didn't like to fly, you know. He didn't like locations. He was never going to do that. The idea of going to India and shooting a film would have been something that Jim would eventually not have done. It was hard enough to get him on a plane to New York when something had to be shot there or for location scouting....
>
> Jim then said, "Let's see if it can be a play." Jim thought it could be a play and this would be a stepping stone to something, and maybe resolve his, I

can't say responsibility, but resolve something about the idea that Chris wanted him to do it as a film.

So Jim then worked with Chris, and Chris's friend Don Bachardy came aboard as a co-writer of this play. Jim oversaw it and worked very hard on it.[3]

By the time *A Meeting by the River* came up, Luckinbill was already well known for his work in Mart Crowley's groundbreaking Off-Broadway play about modern gay life, *The Boys in the Band*. On screen, he appeared in William Friedkin's fine film version of the play. He also had a central role in Otto Preminger's late masterpiece *Such Good Friends*. Asked how he was cast as Patrick, Luckinbill recalled,

> I think the connection was through *The Boys in the Band* and Mart Crowley, I'm not sure. I was an actor that was obviously somebody who took on edgy projects and projects that were kind of "out there." I have always been like that and unafraid to try new stuff. This didn't happen to be very avant-garde, really....
>
> It was the first time I was ever cast in a play at the Polo Lounge. It was not the setting that you would expect Chris Isherwood and Don Bachardy to be in, either! But there we were in the Polo Lounge, discussing matters of the spirit and the flesh, and surrounded by really nothing but the flesh. Jimmy was there, too. I'm sure it came about because of my getting noticed from *The Boys in the Band*.[4]

As Oliver, Bridges cast Sam Waterston. Like Luckinbill, he was an established actor in the theatre, at that point a year away from appearing in two important early screen roles: as Tom in a television version of *The Glass Menagerie* and as Nick Carraway in Jack Clayton's admirable adaptation of *The Great Gatsby*. Of his role in *A Meeting by the River*, Waterston said, "I always carried it around in my back pocket as a sort of accepted theory that it was very much [Isherwood's] story and that therefore Oliver was very much him, but fiction is fiction and I don't know how you would ever be able to pick that apart. Maybe Don Bachardy could have, knowing him so well, but I didn't."[5]

"I was the perfect Patrick," Luckinbill joked. "I was completely solipsistic and completely ego-centered. I didn't even know who was on stage with me! It was me and me and me! So they got the right guy, from that point of view."[6] One imagines that Luckinbill's portrayal likely lived up to *Time*'s description of the novel's Patrick as "one of the most cheerfully decadent characters in recent fiction.... Patrick is fully as alive as Sally Bowles, the heroine of Isherwood's *Goodbye to Berlin*, and could support a longer novel."[7]

The contrast between the two brothers was at the very heart of Isherwood's novel. This remained true in the play, according to its two leading actors, and, as was the case in *The Baby Maker*, Bridges declined to take sides.

Three. Hart and Kingsfield, Bridges and Houseman

Waterston said, "I think it would have killed the play, if you had thought, 'Oh, yes, Oliver is obviously right,' or if you had thought the brother is obviously right and he should pack this all up and go home. It's one of those indigestible things where their purposes can't really both be satisfied. I think its indigestibility is the point."[8]

In his review in the *Los Angeles Times*, Dan Sullivan made note of the way in which the play doesn't favor either Oliver or Patrick: "Oliver is definitely a holy man doing the right thing, but an Englishman in a swami suit does look silly (Waterston's awkwardness is just enough here). Patrick's faith that his sort of enlightened, liberated 20th-century man is what evolution has been straining towards is dangerous — and also comical."[9]

For Waterston, what he called the play's "indigestibility" made it an unusually challenging experience: "Sir John Gielgud came to see us ... and he asked me how long I had been rehearsing the play. I told him and he said, 'It's not enough, is it?' First of all, that is a prize John Gielgudism, because he's famous for saying things like that. But also I think it was true, not just particularly to this play or this production, but that those were two great big parts and my memory is really just being buried in it, just trying to get my head above water and stay there in what was really, really fascinating material that I felt you could have spent a whole lot more time on."[10]

Jack Bender and John Ritter, the stars of *Cherry, Larry, Sandy, Doris, Jean, Paul*, appeared in *A Meeting by the River* in a variety of small roles. Bender recalled,

> We were monks in this monastery where Sam's character goes, we were cab drivers, we were guys at the airport. We'd move stuff around the stage and occasionally put on different little things and play parts....
> One time my car broke down. John Ritter and I were living in Benedict Canyon, which is down Sunset, east of where Jim and Jack were. I called Jim in the morning and said, "John isn't here and I have no ride to rehearsal. Can you pick me up?" And he wasn't thrilled about it, but he did. Then he said to me, "Do you have any idea how early I have to get up to stay ahead of Sam?" It was just a glimpse into the kind of homework you do to show up as a director, which I didn't understand until I directed my first play and realized how early you have to get up to stay ahead of the actors.[11]

Waterston remembered Bridges as being "very, very kind. Very, very smart. Very supportive. Gentle. He was a hugely kind person, which is unusual for directors because they demand and direct. He was more of an evoker and an inviter. 'Come out to play.'"[12]

"He was so respectful of actors; he was more than respectful, he was unmanipulative," Luckinbill recalled. "He knew that actors could do what he wanted them to do. He didn't do tricks on them. And so you would just lay down your life for him and try to do anything that he asked you. He was a rare director in that respect. He had so much faith. I would say this about Jim Bridges: We never discussed religion or spirituality or anything like that, but I'm sure that he was drawn to this because of the spirit. Jim had faith, he had a great deal of faith."[13]

Waterston observed,

> There was an atmosphere of tenderness around this whole play. My antennae were all out for all that anyway because of the part I was playing. I remember really fascinating stories about Christopher Isherwood's experiences in India. I can't remember if this was something that I read or something that he told us, or maybe it was something Jim told us, about Chris's early experiences in India. I think he went out there as a Quaker, didn't he, with a lot of ambition to fix what was broken and get things working properly and heal people and get it all done. He was working extraordinarily long hours and, of course, the problems themselves were gigantic. The sea was so great and the boat was so small and he was right on the verge of a nervous breakdown when a friend of his took him to meet the man who eventually became his guru, who was a chain smoker and a giggler, and struck Chris as being not the least bit holy and not particularly sympathetic. Chris would tell him things and he would giggle. But something drew him to go back and his guru asked him how things were going. He said that he was still working himself too hard, but he was trying to turn over a new leaf. His guru thought that was so funny that he was laughing and choking and coughing. Isherwood was really made very angry by that and he said, "What's so funny?" He said, "Well, just the whole idea that you would be able to turn over a new leaf." Chris said, "So, okay, how would you state this?" He said, "Well, the way we think about it is you look at the leaf and you look at the leaf and you look at the leaf and you look at the leaf and you continue to look at the leaf, and then one morning you get up and the leaf has turned over."[14]

"It was a very lovely experience," Luckinbill said. "Jimmy Bridges and I became friends over it. I'm not sure why. It was just one of those shared connections, I guess, from both understanding the 'good old boy' connection that we had from home. If you meet somebody some place else that is from close to your town, then you know so many things about them that they may not even want you to know."[15] The two Arkansans would have another memorable professional encounter in the years to come.

According to Jack Bender, Bridges did "a masterful job" in directing *A Meeting by the River*: "Basically it was an empty stage. Jim's movement of actors and creating this universe of Christopher's book, which was more of a movie because it takes place so many different places, from New York to India ... it was beautifully directed."[16]

Bridges made a particularly striking directorial choice in a scene in which a vision occurs. As Larson recalled, "Instead of doing something on the stage for them to see a vision on the stage, the audience was suddenly flooded with light. It was wonderful. It was a great *coup de théâtre*. It absolutely worked and then nobody had to wonder about, 'What does the vision look like?'"[17]

Such flourishes usually do not go unnoticed. Both Luckinbill and Waterston remembered the presence of Tennessee Williams at rehearsals. "We used to go to lunch at some little place at the Music Center and Tennessee would come in and join us for lunch from time to time," Luckinbill said.[18]

"I remember Tennessee Williams coming to see a run-through of the play and going out to lunch with Jim afterwards," Waterston said. "I remember it primarily as an example of Tennessee Williams's famous inability to keep anybody in his head for more than about ten minutes. He watched the run-through and then he went out to lunch. This is downtown Los Angeles and there aren't too many places to go for lunch there, so we hadn't been invited to go to lunch with them, but Larry and I wound up in the same restaurant. Larry went over to Tennessee and said, 'Enjoy your lunch,' and Tennessee said, 'Have we met?'"[19]

In any case, the play and its director — if not its performers — made a lasting impression on Williams. Jack Larson explained, "It was considered a very brilliant production. Tennessee Williams saw it and offered Jim to do the twenty-fifth anniversary production of *A Streetcar Named Desire*."[20]

* * *

Before he could get to *A Streetcar Named Desire*, however, Bridges had a film to make. To say that the setting of his second film was a world away from that of *The Baby Maker* is an understatement. *The Paper Chase*, adapted by Bridges from the novel by John Jay Osborn, Jr., was about Harvard Law School, of which Osborn was a graduate.

"I got a little nervous that Jim was going to be the director because I knew about *The Baby Maker*," Osborn remembered. "But then when I met him, I wasn't nervous any more."[21] The author's anxiety is not surprising. There was nothing in Bridges's background or his work to this point to suggest anything like an affinity for *The Paper Chase*. Indeed, *The New York Times* indicated the limited appeal of Osborn's novel to outsiders, noting that he "tells it all as it may have been, in a fine, lean style — but there just isn't enough intramural conflict to attract the innocent bystander."[22]

What, then, about *The Paper Chase* appealed to an "innocent bystander" like Bridges? "Jim was very careful in what he did," Larson said. "[After *The Baby Maker*], he was offered some things that didn't interest him, but this book was given to him out of Fox and what appealed to him was the relationship between the professor and the student, a deep, emotional relationship that would turn out to be that the professor, who contributes with his intensity as a teacher, doesn't know the boy exists. That's what interested Jim."[23]

Osborn contended that Bridges also saw the project as a rare career opportunity: "For Jim, the movie was critically important. His career was on the line. He needed that movie. He desperately wanted it to be a big hit."[24] If that was the case, Bridges was prescient; though not the director's biggest hit, *The Paper Chase* was an unqualified success when it was released in the fall of 1973.

But more about that later. If "the relationship between the professor and the student," as Larson put it, was what persuaded Bridges to make the film, it seems obvious that he saw some of himself in the character of Hart, the law student played by Timothy Bottoms (the star of Peter Bogdanovich's *The Last Picture Show*). It seems equally obvious that he recognized a central figure from his life in the character of the professor (who teaches contract law at Harvard): John Houseman.

Having remained in regular contact with Houseman, Bridges made it a point to inform his mentor of the ongoing saga of casting. "[A]s the weeks went by, I detected a growing anxiety over his inability to cast the essential role of Professor Kingsfield," Houseman wrote in his memoir.[25] "I was aghast at some of the other suggestions," Osborn said.[26] After going through a list of such names — which included Edward G. Robinson! — Houseman recalled, "Bridges laughingly observed that I might end up having to play it."[27] Soon enough, it became apparent to Houseman that his protégé wasn't kidding. Houseman informed Bridges that he would be "delighted" to play Kingsfield "but that if he were foolish enough to mention the idea to the studio he stood a good chance of being thrown off the picture."[28]

Well, Bridges did mention the idea to the studio — and he wasn't thrown off the picture. At Houseman's suggestion, a screen test was made. Remember, apart from an uncredited cameo in John Frankenheimer's *Seven Days in May*, he had never before acted in a motion picture. Osborn recalled,

> I wrote a speech for the movie just before Houseman came up to film his supposed screen test. That's the speech that goes, "You're on an operating table, my questions are the fingers probing in your mind." It's the speech that explains the Socratic method because we had this crazy way of conducting class and we needed some idea of how to explain it. Jim didn't know how to do that because he didn't know anything about the Socratic method, so I wrote that speech, which I really liked. Houseman comes up to Toronto to film what he thinks is this other scene where Timothy Bottoms and he have this interaction. Instead, he's given this new speech to do. Houseman looks at me and says, "Osborn, what are you thinking? I'm like seventy years old. You want me to memorize this in a few hours?" I'd gotten to know him before then. We'd met in New York. So he goes off in a kind of pretend huff that

night to memorize the speech, which he wasn't able to completely do so we put the last part of it on cue cards. He was *wonderful* in it.[29]

"Two days later, Jim called in great agitation. He had just seen the test and it was 'fabulous'!" Houseman remembered. "Within a few days a deal had been made for me to play the role ... for which I would receive fifteen thousand dollars and equal second-star billing, with a starting date of November 12."[30] Houseman received something else, too: an acting career that would occupy him for the rest of his life.

Just as he would later insist upon the casting of Debra Winger in *Urban Cowboy*, Bridges "even with his sort of meek — I don't mean meek, because he wasn't meek — but his quiet way, he demanded that Houseman play that part," said script supervisor Michael Preece. "He was very strong about it."[31]

The decision met with the unreserved endorsement of John Jay Osborn, Jr. "In my family, my wife met Houseman first," he said. "I had a thing I had to go to, so she went to dinner out at Houseman's place, with Jim, and she came back and said, 'John, that guy is Kingsfield.' Then I met him a couple of days later in New York City and I was just like, 'They've got to use this guy.' This was so clearly an opportunity. If you want to know the best thing that Bridges did for that movie, it was to bring Houseman on board. It was such an absolutely right casting choice."[32]

The key point is that no one *but* Bridges would have made that choice. Houseman, acclaimed in theatre and in the movies as a producer and director, was not an actor, let alone a movie star. Only Bridges would have been able to identify the similarities between his friend and Professor Kingsfield. Osborn is quick to point out that "Houseman as Kingsfield is one thing, Houseman as a raconteur and friend is something different. He was actually quite a warm person. I became very, very close with him, much closer than I ever was with Jim.... Houseman was very friendly with Jim. I mean, they were friends. There was none of this imperiousness in that relationship."[33] But if Houseman's manner was dissimilar from that of Kingsfield, I shall argue that Bridges felt that what he learned from Houseman in real life was comparable to what Hart learns from Kingsfield in the film.

In all of his films, Bridges took chances with inexperienced actors, new actors, and non-professional actors. Nearly always, the gambles paid off, but on no film did they reap bigger dividends than on *The Paper Chase*. This is equally true of the supporting cast as it was of Houseman. When it came to selecting the actors to inhabit the roles of the other students, Osborn was given the chance to offer his unique, indeed indispensible, perspective. "I was there when the casting was done, with the exception of Lindsay Wagner, who was put in by the studio," he said. "So I knew what the guys should look like and what they ought to be like."[34]

Edward Herrmann played Anderson, a member of the study group in which Hart and other freshmen participate. *The Paper Chase* was, he said, his "first proper movie."[35] It had been preceded by "a crazy film by a local filmmaker about Indian gurus" and a Sophia Loren picture, *La mortabella*, in which he played a bit part as a policeman. "But *The Paper Chase* was clearly my first real movie with a script and characters and all that," Herrmann recalled. "It was wonderful.... I had an agent in New York. The agency didn't last too long, but there were some wonderful agents in it. I was sent up to interview with James. He was putting together a group for the students and, as is the way when you put together a group, you have Tim Bottoms and then you want to surround him with a group of people that were eccentric and different but were compatible. And I fit the profile for one of the characters that he wanted. I still remember my briefcase with the spring-loaded top that bounced open."[36]

Herrmann was joined by an impressive assortment of young actors, most of whom hadn't appeared in films before and all of whom would go on to fine careers, among them Graham Beckel, James Naughton, and Craig Richard Nelson. Herrmann felt that Bridges may have engineered the casting of this group so that any offscreen "competitiveness" was reflected on screen. "When you're starting out and you're all new, you're all hope," he said. "You're all jockeying for position. You all speak the same language naturally. You're frightened, you want the next job, you want to make it big, you have unlimited faith and belief in your own ability one minute and you're in the trash the next minute — you worry about everything. And we were all very proud of ourselves being in this movie and we were all sort of looking over our shoulders as to who's got the bigger part, who's this, who's that. So there was a natural — and, on the whole, it was benign — competitiveness between everybody: who had the better lines, who was doing this or that. You were also nervous about being in front of a camera for the first time. So that competitiveness and that energy showed up on screen. That may be one of the keys to the way James cast it."[37]

Among the supporting cast, Graham Beckel, playing prep school product Franklin Ford III ("I'm something like fifth generation Harvard," he boasts to Hart), has the most screen time. Osborn remembered, "When I heard him speaking the lines, even though he wasn't a preppy, he had this wonderful preppy quality to him. I think I was helpful with that because I don't think Jim understood that fully. He had it. A lot of the other guys didn't and somebody needed to have that quality."[38]

For his part, Beckel said, "From my perspective, the character [of Ford] was somebody I knew. I came from an Eastern seaboard family whose members have gone to Ivy League schools and all that stuff. I didn't find it too much of a stretch. I just pulled various types I went to prep school with and composited them together. I wasn't thrown by the sociology of the character, what was suggested anyway by Osborn, in the slightest. I kind of got who that was. You know, my roommate in boarding school was named George James Nicholson III. And I think his roots were probably a little deeper than Ford's!"[39]

* * *

Plainly, *The Paper Chase* was not directly informed by Bridges's personal experience, as *The Baby Maker* was, as *September 30, 1955* and *Mike's Murder* would later be. But it inaugurated a trend in Bridges's work. When he directed material that originated with other writers, he was attracted to novels and stories that were themselves drawn from their own authors' lives. To the extent that *The Paper Chase* reflected Osborn's experience attending Harvard Law School, Bridges's film is emblematic of this trend. And as he did with Ray Bradbury's short story "The Jar" a decade earlier, he adapted Osborn's novel with great fidelity. Osborn reflected, "You could not have asked for a more literal and thoughtful translation of a novel."[40]

Osborn said that Bridges did make "one brilliant change from the book, which seems very small, but it's not really. The one thing he did, and it's the only change he made, if memory serves me, is he had Susan having been married and getting a divorce." (Susan is the daughter of Professor Kingsfield, played by Lindsay Wagner.) Osborn continued, "That produces that wonderful line when he says, 'You lied to me. You told me your name was whatever-it-is,' and she says, 'I didn't lie. That's my married name.' It's wonderful. That I thought was brilliant and I've always wished I'd put that in the book. It was like, 'Jesus, why didn't I think of that?'"[41]

Bridges welcomed the presence of Osborn on the set and his participation in the making of the movie; the author is credited as the film's technical advisor. Osborn recalled, "When the movie was in production and it was getting ready to shoot up in Toronto, Jim and I spent three days in a hotel together, just going over the script, but that was very small things: sort of ways to compress things or what to leave out because the script was a little bit too long to really film. That was the time that we really got together. And that was very interesting. He was a very smart guy and a very pleasant guy to spend time with....

"I made a lot of contributions to that script. I wrote two classroom scenes on the set with the actors there, giving them lines. I wrote the speech explaining the Socratic method."[42]

Osborn also pitched in during a scene that called for Ford to reference a case. He remembered, "They needed some sort of case, so we just invented it. I'm sure there are cases like that. But that isn't how it got there. It wasn't like I had a criminal law casebook sitting there! Jim said, 'We need a case. Do you know a case?' I said, 'No, I don't know a case, but I'll write one.' He said, 'Great. So write it now.' But he would say that with a smile. The set was really a nice set where people were having fun."[43]

While Bridges deferred to Osborn when it came to aspects of the screenplay, his confidence as a director had grown by leaps and bounds since *The Baby Maker*. As Michael Preece (who had also worked on the earlier film) observed, "By that time, he knew what he was doing."[44] Bridges's evolution as a filmmaker may be measured by comparing the opening shots of his first two films. *The Baby Maker* begins with a rather graceless zoom shot. *The Paper Chase*, on the other hand, opens boldly and with great theatricality. After the Twentieth Century-Fox logo fades from the screen, an empty classroom is before us. As the titles begin, students — one by one at first and then in great clusters — fill the space. There is no music, just the gradually louder murmurs and chitchat of the assembled body. The shot — still, unmoving — suggests somehow the permanence and solidity of Harvard Law School. The imposing nature of the film's first image reflects the reverence which Hart — a hayseed from Minnesota — has for the institution he finds himself attending. When he later speaks to Susan of the futures he imagines for his fellow students ("This guy is going to be a Supreme Court justice and this guy is going to run Wall Street....") and says, "It's just when I walk down the streets, I get the feeling that behind those doors minds are being formed to run the world," the tone he is expressing to her is one of awe.

Significantly, however, we don't notice Hart as he files into the classroom in the opening shot. We aren't aware of him at all; he enters along with the hordes of others as the camera remains trained on the classroom itself. Also significantly, Professor Kingsfield does *not* make his entrance in this shot. Following a title card that reads

> HARVARD LAW SCHOOL
> Academic Year Begins

we abruptly cut to a close-up of Kingsfield's student chart, followed by a tighter close-up of a photo of Hart on the chart. Then a voice: "Mr. Hart, will you recite the facts of *Hawkins* versus *McGee*?" We cut to a wide shot of the class; somewhere among the mass of students is Hart, but it's not clear where. And then comes one of the great introductions in American movies when we see Kingsfield for the first time. There is a cut to an imposing close-up of him, looking up from the chart after calling on Hart, his head slightly cocked to one side. He continues, "I do have your name right? You are Mr. Hart?" We cut back to the wide shot of the class. An almost whispered voice is heard to say, "Yes, my name is Hart." As Kingsfield then proceeds, again in big close-ups, to repeatedly admonish Hart for not speaking loud enough, Bridges carefully adheres to the visual plan of this initial confrontation between professor and student: enormous close-ups of Kingsfield are intercut with wide shots of Hart.

It isn't until Kingsfield asks Hart to stand up that Bridges gives us a slightly tighter shot of the section of students that Hart is seated in. Hart, in fact, receives no close-ups at all in this first scene; in visual terms, as in narrative ones, Kingsfield dominates. After Hart confesses to not having read *Hawkins* versus *McGee*, Kingsfield gives the facts of the case himself. The camera moves for the first time as he steps away from the podium and walks closer to the students. Suddenly he is seen in another big close-up as he unexpectedly turns to Hart again. When we cut to Hart trying to answer Kingsfield's question, the shot is closer this time, but still dwarfed by the enormity of Kingsfield's overwhelming close-up. After failing utterly to impress in his response to the professor, Kingsfield calls on "Mr. Pruitt."

Moments later, Hart is seen in close-ups comparable in size and impact to the ones given to Kingsfield. But Hart's close-ups emphasize not his domination but rather his comparatively lowly position. Close-ups of Hart's eyes behind glasses are intercut with tight shots of the textbook he is diligently reading (determined not to be humiliated again by Kingsfield for not studying). On the page, highlighted words and phrases pop out at us: "L. HAND, Chief Judge..." and "The court took the view that while...." In some respects, these shots are the most *romantic* in the entire movie. We think, *Here is how lawyers are made.*

To whom do we attribute the visual subtlety and sophistication of Bridges's second film? On *The Paper Chase*, Bridges repaid one old friendship (by casting Houseman), but he also forged a new, equally important professional collaboration: It was his first film with cinematographer Gordon Willis. Though he had been shooting features for only three years, Willis's credits already included classics of the period such as Alan J. Pakula's *Klute* and Francis Ford Coppola's *The Godfather*. A mutual friend of Bridges and Willis, assistant director Howard Koch, Jr., who had worked on *The Baby Maker*, introduced them. "Jim was looking for someone to shoot the picture," Willis recalled.[45] Asked what interested him in the project, he said, "The piece as a whole. I just liked it. Felt very comfortable with it."[46]

And Bridges "felt very comfortable" with what the cinematographer was bringing to the table. Producer Robert C. Thompson recalled, "Jim Bridges worked very, very closely with Gordon Willis in setting up the shots and how John Houseman looms over and how Timothy Bottoms sees this person, how he's enamored with this person, and yet the power that John Houseman presents, the superiority thing that comes through in terms of the relationship between the professor and the student.... Willis is a creative cameraman and, working with the director, created the theme of the movie basically, which is long shots first and as Timothy begins to see [Houseman], how he impresses Timothy Bottoms."[47] Osborn remembered meeting with Bridges and Willis during the making of the film and hearing about Willis's formulation of "a theme for how the movie would look on the screen and the progress in terms of the picture. It starts really with Hart being seen in a long shot and pictorially it's a progression of Hart from being shot in a long shot in the classroom to being shot very up-close so he fills the screen."[48]

In his book of interviews *Principal Photography*, Vincent LoBrutto asked Willis about "the alteration of compositional size," which was most obviously evident in the scene described above. The cinematographer said, "That one was very well thought out. The whole front end of that movie with John Houseman and Timothy Bottoms related to who had command of the situation. We used huge close-ups of John, and demeaning shots of Timothy. Then, as the movie goes along and Timothy begins to get on top of it, you'll notice the shot sizes begin to diminish on John and begin to get a little bit bigger on Timothy—until finally they're equal partners shooting back and forth."[49]

The visual idea that the camera recedes from Hart when he is at his least confident in his dealings with Kingsfield is reinforced in a later scene. A moment of intense embarrassment for Hart (Kingsfield calling on him in class and Hart not knowing the answer) is not seen, but heard off-screen over a long shot of Hart walking back to his dormitory by himself.

Willis's contribution to *The Paper Chase*, as well as the three other films he shot for Bridges, should not be understated. Instantly, Bridges's films had visual gravitas. "There was never a shot list, so to speak," Willis said of how they worked together. "The overall visual structure, the concept, the look, was discussed before we began shooting each movie. The blocking was laid down from scene to scene as we would shoot. Always worked out every shot before filming any given scene. This was actually my way of working, but Jim became very secure with it, as well as everyone else. The same system prevailed on all of the films we did."[50]

"He was formidable," Edward Herrmann said of Willis. "He didn't say anything. He insisted on absolute quiet. Years later, I did a Woody Allen movie called *The Purple Rose of Cairo* and Gordon was tight with Woody at the time and he shot it. And he had the same persona, although he actually smiled. I said, 'Gordon, hello. How are you? It's been a long time.' 'Hi, Ed, how are you? Yeah, *The Paper Chase*.' And I got this sort of cool, wintry smile of his. The guys turned around and said, 'Jesus, you got Gordon to smile!' But he was absolutely focused. He was rigid. He didn't want to communicate to any of the actors except as regards his work. He did his work entirely separately. He wasn't a guy that you chatted with, unlike the sound people, unlike James, unlike a lot of other people. It wasn't that he was nasty. It was just that he was focused."[51]

Even in this, his "first proper movie," Herrmann was savvy enough to detect in Bridges what he later called "a quietness and a dependence, I felt, on Gordon. Not that Jimmy didn't know what he wanted to shoot and how he wanted to shoot it, but he deferred to Gordon on many occasions for how to do the shot or where to put the camera — not in how he wanted the scene acted."[52]

"Jim was very appreciative," Willis offered, "but visual design and blocking, these were not his cup of tea."[53] Be that as it may, Bridges obviously liked what Willis was doing photographically. To his credit, he was smart enough, early enough, to forge a relationship with one of the world's great cinematographers, someone he knew would lend his films qualities he couldn't achieve on his own. It is fitting that Willis and Houseman, alone among all of the others who worked on *The Paper Chase*, would collaborate with Bridges on his final film, *Bright Lights, Big City*, fifteen years later.

An early scene in which Kingsfield explains the Socratic method provides a superb example of Houseman's oratory (and Osborn's dialogue) coalescing with Willis's camera moves to form an elegant whole. In a wide shot, the camera tracks laterally as Kingsfield walks from screen right to screen left, the back of the heads of several rows of students visible in the foreground. "The study of law," he begins, "is something new and unfamiliar to most of you, unlike any schooling you will have been through before. We use the Socratic method here." Cut to a big close-up of Kingsfield as he further explains "this method of questioning, answering, questioning, answering," all the while walking from right to left and back again. Then, in a beautifully evocative matching of word and image, just as Kingsfield says, yet again, the words "questioning and answering," there is a cut to a shot of a group of students looking directly at the camera. As Kingsfield continues with his lecture, the camera pans, ever so gracefully, left to reveal further groups of students in the large, oval-shaped classroom. In actuality, this was not Harvard Law School, but a set designed by George Jenkins. According to Osborn, "The only person who did research on Harvard Law School was George Jenkins, who really got that classroom absolutely right. It looks exactly like one of the oldtime classrooms at Langdell Hall. They're not there any more."[54]

Willis had previously worked with Jenkins on *Klute*. "George had no ego," he remembered. "He did lovely work. We did the most to accommodate each other. He never went off half-cocked. He always showed me the floor plans and would accept changes if necessary. He trusted me and would give way if

I absolutely wanted something changed. He was also from the old school. He knew how to do stuff in motion picture terms. I miss him."[55] Bridges again worked with Jenkins six years later on *The China Syndrome*, which earned the production designer an Academy Award nomination.

* * *

At some point during the filming of *The Paper Chase*, Edward Herrmann found himself "nervous as a tick." He had been in a few scenes and thought to himself, "My God, this is much harder than I thought."[56]

To take his mind off of his work, one day he went to see *Dark Victory*, a 1939 Bette Davis film that was screening nearby as part of a festival devoted to her movies.

> There was Bette Davis chewing the scenery and I thought, "What does everybody see in this? She's just as phony as a three dollar bill." And then there was George Brent, a leading man at Warner Bros. for many years and a co-star of Bette Davis's in many of her films, and I thought, "He's wonderful. He underplays. He doesn't do anything. He's just there. He shrugs, he talks, he's very clear, he's beautifully spoken, but there's no pretension about him, there's no theatricality about him. Goddamn it, these people are *wonderful*, these actors."
>
> That film gave me this profound appreciation for American screen actors that I've cherished ever since. But I tried to take it into the work in [*The Paper Chase*]. So I remember vividly the first close-up that I had in one of those study scenes around the table. Suddenly it was my turn and the camera was in my face with this great big lens. And I was scared to death. But I knew my lines, so I did my performance and I got through it, bang. And Jim said, "Ed, that was great. Print that, that was great, that was great. But I think we could have heard that in the balcony. Can you pull it down a little bit to the..." I said, "To the mezzanine?" He said, "Fine, great, the mezzanine." We did it again. He said, "Great, great, fine. Pull it back a little more. About halfway up the orchestra." And we were finally down to the front row about four takes later! By the time I finished, he got exactly what he wanted, but I felt as if I hadn't done anything. I said, "Jim, I haven't *acted*, I haven't done my thing, I haven't *shaped* the line!" He said, "Believe me, believe me, it's wonderful. Just wonderful. The lens loves you, just speak it, just say it." And it was the gentleness and respect that he showed ... I never forgot the way he handled me and taught me how to pull it back, pull it back, pull it back. The impulses have to be the same. Acting on stage and acting in front of the camera is the same, except in terms of the size. You have to fill a great big room when you're in the theatre and you don't have to fill anything when you're in front of the camera. But his gentleness ... I never saw him lose his temper about anything. He was wonderful.[57]

Herrmann's description of the low-key nature of Bridges's direction is echoed by Sam Waterston's memory of *A Meeting by the River*:

Three. Hart and Kingsfield, Bridges and Houseman

Actors sometimes say about directors that they helped them find things themselves. It's easy to think that that kind of director isn't really having very much of an impact. At the time that you're doing it, you can almost think that you are doing it all yourself. But it's an illusion that you don't really understand until you look back on it. I was delighted with the investigation as far as it got and it was only afterwards that I began to think, "Oh, wow, he enabled this and he pointed it. We just never felt his hand." They're not the same kinds of people or the same kinds of director, really, except that they do share this. I was the assistant stage manager for Mike Nichols and general understudy on *The Knack* and the actors were completely under the impression that they were making the whole thing up themselves. But from the outside it was perfectly apparent that they were in the hands of somebody who really knew where he was going.[58]

That Bridges used a gently guiding hand with Herrmann and other young actors is understandable. But what of John Houseman, who, at seventy-one, found himself in the same boat as those more than half his age? In his memoir, Houseman allowed that he "had a few secret misgivings over my ability ... to memorize the long speeches uttered by the professor."[59] When asked about Houseman, Herrmann remembered a first-time movie actor who was, at least initially, very insecure:

> I remember the first day he arrived. Here was this guy and I had vaguely heard of him. I didn't realize what an enormous reputation he had from the Mercury Theatre and as a producer. I found his manner kind of imperial. His first take was behind a desk with Tim in Kingsfield's office. And I saw him working and I saw that he was scared to death. He was nervous and was just trying to get through the words with this sort of generalized pomposity, this generalized character of Kingsfield. I thought, "This poor old fart. He doesn't know *anything.* We have to be nice to this poor old guy." We'd already heard the story that Bridges had tried to get James Cagney and felt that he had gotten some positive input and then Cagney himself said no. And then Melvyn Douglas, who had heart problems and the studio wouldn't insure him, and then finally Houseman. So I thought, "Oh, this poor guy is coming third string."
> Then when I saw him work in the classroom, I thought, "Well, he's getting more confident." I remember the first rehearsal in there, he came in and he took a look at the room — there were sixty or seventy actors and extras — and I thought he was a little bit bowled over when he first saw it. But he went at it and he focused and he did his thing. I thought, "Pretty good, pretty good. A little monotonous, he's got the same rhythm take after take after take, but, yeah, this is going to work. This is great."
> So the first thing I saw was a man who was struggling to master his own nervousness and his own fear, which he did. Then afterwards when we started to talk and he relaxed a little bit, I found him really interesting.[60]

Graham Beckel recalled, "When we went to work in the morning, everybody would make Eddie Herrmann sit next to Houseman because everybody else was so goddamned intimidated by him! Eddie could at least reel off some crap about the Group Theatre and all of that!"[61]

Whatever Bridges said to Houseman, and whatever inner reserves Houseman drew on as filming progressed, few could argue with the final result. Pauline Kael was tepid in her praise of *The Paper Chase* in her review in *The New Yorker*—except when it came to Houseman's performance: "The movie ... is a job of manufacture—a modern commercial version of a problem play—*cum*—Socratic dialogue—but at its center Houseman, who carries the weight of his years and the stiff elegance of his personal authority, brings the picture his own authenticity."[62] Houseman won the Academy Award for Best Supporting Actor for his performance as Professor Kingsfield. In his acceptance speech, after acknowledging the *Paper Chase* cast and crew, and singling out Gordon Willis, he thanked "thirdly, fourthly, and fifthly" his "dear friend," James Bridges.[63] Within a few years of *The Paper Chase*, Houseman was acting in films left and right: Sydney Pollack's *Three Days of the Condor*, Joan Tewkesbury's *Old Boyfriends*, John Carpenter's *The Fog*, and many others.

* * *

Kingsfield tells his class, "My little questions are the fingers probing your brain." His next line—"We do brain surgery here"—is spoken by Houseman over a close-up of an enraptured Hart. Then, in a profile close-up, Kingsfield continues, "You teach yourselves the law but I train your mind. You come in here with a skull full of mush and you leave thinking like a lawyer." Immediately after the word "mush" is spoken (with great relish), there is a cut to another close-up of Hart, his mouth betraying a hint of a smile. When, a scene later, in the first meeting of the study group, Hart volunteers to outline contract law—in contrast to Kevin (James Naughton), who bitterly proclaims that he "hates that son of a bitch Kingsfield"—his affinity for his professor is confirmed.

Osborn sees it differently. "[Hart] is not grateful to him. I mean, when he throws the grades away, he's saying the whole system sucks and Kingsfield is the personification of the system," he said.[64] But it was Houseman himself who described the ending of the film—which has Hart making a paper plane out of his unopened grades and launching it into the ocean—as "soft and disappointing."[65] It's worse than that; in my view, it's inconsistent with the depiction of the relationship that exists between Hart and Kingsfield, which I take to be a reflection of the relationship that really existed between Bridges and Houseman and therefore contains no element of rebelliousness or discontent. (The ending works better in the novel.)

In *Easy Riders, Raging Bulls*, Peter Biskind argued that Peter Bogdanovich "was aesthetically, at least, quite conservative.... In contrast to authority-bashing, adult-baiting pictures like *Bonnie and Clyde*, *Easy Rider*, and *MASH*, *The Last Picture Show* is reverential toward its patriarch, Ben Johnson's Sam the Lion, who is the film's teacher, law-giver, fount of values."[66] Could not the very same words be said of Kingsfield? No less than Bogdanovich in *The Last Picture Show*, Bridges in *The Paper Chase* presents its "patriarch" reverently. While the film is seen from Hart's point of view — only once do we see Kingsfield alone in a scene not also featuring Hart or others — and while we are certainly sympathetic to Hart's fear, anger, and frustration, we finally come around to Kingsfield's perspective, as Hart does. Even in the film's first scene, it is hard to take Hart's side. Objectively speaking, Kingsfield is correct: Hart *does* need to speak more loudly. Perhaps this is why, much later in the film, Kingsfield commends, rather than rebukes, Hart for standing up to him in class and calling him a "son of a bitch." "That's the most intelligent thing you've said all day," Kingsfield tells Hart. He knows that good lawyers cannot be mealy-mouthed, that they must speak with conviction.

On the last day of class, after Kingsfield says to his charges, "Thank you. Good luck with your exam. You'll need it," Hart stands and applauds. He is joined almost immediately by the rest of the class. Kingsfield turns briefly and acknowledges the applause, but only barely. Close-ups of Miss Farranti (Blair Brown), Ford (who looks to Hart, grinning), and Hart follow, as everyone continues to clap. It is they who have gotten so much from Kingsfield, not Kingsfield from them, and it's nothing personal; it's his job. ("Personal comment is not necessary," he scolds Anderson after the telling of an anecdote in class.) In light of his apathetic response to this outburst of appreciation, Kingsfield's later interactions with Hart — such as the famous scene in which he seems not to remember Hart's name after the student thanks him for what his class has meant to him — seem less callous. "There's one question that Jim asked and John Houseman asked, which is a central question, which is, 'Does Kingsfield really not remember Hart's name?'" Osborn said. "And of course Kingsfield knows Hart's name. He has to. He'd be an idiot if he didn't know Hart's name. But the trick in the book and the movie is to make you think it's possible that he doesn't."[67] By Osborn's reckoning, this act means that "Kingsfield and Harvard Law School are not honoring the implicit contract they made with Hart when they accepted him. They are teaching contract law, but they are violating the principles of the law they teach."[68] I don't think that is the case. Kingsfield is not obligated to be Hart's friend; he is obligated to "train his mind," and since Osborn rightly described Hart as "one of the best students Kingsfield has ever had in contract law,"[69] it seems clear that Kingsfield's methods have succeeded.

To the extent that the Bridges-Hart, Houseman-Kingsfield parallels I suggest have merit, it is inconceivable to imagine Bridges doing what Hart does in the finale: throwing the symbol of his relationship with Houseman-Kingsfield to the wind. Bridges always remained profoundly grateful to Houseman and the others who served as teachers to him. "Before there was Kingsfield there was John Houseman," Bridges later said. "He was the Kingsfield to many of the actors, producers, directors on the American stage today."[70] Conflating Houseman with Kingsfield was a term of endearment, as far as Bridges was concerned. Critic Jay Cocks, reviewing the film in *Time*, found the ending "infuriating" because Hart's "last, too easy gesture of mocking his achievement thus looks not only frivolous and empty-headed but contemptuous."[71] Cocks perceptively viewed this gesture as incongruous with the rest of *The Paper Chase*. In a similar vein, in his capsule review in *The Village Voice*, Andrew Sarris praised the film as a "pro-grind, anti-dropout, postgraduate, anti–*Graduate* reversion to traditional competitive values" but decried the ending as "pure cop-out."[72]

Bridges's friend and collaborator Jack Bender commented, "I think Jim in a lot of ways was cautious. He was very protective, I think, of his brain. He did his share of partying, I'm sure, but I don't think he wanted to fuck up the work. I think that there was something a little conservative about Jim in those ways."[73] Bridges's "conservatism"—which had nothing to do with politics and everything to do with the way in which he chose to lead his life and conduct his career—is obvious from his films, particularly *The Paper Chase*, which depicts Harvard Law School so respectfully. What's more, the film's most fondly remembered character is not Hart, but Kingsfield. Clancy Sigal was onto something when he suggested that the "ambitious young hero, not the professor, is the villain," though I obviously reject completely his assertion that "Bridges seems totally unaware"[74] of this and I am dubious of the notion that any character in Bridges's early work deserves to be called a "villain." (This is not true of some later films.)

Lest we forget that the year of the release of *The Paper Chase*—1973—was also the year that another product of Harvard Law School, Attorney General Elliot Richardson, an establishment figure if there ever was one, became heroic in the eyes of many Americans for his courageous defiance of President Richard Nixon, resigning his post rather than following the president's orders to fire Watergate special prosecutor Archibald Cox. As author Geoffrey Kabaservice noted, "Amid the whole sordid business ... Richardson and Cox stood out as shining examples of public virtue, defenders of a government of laws not men, and representatives of an older, less crass and self-centered tradition of American leadership."[75] A fictional creation of the same cultural moment, Houseman-as-Kingsfield possesses many of the same attributes of Richardson and Cox, as described by Kabaservice.

* * *

Osborn had nothing but admiration for the way Bridges expanded the character of Susan. Her having been married and divorced prior to meeting Hart adds to her exoticism, which is expressed in visual terms, too. Consider the way Bridges and Willis introduce her: Hart is seen exiting a pizzeria one night after class, the camera dollying along with him, when, walking at a faster pace than he is, Susan seems to float into frame from behind him, saying she's being followed and requesting that Hart accompany her to her door. Even Pauline Kael had to admit to the beguiling ambiguity of Lindsay Wagner's portrayal of Susan when she wrote that "you can't decide whether she's hateful-looking or beautiful or both simultaneously."[76]

If Willis brought a new level of distinction to Bridges's films photographically, a familiar presence joined him in the editing room. The editor of *The Baby Maker*, Walter Thompson, returned to cut *The Paper Chase*. Osborn remembered him as "a real sweet guy. Very, very nice and always like, 'This is what I'm doing. What do you think? Let's talk about it.' He was terrific. He was very methodical."[77]

Thompson's filmography has a beautiful symmetry to it. He has one film about a lawyer in the making (John Ford's *Young Mr. Lincoln*) near the beginning of his career, and another (*The Paper Chase*) near the end. There is that immortal scene in Ford's classic depicting Lincoln (Henry Fonda) reading *Blackstone's Commentaries* under a tree. He says to himself, "Law. That's the rights of persons and the rights of things. The rights of life, reputation, and liberty. The rights to acquire and hold property. 'Wrongs are violations of those rights.' By jing, that's all there is to it. Right and wrong."

Professor Kingsfield couldn't have said it better himself. In an altogether delightful coincidence, Osborn, who now teaches at the University of San Francisco School of Law, shows *Young Mr. Lincoln* as part of a class called Law and Literature.[78]

* * *

Following its release in October 1973, *The Paper Chase* received three Academy Award nominations: Houseman for Best Supporting Actor, Bridges for Best Screenplay Based on Material from Another Medium, and Donald O. Mitchell and Larry Jost for Best Sound. Houseman was the only one to walk away a winner, but for Bridges the cliché must have rung true: It *was* an honor just to have been nominated. Only a few years earlier, he had to persuade National General Pictures that he was capable of directing at all. Now he was an Oscar-nominated director (even if he was being recognized as a screenwriter).

For Osborn, the saga of *The Paper Chase* didn't end with its release. A successful television series derived from the novel followed and, along with it, so too did a "wonderfully friendly" relationship with Bridges. Osborn recalled,

> I went to his house, which was great. Jack Larson and he went to our house many times. We saw each other when he would come to New York. I wasn't a close friend with him in the sense that Gordon Willis was. I wasn't in the business and I didn't want to be in the business. By accident, I ended up writing quite a lot of television, but I've never lived in Hollywood, had no desire to be anywhere near Hollywood.
>
> There are whole different kinds of levels that are operating here and I'll give you an example. Houseman was a member of a club in New York called the Century Association. Well, my grandfather, my uncles were all members of that club. It's a very old time New York club. Houseman and I had lunch there I don't know how many times. So we shared a certain thing that Jim and I didn't share and he wouldn't have been interested in anyway. I'm not quite sure of the point I'm trying to make. We were friends, but we had limited shared interests.[79]

Edward Herrmann's film career was launched. After *The Paper Chase*, plum roles in Mike Nichols's *The Day of the Dolphin* and George Roy Hill's *The Great Waldo Pepper* soon followed. "I find it a very important step because it was the first fully rounded character integrated into a very good script, an intelligent script, with intelligent dialogue and beautifully shot. It was an adult movie; it was a movie for grown-ups," Herrmann said. "And it was shot in a way that showed tremendous respect to what I had to offer. It made me feel as if I was a competent film actor when I left. I'd done a film that I could say, I didn't just drive a car through a wall, I wasn't a zombie, I wasn't something I need be embarrassed about. This was a film in which I had to speak and interact with other actors. I had intelligent dialogue. And I was treated as an artist. It made me tremendously confident the next time I went in to audition."[80]

Herrmann also remained grateful for the latitude Bridges gave him to create one of the most memorable characters in *The Paper Chase*. His Anderson isn't the star, like Bottoms's Hart is, and he doesn't have as many scenes as Graham Beckel's Ford. But he makes an impression. For example, Anderson is seen smoking a pipe in nearly every scene set outside of the classroom. "I plead guilty to that," Herrmann laughed. "It's such an impossible pretension for a college kid to be smoking a pipe. He wants to be thirty-five or forty in his Turkish velvet smoking jacket. It's just silly. And he's smoking Mixture Seventy-nine in some heavily aromatic blend.... Well, I wouldn't have done it if [Bridges] didn't like it. I was the only one who had it, so he liked it."[81]

"He was non-demanding," Beckel remembered. "He listened like few directors I have worked with since. He just listened. He dignified everything that was being said and any need that was being expressed. Jim didn't give off any fear.... Not once did I see him be judgmental with anyone. He was very easygoing, very mild-mannered. In this way, he was very assured."[82]

Every actor in *The Paper Chase* made a success of themselves. Beckel became familiar to audiences from such films as Curtis Hanson's *L.A. Confidential* and Ang Lee's *Brokeback Mountain*. James Naughton has been a fixture on network television for many years, and he made a particular impression playing the gentleman caller in Paul Newman's masterful screen adaptation of *The Glass Menagerie*. Lindsay Wagner was, of course, *The Bionic Woman*. Even Bottoms, whose career in many respects peaked with *The Paper Chase*, had several more noteworthy films in him, including Philip Kaufman's *The White Dawn* and Peter Bogdanovich's sequel to *The Last Picture Show*, *Texasville*.

John Houseman was prolific, too. In 1988, the year of his death, he appeared in no fewer than three films, including Bridges's own *Bright Lights, Big City*, and two made-for-television movies. And it was all thanks to the man whom he thanked "thirdly, fourthly, and fifthly."

* * *

The television version of *The Paper Chase* debuted five years after the film was released, airing first on CBS, then on public television, and finally on Showtime during the course of its four seasons. "I was shocked at how long the *Paper Chase* TV show went on," Osborn said. "The first three seasons, I wrote a lot of it. And then I got tired of it. I was like, 'Wait a minute. I can't keep doing this my whole life.' If you look at the credits, you'll see that that fourth season, I think I wrote one [episode]. I could write one any time I wanted. But it kept going! Houseman was unstoppable! I was like, 'We can't keep doing this, John!'"[83]

Bridges's involvement in the show was, according to Osborn, "peripheral," especially after the first season. As Jack Larson explained, Bridges lent his name and time to the show primarily as a favor to Houseman, who "wanted to make every penny he could after he became a star. He had two sons and a very expensive, wonderful wife, Joan. He'd given up everything to go found Jilliard. He'd never made big money. They had sold their lovely house in Malibu. He wanted to make money. This offer came to turn it into a television series. Jim would have done anything for John on Earth. He absolutely loved John, worshipped John, who was worshipful. Fox would go with this whole thing if Jim would create the series, so Jim did. He created the series. For at least the first season, he read all the scripts and helped the writers and suggested writers. He did everything you were supposed to do. It was a successful series up to a point."[84]

Bridges wrote the pilot for the series, the idea for which was supplied to him by Osborn. Osborn said,

> It was important for Jim to write the pilot to get the thing made. He couldn't think of anything to write it about because he didn't know any more about law school, you know? All he knew about law school was *The Paper Chase*. So there's a famous story at Harvard Law School about the shrouding, which is a true story. Way before my time, a professor actually does what Houseman did in that pilot episode. "This is a shroud and I will never call on you again." So Jim took that idea and produced that episode. That was a good episode. That helped. But then we had to produce two other episodes. One of them was all right and the other one, the screenwriter completely didn't know what he was doing. He just had no idea what law school was about, so Houseman sent him down to my house. For two days, we essentially wrote a screenplay, which became one of the episodes in the package that went to CBS.[85]

Beyond this, however, Bridges "was not at the TV show," Osborn said.

> And he didn't want to be. He did one more script, but only because Houseman sat on him. He didn't want to do it. One thing I'll never forget: The TV show got in trouble, so Houseman said, "Osborn, you've got to come out here." Houseman had basically fired everybody except the actors and one wonderful oldtime producer who was around until the bitter end. He was great. But Jim picked me up at the airport, which was kind of cool. He was driving this Volkswagen Beetle. And that was it. He took me to the hotel and we went down and I don't remember if we had a drink or we had tea or something at the hotel. We kind of caught up. He was like, "Well, I'm not going to have anything to do with the TV show. I've got other things to do. I've got to get out of here before Houseman comes over!"[86]

Bridges used the series as a way to give opportunities to old friends like Jack Bender. As Bender recalled, "John Houseman came from the time when he was producing great films for MGM when there were dialogue coaches. Guys like George Cukor would come out from New York to direct the actors and the 'camera directors' would direct the camera, and then that became one job. John Houseman had a very young cast on *The Paper Chase* and felt like he wanted a dialogue coach to work with them, not only to run their lines, but just help them out and support them."[87]

Bridges suggested Bender, who had by now resolved to become a director. To fill the slot, "John thought it was a brilliant idea and called me at like six in the morning," Bender said.

> I had no money. I was living at my parents' house. It was a transition between living with Ritter and finding out where I was going to live next. John called me and said, "Bender! How would you like to do this?" "Oh my God, that sounds wonderful!" So I went to work on *The Paper Chase*....
> Because John Houseman was John Houseman, and because I had written

and directed a short film that got a lot of attention simultaneous to that, he was able to force Fox Television to allow me to direct, which of course Fox Television didn't want any part of.[88]

Bender ultimately directed eight episodes of the show. It was his first big break as a director and the beginning of a long and acclaimed career in film and television. In May 2010, Bender directed the much-anticipated series finale of *Lost* on ABC. Bender said:

> I remember just breathing that rarefied air, being around Houseman and Bridges, sitting around the office together drinking Scotch at the end of the night. I just learned so much from the way Houseman worked. He was in his seventies at the time. I remember it was when I was about to direct my first episode and they threw it out and the network didn't like it. And John Osborn and Houseman and Bridges had come up with another idea. I was supposed to start directing like the next day. They were furiously re-writing this script. Houseman was at the office, after acting, editing, and everything until 10:30 at night, and we were all having a drink. Then he left and got in his car. And it was raining. Suddenly, five minutes later, we heard this furious honking of a horn and we went down and stood on the balcony of the writers building at Fox. We looked out and Houseman was standing with his umbrella in front of his headlights in the rain and said, "Bender, I have one more idea!" I thought that was so inspiring. There's always one more idea.[89]

Four

Going Home: September 30, 1955

James Bridges must have known that his third film would have to be important — look at how long he took to make it. Five years passed from the release of *The Paper Chase* in 1973 to the release of *September 30, 1955* in 1978. This was to be the longest period between films in Bridges's career. (By contrast, starting with *September 30, 1955* in 1978, he kept a John Ford–like pace for several years: *The China Syndrome* was released one year after *September 30, 1955*, followed by *Urban Cowboy* in 1980.)

If Bridges had only directed *The Baby Maker* and *The Paper Chase* or had continued to make films on the level of those films, it's doubtful that a book on his work would ever have been written; I certainly wouldn't have written this one. Instead, what Bridges produced in his third film was, as the headline of a *New York Times* piece by Janet Maslin put it, "A Great Movie — If It Comes Out."[1] As much as *The Paper Chase* was an improvement over *The Baby Maker*, *September 30, 1955* was a major advance over *The Paper Chase*, in theme, in style, in personal expression. *September 30, 1955* is, with Bob Rafelson's *The King of Marvin Gardens*, Peter Bogdanovich's *Daisy Miller*, Charles Burnett's *Killer of Sheep*, and a few select others, among the very greatest of American films of the 1970s — simply put, a masterpiece.

The years between *The Paper Chase* and *September 30, 1955* were not spent idly, however. Eight months before *The Paper Chase* was released, *Carola*, which Bridges adapted from a play by Jean Renoir, the director of *Le regle du jeu* and *The Golden Coach*, aired on Los Angeles public television. It reunited Bridges with Norman Lloyd, who was the show's producer and director. Lloyd explained the genesis of the project:

> Renoir had written the piece originally in French. It had been translated a number of years before by some professors up at the University of California at Berkeley. I was very impressed by the piece — wonderful piece. I wanted Jean to do it, but he was not well. It was the last years of his life and his

health was very bad. So Jean asked me to produce and direct it, which I readily consented to do. Now the translation was, in my view, not very smooth. I thought about putting someone on it. I did think about Jim, and Jim — and I quote him now — said, "I want that credit." He wanted to be identified with Jean Renoir, as the world did. Renoir was one of the greats.[2]

Bridges's credit—"Adaptation by James Bridges"—is in some respects misleading. After all, Bridges lacked familiarity with the subject matter (as was the case on *The Paper Chase*). "It was a story about the occupation in France in the Second World War, and Jim's knowledge of it was remote," Lloyd said. "But he did have a sense of the writing and he smoothed out the awkwardness in the actual text. He didn't reconstruct anything, didn't rewrite anything in the sense of changing character. The story is all Jean.... Jim's job was sort of adapting the language. Jim wrote lovely dialogue that was very speakable. In that sense, that's what he did with the Renoir thing, but he left the story, the structure, the characters all the same."[3]

Leslie Caron, the iconic star of *An American in Paris* and *Gigi*, played the title role. Jack Larson said, "Jean was here and hadn't worked in years. He'd written this play really for Ingrid Bergman. He'd written two plays, one that Leslie did in Paris and he wrote this one for Ingrid Bergman, who was also a friend, but she never did it."[4]

The matter of the part having been intended for Bergman proved to be a sticky one, said Norman Lloyd:

> When I read it, I thought Leslie would be absolutely perfect. But in the course of that time, Ingrid Bergman was very close to the Renoirs, as was Leslie, and Ingrid heard about the piece. We hadn't gone into rehearsal yet and I hadn't really firmed up the casting. However, one afternoon, shortly before we were to really settle on the cast, Ingrid Bergman was at the Renoirs. Mrs. Renoir called me and said, "Ingrid is here and she'd love to see you." And I knew what she wanted. I knew her because I spent ninety-nine days as [Lewis] Milestone's associate on *Arch of Triumph*, which she did with [Charles] Boyer and Charles Laughton and Lou Calhern. So I ducked. I never showed up. I loved Ingrid, I think she's done some wonderful work, but this character was Leslie to me. So the Renoirs just rode with the situation. Ingrid left and I think she went back to Sweden shortly after. As far as Leslie was concerned, she was eager to do it and was wonderful while we did it. So that's the story of *Carola*. Jim wanted that credit — and he got it![5]

* * *

One example of the rarefied company Bridges kept in those days is that he seamlessly went from adapting Jean Renoir for television to directing Tennessee Williams on stage. In March 1973, the twenty-fifth anniversary production of *A Streetcar Named Desire*, which Bridges directed at the invitation

Bridges and Helen Owens performing at a homecoming parade. Bridges shot the opening and final shots of *September 30, 1955* on this very street. (Courtesy of the University of Central Arkansas Archives.)

of Williams, opened at the Ahmanson Theatre in Los Angeles. Larson said it was "the most commercially successful production they ever had at the Ahmanson," but that Bridges "was very reluctant to do it."[6]

"One of the difficulties in working with this play is that you know too much," Bridges told the *Los Angeles Times*. "It's been performed so many times in so many places.... But our *Streetcar* is being made out of the solids — out of Faye [Dunaway], out of Jon [Voight], out of me."[7] Dunaway and Voight played Blanche DuBois and Stanley Kowalski, respectively.

Bridges stressed the novelty of his staging: "We went back to the Signet paperback which has only Tennessee's directions," he said.[8] As Dunaway explained in her memoir, *Looking for Gatsby*, "When we began rehearsals, Jim Bridges said he wanted to try to return, as much as possible, to Tennessee's original vision for the play. He had unearthed an early version of the play that included Tennessee's first ideas on stage direction."[9]

Bridges said that the production was to be "very romantic. It's a red *Streetcar*. The set (by Robert Tyler Lee) is very realistic but full of hot, sexual colors — a plum living room, a red bedroom like the inside of a mouth or womb."[10]

Inevitably, however, much of the critical attention focused not on matters of dramatic interpretation but on "Faye and Jon," who were then two of the biggest stars in Hollywood. The consensus seemed to be that she was better than he. "If Miss Dunaway could bring a little more moonlight into her performance without obscuring Blanche's basic honesty, this would be a great performance," Dan Sullivan wrote in the *Los Angeles Times*. "It stands now as an individual, sympathetic and, as I have indicated, very funny one."[11] *The New York Times*'s Stephen Farber was also impressed: "It must be a rare production when Blanche gets more laughs than Stanley, but that happens here. Dunaway's timing is expert," he wrote.[12]

Like all actors, Dunaway loved working with Bridges, and it is obvious that she flourished under his gentle hand. "Jim Bridges was the sort of director who trusts his actors," she wrote. "He was a lovely man. A director, he said, had a place, but it was never to overtake the rest of us."[13]

"I think Jim had an extraordinary gift of Zen directing," Jack Bender said. "He said to me once, when he was doing *The Paper Chase*, that the publicist from Fox came up and said to him at one point, 'What do you do?' Jim was amused by that. This guy felt like you've got to be shouting and you've got to be standing on top of the camera and doing all of that Otto Preminger directing! Both in the theatre and in film, that was not Jim's style at all. Jim's style was much more like a patient gardener who would plant the seeds and let them start to sprout and then probably, unbeknownst to you, direct the way the sunlight was coming in based on how he wanted it to grow, but he still allowed you to grow."[14] (Dunaway would appreciate Bender contrasting Bridges with Preminger, who directed her in his film *Hurry Sundown*, an experience she described in scathing terms in her book.)

Voight's performance elicited a more muted response, not unlike the performance itself, if the critics' accounts are to be believed. Sullivan decried its "boyishness."[15] Farber wrote that the actor's "studious attempt to underplay the role" was "disastrous."[16] Years later, Bridges was ungallant when he called working with Voight and Dunaway "positively the worst experience I've ever had in my life."[17] It couldn't have been *that* bad, given the near-unanimous praise Dunaway received, and the kind things she would say about working with him.

Williams himself was never anything but generous in talking about the production. As he gushed in a 1973 essay, "Having Faye Dunaway, Jon Voight, and Earl Holliman in *A Streetcar Named Desire* under the brilliant, young director James Bridges, is not an occasion for me to take at all casually, and that is one thing, for sure."[18] Let's let him have the last word.

* * *

Other projects arose during these years but none came to fruition. There was, for example, Bridges's adaptation of John Updike's 1965 novel *Of the Farm*. Larson contended that the screenplay "is absolutely equivalent to *The Glass Menagerie*."[19]

Bridges became aware of the novel, published in between two far better—remembered Updike novels, *The Centaur* and *Couples*, through his friend Joe LeSueur. "Jim got Joe the job of looking for properties through Bob Wise's company," Larson said. "Joe had been an editor at a book company in New York and was also a writer and sometimes wrote soap operas. Joe found this property and thought it would make a good film.... Jim read [*Of the Farm*] and I read it, and we thought it would be a very good movie."[20]

Coincidentally, the co-star of *A Meeting by the River*, Laurence Luckinbill, had optioned the rights to *Of the Farm* in the mid-seventies. According to Luckinbill,

> The rights had been negotiated by Tim Seldes, who is Marian Seldes's brother. I wrote a film based on the book, very closely connected to the book. I started shopping the film and I got some interest, but not a lot, just on the basis of the script. Then somebody said, "Get a star attached to it," so I called Katharine Hepburn, because I happened to be on Broadway and knew people who knew Katharine Hepburn. And she invited me to her house on 49th Street. I went there and I spent six hours with this extraordinary human being. She refused to let me put a log on the fire: "I can do that!" It was just astounding. She told me how shitty the script was and how poorly written and how Updike was a weasel and a wimp and how this was a very unmanly leading man. Finally, I'd had enough of this and I said, "Miss Hepburn, that is the *point* of the whole story: that you are a domineering mother who won't take no for an answer. This man brings a new wife home to the farm to save your ass because you've gotten too old to handle things. He handles things and you try to break him up with his wife. And lo and behold, he takes his wife and goes back to New York once things have been handled." That's the story and that's the key thing. And she said, "You may use my name, but you won't have any success with it." Meaning, her name.
>
> And it was so true. I had meeting after meeting with the biggies and they said, "Katharine Hepburn? No, thanks a lot. She's not box office." I mean, it was *astounding!* So I kept the rights for another year or so after that experience. I kept renewing them and it wasn't cheap. Tim drove a hard bargain for Updike, of course.
>
> Anyway, I get a call one day from James Bridges. He said, "Larry, you've got something I want." I said, "I do?" He said, "Yeah, it's *Of the Farm*. I know you've written a good screenplay of it because—believe it or not—I've read it." I said, "Oh, really?" He said, "Are you done with it? Because I really want to get it and make my own movie of it." I said yes and so it went to him. I said, "Take your shot." He took a shot and couldn't do it either.[21]

Bridges encountered the same peculiar difficulty as Luckinbill in getting the film off the ground: the presence of Hepburn. Larson said, "Several of the studios said if we could get Bette Davis ... but Kate was a friend, number one. We knew her through Salka Viertel and Peter [Viertel], and she was a friend and she was committed and she wanted to do it. We could not get it made with her."[22]

"It would have been a sensational part for Miss Hepburn," Luckinbill lamented. "But I actually thought at the time that probably Jimmy would do a better job on the script than I had, although I liked my script."[23]

Of all of the film projects Bridges wasn't able to realize, and they are legion, perhaps it is *Of the Farm* that one longs most to see, and not only because of the possibilities suggested by a Bridges-Hepburn collaboration. Updike's work is terribly underrepresented on the screen; only two of his novels, *Rabbit, Run* and *The Witches of Eastwick*, have been made into films, and the results were middling in both cases. Fielder Cook's television adaptation of the author's famed Maples stories, *Too Far To Go*, is substantially better, and probably more along the lines of what Bridges would have done, in terms of its faithfulness to Updike. Indeed, it seems safe to assume that the man who successfully transmitted the disparate visions of such authors as Ray Bradbury, John Jay Osborn, Jr., and Jay McInerney to the screen was more than up to the challenge.

* * *

In a 1979 *New York Times* profile of Joan Didion, literary critic Michiko Kakutani quoted from Didion's collection of essays *The White Album*: "Kilimanjaro belongs to Ernest Hemingway. Oxford, Mississippi, belongs to William Faulkner ... a great deal of Honolulu has always belonged to James Jones.... A place belongs forever to whoever claims it hardest, remembers it most obsessively, wrenches it from itself, shapes it, renders it, loves it so radically that he remakes it in his image." Kakutani then added, "California belongs to Joan Didion."[24] She was right, of course, and I can say with every bit as much surety that Arkansas "belongs" to James Bridges.

Striking a similar chord, the novelist Frederick Buechner once defined the word "home" as "a place where you feel, or did feel once, uniquely *at home*, which is a way to say a place where you feel you belong and that in some sense belongs to you, a place where you feel that all is somehow ultimately well even if things aren't going all that well at any given moment."[25]

"I love coming home," Bridges told *The Log Cabin Democrat*.[26] Twenty years after moving from Arkansas, he returned home to artistically claim the place he was from in the same way that Hemingway and Faulkner and Jones and Didion had. In 1976, Bridges shot *September 30, 1955*, his most explicitly autobiographical film, in and around Conway, Arkansas. The origins of the project were modest enough. He told Janet Maslin that he wrote the screenplay in three weeks,[27] perhaps owing to the fact that it wasn't the first time he had grappled with the material. According to Lee Grant in the *Los Angeles Times*, it "came out of a play Bridges wrote a few years back." Bridges explained, "I called it *How Many Times Have You Seen* East of Eden? and did it in 1966 in North Carolina. Then I put it aside. After *Paper Chase*, I picked it up again and wrote a screenplay."[28]

In truth, Bridges had been contemplating making a film about his days as a James Dean-obsessed undergraduate at Arkansas State Teachers College for a very long time. His friend from those days, Tom Bonner, recalled, "Jim was always saying, 'I'm going to write a movie someday about this whole experience and then I'll direct it. So we'll all be in a movie.' We all laughed and it was a big joke. But sure enough, he did."[29]

September 30, 1955 "got off the ground very quickly with a producer, Jerry Weintraub, who had a deal at Universal and was very interested in Jim's work," Larson said. "It was quite quickly greenlighted and Jim went back to Arkansas and shot it."[30] Bridges spoke glowingly of Weintraub, whom he compared to John Houseman, which was high praise indeed. "Both get you working with a kind of positivism and not the sort of bickering negativism so many producers use to provoke people," he said.[31] Weintraub, formerly a music producer, would go on to produce a string of hits in the 1980s, including *Diner* and the *Karate Kid* series. But in 1976, he had one feature film to his name, Robert Altman's *Nashville*, making *September 30, 1955*, Bridges's third film, Weintraub's second. "The film was not something that Universal wanted to make," said Gordon Willis. "It had no commercial appeal, as they saw it, and as a result, the final go-ahead was barely given, and the money was nothing. Shoestring productions." Nevertheless, Willis remembered the set as "a rather friendly and cozy atmosphere surrounded with a lot of nice people and Jim's friends."[32]

As Jimmy J., the film's protagonist and the stand-in for the youthful Bridges, the director cast Richard Thomas, best known as John-Boy on TV's *The Waltons*, who had a three-picture deal at Universal. "I think I was one of the last stable actors—and I'm not talking about emotional configurations, I'm talking about contractual obligations," Thomas joked. "My first picture there was called *Winning* and then I did a picture called *Red Sky at Morning*, and then I owed them one picture. When this came up, Jim wanted me and it worked out. I'd met him a few times in company and just socially, as you do out there. But we became good friends, as I think most people did who worked with him. He developed very, very good personal relationships with colleagues and especially actors, who really liked him a lot."[33]

Thomas found himself in the odd position of portraying a fictionalized version of his director. Yet he didn't feel hemmed in by this fact.

> Jim never put a grid over the piece. Maybe some directors would have: "This is me when I did this" and "This is how I felt about that." I think that would have been a little hobbling for an actor. He had been an actor, he was a writer and a director, and he really did have a multivalent point of view about the process. He could see it from many different people's perspectives, which is one of the reasons he was very good, I think, to work with. I think he knew that giving one-to-one correspondences would be probably not the best thing.
>
> But it was very clear that this was a personal piece of material. He said that he was influenced by James Dean. I knew that he was from Arkansas and I knew that it was about Arkansas and I knew that it was sort of a fictional account of leaving home and how the inspiration that you take — for some people it's writers and it doesn't have to be even in the arts. My dad left a mining town in eastern Kentucky to become a ballet dancer. He would go to the movies and he knew that those were real people out there doing that. It was that story of what gets you to leave home and move on and find the life you want to have.[34]

Wielding the clout he won with the success of *The Paper Chase*, Bridges persuaded Universal to allow him to make the film in Conway, when most studios would have insisted on finding a West Coast substitute. Bridges said, "We were going to first shoot the picture in California and say it was Arkansas. I looked and looked and looked all up and down the coast and just could not find anything that looked right."[35] His quest for authenticity did not end here. The three main female roles — Billie Jean, Charlotte, and Pat — were played by Arkansas natives: Lisa Blount, Deborah Benson, and Mary Kai Clark, respectively. Bridges said, "I looked in L.A. and New York and just couldn't come up with the right girls."[36] As Jimmy J.'s mother, Bridges cast longtime collaborator Collin Wilcox, who, though not an Arkansan, was at least a Southerner.

Cinematographer Gordon Willis returned, as did script supervisor Michael Preece; both of their careers had blossomed since *The Paper Chase*. Willis had shot the first *Godfather* sequel and two more films for Alan J. Pakula, *The Parallax View* and *All the President's Men*. Preece was no longer just a script supervisor; he had begun to direct episodic television. He remembered, "They called me and said, 'Do you want to go down to Conway, Arkansas, and work on this movie?' I had directed one episode of television, but the season was over and I remember the first assistant director had directed one episode of a television show. We both went down there and I said, 'Oh God, it's hard to go back.' I was a little bit not the happiest person to be doing that job. Jim by that time — and Gordon Willis was on it — it was more their movie. I was just along for the ride and to do my job, even though

Jim and I were quite good friends socially. But I really didn't want to be there."[37]

Then something happened that changed Preece's involvement in *September 30, 1955*, and changed the course of the film itself. Near the end of the movie, Jimmy J. is seen riding a motorcycle he has purchased after cashing in his war bonds, inspired by having just viewed *Rebel Without a Cause*. Richard Thomas said,

> I do not ride motorcycles, I am not a motorcycle guy. I think the fun thing about the movie is that Jimmy J. isn't either. And neither was Jim Bridges. They're just not motorcycle characters. He sort of dreams himself into that role at the end.
>
> But here I am ... and it wasn't just a motorcycle, it was a big-ass motorcycle! So I worked with the Teamsters and they taught me how to ride. I didn't have a lot to do. I just had to ride out of town very quietly and sort of pull in and pull out. I worked on it and I rehearsed with the thing. If it had been a horse, it would have been no problem. I've been riding my whole life. But this was a horse of a different type! We did this scene where I came up to the chain-link fence to tell somebody I was leaving. I pulled out and pulled away and the thing got away from me and went under a truck. I had to ditch it because if it had gone under the truck with me sitting up, it would have been a very bad story altogether. So I just laid it down and broke my ankle, which is really all it was. Everybody came running up and I stood up. "I'm fine, I'm fine." And the minute Jim got to me and said, "Are you okay?" I just fainted dead out. It was very dramatic.[38]

Preece said, "We had only shot I think for five days. We didn't even finish that day's work. They said, 'We're all going back to Los Angeles. We'll let the leg heal and we'll start shooting again in a few months.' I was thrilled. I mean, I was relieved. I went back and I got a job as a director."[39]

Also relieved was Richard Thomas, who to his amazement was not replaced by another actor during his convalescence. "I had to go back and start *The Waltons*, so they had to start up again much later," he noted. "I had to heal, then I had to do *The Waltons*, and then I had to go back and finish the movie. I couldn't believe it that he didn't replace me. And Universal ... 'Come on, get another twenty-one-year-old.' But he didn't. He stuck by me. He came to the hospital and he said, 'I'm not going to replace you. I want you to get well and we're going to wait and when you're ready, we're going to do it.'"[40]

So Thomas stayed and Preece didn't. In the meantime, others joined the production when filming began again, including one person who would be integral to Bridges's films over the next decade: second assistant director Kim Kurumada. He remembered,

> As often happens, when the show resumed they were going around trying to get the crew together and the second assistant director who had been on the

show was not available for some reason and they couldn't get him back. So they needed another second assistant director. Coincidentally, I had a few months earlier finished shooting *All the President's Men* and that's where I had met and worked with Gordon Willis. For some people, Gordon was a very, very difficult person to work with. He was a very demanding person. He was a terrific artist, a terrific cameraman, but not everybody could get along with him. So when they were looking for a second assistant, basically I think it was because of Gordon, they said, "Well, let's get somebody who has worked with Gordon before." And the second assistant who had most recently worked with Gordon was myself on *All the President's Men*.[41]

As *September 30, 1955* was being made, Bridges boasted that it was "Willis's best work,"[42] and to that point, it was. Thomas recalled,

> Gordon, of course, was a complete master and genius, especially of darkness and chiaroscuro. It was very clear early on that Jim and Gordon had decided to shoot the movie like a 50mm snapshot. The point of view of the film is always the point of view of something you would have seen in a scrapbook. As you watch the movie, I think that creates a slight sense of claustrophobia, which I think is good because it's a claustrophobic world that he wants to get out of. I'm not sure anybody ever really knew that it was that carefully thought-out. This is one of the things that kind of made it an art film. They did something with the camera without calling attention to it. It wasn't like shooting things in sepia or like in *Traffic*, color-coding the stories or something that's so visually obvious. It may be a good thing, but it advertises itself. This particular decision I don't think advertised itself at all. In fact, I would say that ninety-five percent of the people who go to the movie would never even have known what they were looking at in terms of that.[43]

Nevertheless, the decision was totally conscious. Janet Maslin reported that Bridges asked Willis "to copy the color scheme of his college yearbooks." The director said, "I don't remember the past in close-up; I remember it as a series of snapshots."[44] Kurumada described Willis as "one of the best cameramen I've ever worked with," and his knowledge of how the cinematographer affected a film set proved beneficial. "Gordon was in the air force," Kurumada (also a military veteran) explained:

> He kind of had a militaristic approach to how things had to be done. Oftentimes, it was an uncompromising approach. I understood that because I had worked with him before, so I got along with him.... As an assistant director, your job is, you're supposed to run the set. You're supposed to tell the crew, "This is what we're shooting. We need to get this ready in five minutes." If you see the crew not working as hard as they should, you talk to them. You say, "Get this ready. I want this ready in ten minutes." Well, when I was an assistant with Gordon, I never had to do that because *Gordon* did it! I never had to complain to producers that the crew wasn't working hard enough or expending their effort because Gordon would do it.[45]

Of Willis, Thomas reflected, "His influence was very strong on the set. If a shot didn't go the way he liked it, he was just as opinionated and strong about it as Jim — in fact, more so, because Jim was always very gentle about things and Gordon would be a little bit more irascible when things weren't right and had more of a temper than Jim."[46] By Kurumada's reckoning, however, Bridges was cognizant of the "good cop-bad cop" dynamic that existed between him and Willis: "Jimmy was very, very smart. He knew that in certain instances there was no reason to have two pit bulls on the set; one will do. So Gordon would do it. But Jimmy was very smart because he knew that while it's good to have a pit bull, you don't want the pit bull to bite your own children. So he would make sure and he would work with me to make sure that it's great to have that pit bull when you need it, but watch out for our baby. The pit bull could bite our baby and we don't want that."[47]

Kurumada maintained that the actors had to be on their toes when appearing in a film photographed by Willis. Because Willis rarely shot with two cameras at once, Kurumada said, "the actors had to replicate their performances even when they were not on camera because they had to do it for the benefit of the scene and also for the benefit of the other actor. That can be a little bit unnerving sometimes for actors. That can mean that an actor may say, 'Well, gee, can't I just breeze through it and then when the camera is on me is when you'll see my best stuff?' With Gordon, you couldn't do that."[48]

* * *

Kurumada would be with Bridges on the director's next four films. He rose through the ranks, graduating from second assistant to first assistant and eventually to executive producer. Perhaps no one I interviewed for this book had more firsthand observation and insight about how Bridges's sets were run than Kurumada. I spoke with him about the day-to-day routine on *September 30, 1955*. He remembered that, during rehearsals,

> I would be standing with Jimmy and next to me would be Gordon, the actors, and the script supervisor, and no one else. The reason there was no one else is because it was done in silence — complete silence but for the dialogue. There were no distractions. It had to be silent so we could concentrate....
>
> What I noticed and what Jimmy noticed was that it kept people focused. What happens sometimes on a film is the novelty of a project starts to wear off for different people at different times. And they don't know that on the second day you may be shooting a fairly inconsequential scene, but on the twentieth day you're shooting a critical scene. You need the crew's attention and focus on that twentieth day much more than you need it on the second day. How do you make sure that you can keep that happening? Well, by forbidding any extraneous talk, you do wind up keeping people focused because

everything is always new. They don't know what's happening. Everything demands their attention. People used to walk onto the sets and say, "Are they shooting?" And we wouldn't be shooting at all! But it would be just as quiet as if we were! The only people who were talking were people who needed to say something....

The actors would go ahead and rehearse. Jimmy would be walking around looking at it. He would be nodding to Gordon where he thought the scene was breaking up into different shots. They'd run the entire scene and he'd be walking around with Gordon and they'd be looking back and forth at each other, like saying, "Okay, this is going to be our master shot. We're going to do coverage here. This is going to be a second master. We're going to do coverage here."

After we had rehearsed it until we felt we had the mechanical moves done — not the performances, but the mechanical moves done to where everything was supposed to be — Jimmy would say to either Fred [Gallo] or me, "Okay, let's mark 'em." When he would say that, I would bring in our marking team. The marking team was the stand-ins, the camera assistant, the dolly grip, the key grip, and the gaffer. Just them — those were the only people who were allowed to come in because it had to be very quiet and there was not room for extraneous talking. These people would then come in and we would run the scene again. While we were running the scene again, as the actors were going through it, Gordon would be looking through the viewfinder. He'd be sitting at a viewfinder and he'd say, "That's number one." When he said, "That's number one," everybody would stop. The actors would stop. And Gordon would allow maybe five seconds for questions. He'd say, "That's number one," there'd be silence, and then Gordon would say, "Okay, continue." The actors would continue with the scene. Gordon would move to another spot, looking through the viewfinder. He'd say, "This is number two." That would be the end of that. Then he would basically say, "That's it."

When he said, "That's it," I would tell the actors, "Go finish your makeup, your hair, and your wardrobe." Gordon would sit down and get a cup of coffee. When he came back, five or ten minutes later, where he said, "That's number one," the dolly grip better have measured and marked exactly where Gordon was standing and where the lens was. So the dolly grip would be standing unobtrusively to the side with a tape measure. As soon as Gordon said, "That's number one," the tape measure would fly in and he'd get the measurement exactly where Gordon was and he'd mark the spot on the floor where it was and how many inches above the floor where it was. Now when Gordon came back after getting his coffee, the camera had better be on the dolly on that spot, exactly where Gordon was, at the height exactly where Gordon was holding the viewfinder. And the camera assistant had to look and see what focal length Gordon was looking at and have the camera already set up. Then Gordon would come back after he got his coffee and sit down on the camera, which was now in position. I would have the stand-ins on the positions of the actors and have the prop man and the script supervisor standing by to tell them exactly what to do. They would make the physical moves and the gaffer and the grip would start lighting the set.

Jimmy would then go off and either work on the script or just converse with the actors. He would talk to them about what was happening. Because I'd worked with Gordon before and would watch him light, and Fred had worked with Gordon before on *The Godfather*, we didn't have to ask him, "Are you done yet? How much longer?" We knew because we could tell by what equipment he was starting to use, and how his adjustments were getting finer and finer, that he was getting close to being finished. I would then go tell the actors, "It's going to be pretty soon." I would go back to Gordon and say, "What do you think? A couple more minutes? Little while longer?" Obscure, you know, just, "What do you think, Gordy? We're getting close now, aren't we, Gordy?" Not "Are you going to be ready in five minutes?" He would have bit my head off if I'd said that! Gordy would nod to me, I'd go get Jimmy, and we'd come back. Then we'd run it again.

I don't know if you want to call it military or whatever, but that kind of procedure basically was what Jimmy liked. He utilized it because he was a third-time director. He was able to command a certain presence and get a certain professionalism out of everybody.[49]

* * *

This "third-time director" had grown in so many different ways since *The Baby Maker*. "Jim definitely was in the school of great American filmmaker storytellers, the William Wylers," observed Jack Bender. "Jim's films are really about the story that he's telling and the characters on the screen, and much less about, 'Look at me, I'm the director.'"[50] Bridges's style had no traces of flash to it. As in *The Paper Chase*, the visual handiwork he and Willis devised emanated quiet authority.

Starting with *September 30, 1955*, the director usually began his films with a scene before the main titles. This was the case in *The China Syndrome*, *Urban Cowboy*, *Mike's Murder*, and *Perfect*. These pre-credit scenes instantly immersed the audience in the world Bridges was creating. They also served as a kind of warm-up to the story he was about to tell. They usually grabbed an audience's attention, as in *Mike's Murder*, when a dissolve takes us from a couple (Debra Winger and Mark Keyloun) playfully flirting on a tennis court to shots of the two of them together in bed—all before a word of dialogue has been uttered.

The pre-credits scene in *September 30, 1955* does all of the above. The film opens with a wide shot of the exterior of a movie house at night. The marquee tells us what is playing: JAMES DEAN IN EAST OF EDEN. Inside the darkened theatre, we find Jimmy J. watching the end of Elia Kazan's adaptation of the John Steinbeck novel, starring James Dean and Julie Harris. Bridges cuts between clips from *East of Eden* and a close shot of Jimmy J. looking straight ahead at the screen.

As he watches *East of Eden*, Jimmy J.'s face registers a variety of emotions.

When we first observe him, he is smiling slightly. It's a smile of appreciation and anticipation; we know instantly that he has seen *East of Eden* before — perhaps many times before. During the final moments of the film, Jimmy J. finds himself profoundly moved, and his eyes begin to fill with tears. But the tears seem to be buoyed by a sense of ecstasy.

We next see a sober, serious Jimmy J. exiting the theatre. Then — in a magical moment — Leonard Rosenman's score to *East of Eden*, which so far has only been heard diegetically as part of *East of Eden*, swells up on the soundtrack of Bridges's film. Jimmy J. turns to screen right, pauses, and gazes at the poster of *East of Eden* which adorns the front of the theatre. The theatre's lights dim and the opening title sequence of *September 30, 1955* commences. The credits are set against shots of rural and small town Arkansas. We eventually find ourselves in Conway, Arkansas, on the handsome, red-brick campus of Arkansas State Teachers College, where Jimmy J. is going to school.

The great majority of *September 30, 1955* takes place on a bright, hot, early fall day. In the first scene following the credits, two students — a boy and a girl — are seen talking in front of a chain-link fence. Behind them is the ASTC football team conducting a practice. The boy is holding a radio, but neither of them is listening to it very closely. Here, and in other places in the film, Bridges makes masterful use of overlapping dialogue, as the chitchat of the two students, the voices on the radio, and the commotion being made by the football players compete for our attention all at once. We must strain to hear the radio announcer clearly when he says, "James Dean, the movie star, who was in *East of Eden*, was killed late yesterday afternoon."

As these words are heard, we see Jimmy J. for the first time in the "normal" context of his everyday life, his life as it is outside of the movie theatre. He is on the football team, a fact that critic Molly Haskell, reviewing the film in *New York* magazine, saw as indicative of his ability to "pass in both worlds" of "the hips" and "the squares."[51] (Though Haskell regrettably misidentified Jimmy J. as a "basketball player," when his sport is obviously football.) As he runs off the field trying to catch an errant pass from the quarterback, he overhears the tail end of the radio news item, just as we do. Bridges and Willis capture all of the aforementioned action in a single master shot, effortlessly timing Jimmy J.'s entrance in the scene to the precise moment when the radio bulletin about Dean is heard on the soundtrack.

Jimmy J. isn't sure of what he has heard. He asks the couple with the radio, "What'd he say? Who'd he say die?" The girl answers, "I wasn't listening." "Something about some movie actor," the boy says.

Even at this early point in *September 30, 1955*, the couple's nonchalance is offensive to us, as Jimmy J.'s connection to Dean has already been definitively established in the pre-credits scene. Jimmy J. says nothing in response to them, knowing (or fearing) who has died. He darts off the field. Willis's camera has so far remained stationary throughout this shot, but as Jimmy J. runs, the camera moves with him, tracking laterally from right to left, past the chain-link fence, and then panning with Jimmy J. as he runs by an adjacent field where the ASTC marching band is practicing. His friend, Eugene (Dennis Christopher, later the star of *Breaking Away*), is in the band.

Jimmy J. then runs into his girlfriend, Charlotte (Deborah Benson), an attractive and personable blonde from an upstanding local family, who is playing tennis. Jimmy J. addresses her, as he did the couple with the radio moments earlier, from behind a chain-link fence, which provides a visual metaphor for his isolation from his fellow classmates, even from Charlotte. He asks her for a dime. "What's the matter?" she asks. "I just heard something on the radio — I can't believe it," he replies. "What?" "They're saying Jimmy Dean's been killed."

Charlotte tells him that she doesn't have any change. Jimmy J. next spots Eugene, who is practicing with the band, and successfully extracts a dime from him. Eugene attempts to follow Jimmy J. as he goes to find a telephone booth, but is reprimanded by the band director, who yells, "Eugene, get back in line!"

Across the tennis courts to the phone booth, the camera again tracks laterally with Jimmy J. Richard Thomas sustains a level of frenzy in the early minutes of the film that is remarkable to behold. Jimmy J. tries to call Billie Jean (Lisa Blount), an ex-girlfriend from "the wrong side of the tracks," who, we come to learn, shares his passion for James Dean, but she doesn't answer the phone. Still in a state of tumult, Jimmy J. runs across the street to the campus radio station. Charlotte follows him, joined by Frank (Dennis Quaid) and Pat (Mary Kai Clark), who are walking together on the sidewalk as Jimmy J. rushes past them. They ask Charlotte what's wrong. "James Dean is dead," Charlotte says plaintively. Frank and Pat do not say anything in response. The three of them follow Jimmy J. into the radio station.

All of this really took place. Bridges said, "I wasn't on the football field when I heard the news of Dean's death, but I was nearby on the stage of the auditorium building a set. The Charlotte character and I went straight to the radio station and stood just where Thomas stands. From then on, it all happened in one variation or another."[52]

The station's announcer (a cameo appearance by Tom Bonner, who was by then working at KARK-TV in Little Rock) is reading the morning's headlines from behind a glass pane. Jimmy J., Charlotte, Frank, and Pat cluster in front of the window as they wait to hear word of Dean. Bridges is careful to place Jimmy J. and Charlotte in the foreground of the shot, with Frank positioned in the background between them; the responses of Jimmy J. and Charlotte are the ones we are meant to care most about.

After a while, the announcer says, "Hollywood: Rising young film actor

Four. Going Home 77

James Dean was killed as his sports car collided almost dead-on with another car at an intersection near Paso Robles, California. He was twenty-four." As Jimmy J. hears this, his face turns from agitation to shock. It is crucial that Bridges at no time cuts to a close-up of Jimmy J., as it is clear that Bridges regards Charlotte's reaction to the news to be as significant in its way as Jimmy J.'s. At first, she is seen looking straight ahead at the announcer, as Jimmy J. is, but she looks to him as the item about Dean is being read. Jimmy J., concentrating on what he is hearing, doesn't see Charlotte to interpret her obvious concern, but we do. While Charlotte manifestly lacks Jimmy J.'s near-manic enthusiasm for Dean, and at times has difficulty even comprehending it, she is worried about *Jimmy J.* in this instant, and what this catastrophic (as far as Jimmy J. is concerned) news means to *him*.

It's a moment of great sensitivity, captured by Bridges in a Preminger-like group shot, and beautifully played by Deborah Benson, who had never before appeared in a film. "Debbie was just the most adorable," Thomas remembered. "You can't manufacture that. If a girl from L.A., unless she'd been born and raised in that area, and this shortchanges actors and actresses, which I don't really mean to do ... it would have been very difficult for a different kind of actress to go in and create that performance without satirizing it, without it being a comment. The thing about her character, Charlotte, is she's completely adorable. Yes, she's a homecoming queen, yes, she's ultimately conventional and can't go the distance, even though she liked to play at it when she was little, but there's so much sweetness in that performance, and naturally in her, that it would have been very hard for someone else to do that and not comment on it as though it were somehow a kind of shallowness. Because Charlotte isn't shallow."[53] Of all of the characters in *September 30, 1955*, Charlotte alone can be said to have the world by the tail.

Benson said, "I think I came in with an idea of who this girl was, which probably wasn't that far from who I was at that time. So all I had to do really was to bring that and then just tweak some things here and there."[54] A recent graduate of Arkansas State University, she left Arkansas for New York to pursue a dancing career. Then she received a call from home: "I'd only been there about a month. And it was rough because I was from a small town and was very unsophisticated. New York was just eating me alive. I think I was at a party at the apartment of Princess Yasmin Aga Khan. I didn't even know her, but someone that we knew did and I was at her party. My roommate called me and she said, 'Your mom is trying to get in touch with you.' When I spoke to my mom, she said that they were doing a film in Arkansas and they either wanted me to be the lead or the second lead in it, or to read for it. And I was just like, 'What?' She said, 'And they're sure that they can have you work on it somehow.'"[55]

Benson had a cousin who was a photographer and had taken headshots of the aspiring actress. Bridges saw the photographs when he was meeting with the state's governor to discuss hiring local actors. "My cousin heard about them, and he knew that I had just gone to New York, so he gave them a headshot. I guess they contacted my cousin and my cousin must have contacted my parents and then they called me," she said.[56]

After reading for Bridges and Jerry Weintraub, it was only a matter of weeks before Benson was offered the part of Charlotte: "I had no agent, so I just represented myself. They gave me SAG minimum, but that allowed me to get into the union, which is a big obstacle for new actors. So I thought, 'Woohoo! I don't care what they pay me! I get to get a screen credit and get into the union.' It just stripped my gears that I had left Arkansas to go to New York to try to make my career and then I'm back in Arkansas doing a lead in a film for Universal Pictures!"[57]

Benson's performance is one of the joys of *September 30, 1955*, but credit is also due to Bridges's conception of her character, so free, as Thomas said, of "comment" and "satire." That Charlotte was written so sensitively is another instance of the evenhandedness referred to by David Shipman when he praised *The Baby Maker* for being pleasing to "preppies and hippies alike."[58] "Jimmy wasn't a judging guy," Thomas explained. "Believe me, he had his opinions and they were strong, but he was a humanist and he also loved the variety and the sort of crazy diversity of human inclinations. He was not one to judge. He could appreciate it when it was buttoned-up and very proper and he could appreciate it when it was crazy and wild and out of control. He could go in any direction in terms of appreciating life, and I think you see that in the roles."[59]

Such expansiveness is also apparent in Bridges's empathetic depiction of Jimmy J.'s mother, played by Collin Wilcox in a last-minute substitution for Geraldine Page. "Geraldine Page was a mentor of mine," Wilcox recalled. "She had some conflict maybe a week or ten days before shooting. Jim called me and of course didn't fudge around. He said, 'Geraldine can't do it. Will you please come and do this?' Of course, I was flattered out of my mind that he would choose me as a replacement for Geraldine! It took me one-half of a second to say, 'I'll be there.' I was, I felt, a little young for the role, but he said, 'You're going to be fine, you're going to be fine.' And I was."[60]

Wilcox was beyond "fine"; her one scene, opposite Thomas, is a highlight of the film. "She's a wonderful actress," Thomas said. "She's an actress with a serious spine."[61] In fact, the two actors went back quite a few years: They met when they both appeared in the New York production of Eugene O'Neill's *Strange Interlude*, directed by Jose Quintero, also starring Geoffrey Horne, to whom Wilcox was about to be married. "I was the ring bearer at her wedding,"

Thomas revealed.[62] Wilcox felt that the "familiarity" they had with each other helped them in their scene: "We hadn't known each other intimately, but you know how actors are. If they've been in a production together or a film together, they have a little history."[63]

Jimmy J.'s mother shows up at a most inopportune time. Jimmy J. and Charlotte, along with Frank, Pat, and Jimmy J.'s best friend Hanley (Tom Hulce), have spent the afternoon on the banks of the Arkansas River. At the midpoint of an extraordinary scene, as the others carouse, Jimmy J. strips down to his underwear and covers himself in mud. He then sits at the center of a "circle of prayer," an Academy Award molded out of sand and mud before him, and recites the Lord's Prayer, prays for "the loved ones and the friends and the relatives of James Dean," and calls out for a "sign" from Dean. (A dog is heard barking, which Jimmy J. interprets as said sign.)

Before Jimmy J. has a chance to shower and change, he finds his mother, aunt, and little brother Dickie waiting for him at the steps of his dormitory, where Hanley has dropped him off. The four of them are scheduled to go to a show in Little Rock that evening; Jimmy J. has forgotten all about this.

His mother expresses surprise and disappointment at the state she finds her son in. She greets him by asking, "What on *Earth* have you been doing?" She accuses him of drinking (which he was). When Jimmy J. explains that he can't join them in Little Rock because James Dean has been killed, her response is painful — and reasonable. "I'm very sorry when anybody dies," she says quietly, "but I don't understand for the life of me what that death clear across the country has to do with you." Bridges never lets Jimmy J. get too carried away with his infatuation with Dean; there is always someone, such as his mother in this scene, to give him a dose of reality. Sometimes we identify with him in these situations, and sometimes not. In his laudatory review in *Newsweek*, critic David Ansen insightfully observed that "one of the many accomplishments" in *September 30, 1955* is that Bridges allows the audience to "see the truth in all of [the] conflicting assessments" of Jimmy J.'s friends.[64]

At one point, Pat condemns him as "sick, affected, and weird." She is being terribly harsh. (Her careless insensitivity is akin to the piercing moment in *Rosemary's Baby* when Guy reveals to Rosemary that he has thrown away a book she received as a gift from her deceased friend: "Oh, I put it in the garbage. I didn't want you upsetting yourself.") But Bridges's genius is that some of what Pat says rings true. If he is nothing else, Jimmy J. surely is "affected." Thomas admitted, "You can't help but feel the way his friends feel sometimes — why is he beating his head against the wall about this thing?"[65] Perhaps Ansen put it best: "We can be moved by Jimmy J., as he was by Jimmy Dean, even as we smile at his narcissistic role-playing and are appalled by the tragedy his irresponsibility helps bring about."[66]

For every adult character who is depicted cartoonishly — such as Jimmy J.'s aunt, who tells him to go to church and ask the Lord for forgiveness after the encounter with his mother, or the blowhard football coach who lectures him about running out on practice — there are adult characters who are written and played to sound extremely sensible, and none more so than Jimmy J.'s mother. Before the scene is over, he has tussled with Dickie, who has been taunting him, in the process ruining his brother's new white suit. In the face of such behavior, she is in many ways the picture of restraint. "Just look at you," she says, almost whispering. After she scolds him, she delivers his monthly allowance, as well as a pound cake, a batch of cookies, and a jar of his grandmother's chili sauce. She also returns a jacket of his, freshly affixed with new leather patches. All of these actions speak to her authentic concern for him. On the other hand, from her perspective, he demonstrates, in appearance and behavior, a complete *lack* of concern for her or what she might think. When she cries out, "Oh, Jimmy J., why can't you be good?" we feel for her.

Wilcox "delivers the Southern mother, a certain type of Southern mother," Thomas said. He added, "This is like the worst thing a mother could be facing. I have a bunch of kids and you just want to shoot them when they do this thing that they do when they're adolescents."[67] This is why *New York Times* critic Vincent Canby's judgment that the film "lacks the edge of satire that can make the difference between a good film and a great one, between a film that is somehow in thrall to its sentiments instead of being in charge of them,"[68] is so wrong. Bridges is aware of how absurd Jimmy J.'s behavior looks to others — and so, in rare moments, is Jimmy J. "I feel like someone I've known my entire life has died, and I've never met the man," he tells Charlotte. "It's so dumb." Kind, understanding Charlotte says that she disagrees, offering the example of her father's reaction to the death of Franklin Delano Roosevelt. "He went into his room, closed the door, and threw a chair against the wall," she says. "Over and over, he just kept throwing this chair against the wall." One is reminded here of the famous *Look* magazine photograph taken by a young Stanley Kubrick, depicting a newsstand vendor surrounded by headlines announcing FDR's death. In his biography of Kubrick, Vincent LoBrutto described the scene well: "A saddened and defeated-looking dealer sat, his hand at his face, his eyes downcast and full of the grief communally felt by the country."[69] Thomas said, "You don't have to be a Dean fan to be affected by the movie. That's why there's a line about one of the kids' fathers having felt the same way about Franklin Roosevelt. And that's why at the end of the film, as he drives past the local movie theater, Marilyn Monroe in *The Seven Year Itch* is playing. She was the next one."[70]

Andrew Sarris comprehended the film better than Canby did when he wrote in *The Village Voice* that "Bridges mocks himself as well, and he does not try to score any easy points on the wasteland of Middle America in the '50s."[71] Indeed, there is nothing in the film to suggest that Bridges *did* consider the town of his youth a "wasteland." He was laudatory in describing the education he received at Arkansas State Teachers College, and the very fact that Jimmy J. finds an outlet, as Bridges did, in cinema suggests some rudimentary cultural life, however incomplete it may have been. Critic Armond White denounced the "immodest stereotypes about '50s conformity" in the recent film adaptation of Richard Yates's great novel *Revolutionary Road*, properly noting that mainstream American films from that very period, such as George Cukor's *The Marrying Kind* and Vincente Minnelli's *Some Came Running*, "already acknowledged social complexities."[72] The same is true of *East of Eden*, which is, after all, quite a serious and sophisticated movie for Jimmy J. to attach himself to. He has none of the cultural philistinism of, for example, Sandy and Jonathan in Mike Nichols and Jules Feiffer's *Carnal Knowledge*; they boast of reading *The Fountainhead* and other "classics" mainly to impress Susan, the object of their affections.

Speaking about the closing of the theatre in *The Last Picture Show*, Samuel Fuller once observed, "That movie house ... it means entertainment and it also means *life*. Anything in that house was *living*. People came in, people went out. That's what I liked about that theatre. And when they close that, that's the closing of a lot of ideas, a lot of independent thinking, whether it's political or not, and art."[73] But unlike *The Last Picture Show*, the movie house does *not* close in *September 30, 1955*; even as Jimmy J. has sped out of town at the film's conclusion, the theatre remains open, alight in the dark of the evening to inspire others as it did Jimmy J. A town with a movie theatre and a college campus can hardly be described as a "wasteland."

"Obsessions with movie stars go all the way back," Thomas noted. "It was obsessions with opera singers at one time, with pianists, with whoever the sensations are culturally, whether it's Chopin or Clara Bow or Valentino. This kind of identification is something that people understand at one level. It seems a little strange in the movie, but I think it's something that people can identify with across the board."[74]

* * *

In the earlier scene at the Arkansas River, the extent of Jimmy J.'s remoteness from his contemporaries became clear to us. As Frank and Pat make out (with Hanley looking on), Jimmy J. and Charlotte sit together near the river's edge in the distance. Frank, Pat, and Hanley are in the foreground of the image. It isn't clear what Jimmy J. and Charlotte are up to.

"What's he doing?" Frank asks. Pat replies, "I can't tell. Can you see what he's doing?" Frank yells, "Hey, Jimmy J.! Jimmy J., what're you making?" "Something out of mud," Hanley offers.

Jimmy J. just now emerges from the background of the shot to join Frank, Pat, and Hanley in the foreground. He holds the "mud Oscar" in his hands. The composition of the shot, and the blocking of the actors, recalls the earlier shot in which Jimmy J. approaches the young couple with the radio from behind. In both cases, Jimmy J. is, in a sense, "intruding": Frank, Pat, and Hanley are having a fine time — they are all inebriated to one degree or another by this point — and Jimmy J. upsets the fun-loving good times with his solemn intensity.

After explaining to them what it is that he has sculpted, he says, "Billie Jean says we ought to get in touch with him." His suggestion isn't taken seriously by Frank, Pat or Hanley, who, along with Charlotte, are quickly distracted. While they are off cavorting on their own, Jimmy J. goes down near the water, takes off his shirt and slacks, and covers his body in mud. When the others spot him and wonder what he is doing *now*, Hanley gets it right on his first guess: "I think he's turning himself into one of those mud natives we saw in *National Geographic*. It has to do with funerals and grief."

Jimmy J. may be alienated from his mother and most of his peers when it comes to his passion for James Dean, but the unshakable bond he has with Billie Jean was formed on that very basis. Significantly, Billie Jean is the sole person Jimmy J. tries to contact after he has heard the news; he only tells Charlotte of Dean's death after she asks him "What's the matter?" He knows that Billie Jean is just as obsessed with Dean as he is, and that she will be just as forlorn. Indeed, while Jimmy has seen *East of Eden* four times, we learn that Billie Jean has seen the film on 22 different occasions.

When Jimmy J. and Billie Jean speak on the phone for the first time, Bridges only shows us her side of the conversation. He never cuts away from the medium shot of Billie Jean sitting on the staircase of her mother's house, cradling a radio in her lap as she talks to Jimmy J. In so doing, Bridges privileges *her* experience of losing Dean; if the film had cut back and forth between shots of Jimmy J. and Billie Jean, it would risk letting Jimmy J.'s perspective take over the film. Indeed, Billie Jean becomes increasingly complicit in the events to come.

The dialogue Bridges gives Billie Jean in this scene is both subtle and witty, delivered with just the right inflections by Lisa Blount in her feature film debut. "Jimmy? Did you hear what happened?" Billie Jean asks as she gets on the phone. "You were the first one I tried to call when I found out.... No, I'm not all right at all. Really, I'm about to fall to pieces.... Well, I've just been looking at pictures of him and thinking about him and trying to contact his spirit...."

Bridges's dialogue — some of the best in an American film since *All About Eve* — is pitch-perfect in its authenticity. Thomas observed, "I think that one of the things that is so charming about the picture, and one of the autobiographical aspects of it which doesn't strictly have to do with Jim, is the fact that he was such a keen observer of, and writer about, Southern people. The movie has a regional feeling about it. There's definitely a feeling of locality. It isn't like somebody wrote a script that takes place in Arkansas so that they could sort of make fun of a certain lifestyle or satirize. No, he wrote from the inside out about the relationship with the parents and how these kids talk and the sort of boredom of those summers."[75]

The actors appear to delight in speaking their lines. Perhaps no one had better lines to speak than Blount as Billie Jean. Born in Fayetteville, Arkansas, she was attending the University of Arkansas when she found out that auditions for the film were being held:

> I thought, "Oh! This is perfect because I'm not going to ace these midterms, so I'll just go get this movie and go to Hollywood!" I mean, that was my thinking! I knew it wasn't going to be easy.
>
> I read for extras casting, but they had to read something so they had me read this role. I didn't know that that wasn't the role I was actually being considered for. So when the time came, I went into my costume department at school and did the whole Vampira makeup and costume. I took myself up to Toad Suck Ferry, Arkansas, where they were casting. I guess they just honestly thought I was crazy. There I sat. This was very extreme makeup and outfit, because that's what Billie Jean does. I sat on the steps all day long. As I remember, I never gave up. I *knew* they would get me in there some way. They *finally* let me go in and he really liked it. They didn't tell me at that moment that I had the role. I found out later that they had actually had somebody in L.A., but they liked me better. So I got the job and got out of midterms.[76]

Inexperienced as she was, Blount earned the immediate endorsement of Richard Thomas. "I was a huge supporter of Lisa Blount," he said. "There was something that Lisa had. She had a kind of unvarnished, edgy, girl-from-the-wrong-side-of-the-tracks feeling and that accent, the way her accent worked. When we did the tests, I was in the room with Jim afterwards and I was very, very, very supportive of her because, as untutored as it was, it had a kind of wonderful homeliness to it."[77]

Blount noted, "The only other really, truly local girl was Mary Kai Clark, who was from right there. I thought she had such an authenticity about her. The Hollywood guys, they tried, but even back then, I thought, 'A lot of people who aren't from the South think that if you just put on a certain accent, you'll pass.' But there are so many accents."[78]

Like Benson, Blount didn't have an agent and received SAG minimum for her work in the film. But it wasn't about the money — it was about working with James Bridges. "We had a lunch, just the two of us, and he wanted to know my aspirations and all of this," she recalled. "I was amazed at how he treated me, like an equal and a human being. You've got to realize I was out of high school maybe a year and a half, where I was treated like a mean child, and then here's this big Hollywood director wanting my opinion on things. If you think about it, this movie was about him breaking out of this small town and making his dreams come true through a series of events, and in a way, he was giving me exactly that, exactly what the movie was about. He gave me my red jacket."[79] (In the film's last scenes, Jimmy J. wears a red jacket patterned after one worn by Dean in *Rebel Without a Cause*.)

Blount never forgot the opportunity Bridges gave her. She said, "The fact that Jim had the courage to cast a little girl from Arkansas who was as close to Billie Jean as he was *ever* going to find, to trust that I could hit a mark and say these lines and carry the emotional line that I needed to carry, he had to make that decision fairly quickly. He didn't put me through the wringer over it. He just had a sense that I could do it and cast me and all went well. It's a piece that I'm very, very proud of."[80]

* * *

The "other really, truly local girl" referred to by Blount had links to Bridges that went much deeper than her simply being from Conway. Mary Kai Clark is the daughter of Jane Wilson, Bridges's best friend from high school. Wilson remembered:

> He called me before he was going to do it. He was excited and he said, "I'm coming to Conway and I'm going to get to spend some time with you!" He told me a little bit about the movie and he was going to do some casting with local people. I said, "Oh, good Lord, Jim Mac! I don't want to be in the movie!" After they actually came to Conway, they were at my house having dinner one night, Jim Mac and [producer] Bob Larson and some of the other people who were involved in the movie. Of course, it was in the paper that they were casting these roles and you'd go to this place and whatever, and my Mary Katherine got really excited about it because she was big into theatre, anything that called attention! You know how you are when you're seventeen years old. So I said, "I want you to promise me one thing. You are my dear friend and you have to promise me that you will *not* let Mary Kai be in this movie!" And he said, "Okay. That's a deal."[81]

Clark recalled that her mother felt she was "so impressionable" that if she was cast in *September 30, 1955*, "it would probably change my life and I would have bigger stars in my eyes and jump on the bandwagon and go to Hollywood, which is not what I did, but that's what she was thinking. She thought it would really not be in my best interest to have a part in the movie."[82] Nevertheless, she auditioned anonymously — she had never met Bridges and wasn't sure he knew who she was because she and her mother had different last names — and received several callbacks. "I was *really* surprised because I was just so young," she said. "And I wasn't a beauty queen-type or anything like that. In my mind, you have to be like a Marilyn Monroe-type person to be famous! I started reading for the part and then they brought in Dennis Quaid. I read with Dennis and we really clicked. There was some magic there when we read together and I think that was the deciding factor."[83]

Bridges then had to break the news to his old friend. As Wilson recounted, "The next thing I knew, he was back at my house, on bended knee practically, saying, 'Jane, I know you don't want her to do this, but I'm telling you: She was the very best. She was so good. We all want her.' Well, I mean, what's a mother to do?"[84]

If anything, Bridges's friendship with Wilson would have discouraged him from casting Clark as Pat in *September 30, 1955*, making his resolve a sign of his faith in her ability. As Wilson noted, "I mean, I begged him not to put her in the movie."[85] Clark, who later became a professional singer, never appeared in another film. "It was the experience of a lifetime," she said. "I wish that I was a better actress and I wish that I could have gone to Hollywood and done more. When I talked to Jim about it, he said it would be very tough and he would give me the names of some casting agents. Nobody was real encouraging that they thought it would be the greatest thing for me to do. But to be a co-star in a movie when you're seventeen years old, from a little town like Conway, Arkansas, is an experience most people in the world don't get to have."[86]

Pat is not as showy a role as Charlotte or Billie Jean, but Clark acquits herself admirably, contrasting nicely with Benson's homecoming queen refinement and Blount's rough-around-the-edges single-mindedness. Clark imbues Pat with an ordinariness also possessed by her on-screen boyfriend, Dennis Quaid's Frank.

* * *

The entire young cast of *September 30, 1955* loved working with Bridges. Deborah Benson:

> He was so loving and kind. I think the director sets the tone. I was so spoiled by this being my first production. He was so lovely and so patient and so gentle. He understood actors and liked them. It trickles down from the top. Even though sometimes we were chasing the sun or running out of time, you didn't get that panicked, "We gotta go, we gotta go, we gotta go" feeling. He would run his fingers through his hair, though.... It would kind of stick up straight, I remember. He had sort of a flattop at the time. That was the only thing that

gave away that he was getting a *little* nervous. But he was lovely. He was just the best. It was fun. We got to play and he kept us all very creative with him having such a safe environment.[87]

Lisa Blount:

He rarely gave me notes. He just let me sort of do what I wanted to do. Like in the scene where Richard and I were kissing, when the candles are lit and it's all so dramatic and she says, "We're going to get down to brass tacks," and I just attacked him. I mean, not jumped on him, but I kind of began to take it a little too far and they cut it back. Richard was laughing about it. I just didn't know. I didn't know how far you were supposed to go with these things, it really wasn't clear to me in the script. So we got that ironed out....

The more he would let me think that I was an adult and had valid thoughts to contribute, the more I came up with. They didn't all work, of course, but goodness gracious, if it had been any other scenario, when I think of all of the awful directors that I've worked with that truly were rude, I probably would have never gone into this business or at least not in the direction that I did. He just simply was so much fun. How much fun is it to be working with wonderful, talented friends and creating art? He's the one, though, that made it magic. He's the one that just made it all wonderful.... For my first acting experience, it was just like God-given. It was truly, truly great.[88]

Mary Kai Clark:

Since I was not experienced as a professional actress, there were scenes that we would do where I thought I was giving my all, and it might not have been working just right. So Jim would come over and put his arm around me and say, "Let's take a walk." We'd walk and he would put his arm around me and talk to me about the scene and about what he had envisioned. He would say, "You're doing such a wonderful job. I love what you're doing. I'm just wondering if we could try it another way. How would you feel about that?" He always considered how I was feeling and how I was playing the part. But I knew I wasn't giving just exactly what he wanted and he was trying to bring out the best part of me as an actress for what he wanted for the role.

I always knew that he loved me personally. I knew that, no matter what, whether I was good or not, he was still going to love me, Mary Kai, the person. That made it better all the time. I knew I wasn't very experienced and so I had a lot of confidence problems. Somehow, in his way, he would make you feel like you were the best actress who ever lived, just because he had the confidence in you.

Since that time, I've been in a lot of recording studios and I do a lot of productions and I'm being directed by a musical director. And I'll tell you, they're not all that way. It's a hard world out there! None of them are like Jim. They would say, "Do it again! Do it again! That's not right! Nope. Cut. Next!" Just very cut-and-dried. They could zap your confidence in a matter of sixty seconds. When you're an artist, whether you're acting or singing, that's not what you need. You need somebody to love you and to help you through it so that you can be your best. That's what he could do and I think it's a gift that not a lot of people have, that tenderness that he had.[89]

Bridges was unafraid to tweak his dialogue to suit the particular talents of his actors. As Kim Kurumada remembered, "When we did *Urban Cowboy*, I would meet Jimmy every morning and we would ride out to the Gilley's set in a motor home. The reason we would ride out there is so that we could sit at a table and we could talk and go over the work that he wanted to do. What Jimmy would do sometimes is he would listen to what an actor was doing and if it didn't work, he would say to Gordon something like, 'Can you shoot the insert?' or 'Can you shoot the sunset? I want forty-five minutes.' And he would go in and re-write the dialogue, changing the syntax. He would give it to the actors and have them say it. Then, for somebody who was trying to put a dialect on his performance, like Dennis Quaid or somebody, it sounded better. So he was able to re-write at the moment to either make the performance come out better or to make it sound better or to make it more alliterative. He had a very musical, rhythmic ear. And that's what a librettist does! But back in the seventies in Arkansas, you don't talk about librettists!"[90]

No one in the cast had a more profound rapport with Bridges than did Richard Thomas. That much might be expected; he was, in essence, *playing* the director in the film. But it went beyond that. Thomas, though born and raised in Manhattan, had rural roots on his father's side and so could relate to the setting of *September 30, 1955*. "My father's background is in eastern Kentucky and we had a farm and I spent all of my summers in the country, in rural areas. I understood very well that life and those people. And he knew that. We talked about that," Thomas said.[91]

They had other points in common, too, reflecting the bifurcated nature of Bridges's life: an Arkansan by birth and temperament, an artist by choice and affiliation. Thomas explained, "We had a connection through Jack [Larson] and my early, early work as a poet and my connection with certain writers and poets from New York, like Kenward Elmslie and John Ashbery.

Jack and I talked a lot about poetry, and Jim and I talked a lot about the Off-Broadway theatre in New York in the sixties, which I was very much around and a part of the theatre world in New York at that time. We had mutual connections that went way back before that, into that whole period of Terrence McNally and Edward Albee's work, and also the work in the early days of the Mark Taper Forum. I was working at the Ahmanson at the time, but I was very much present during that period when he was doing that work at the Taper. So we had a connection through the theatre and Jack and I had a connection through literature. It was an interesting relationship in that respect."[92]

* * *

Critic Charles Champlin, in a perceptive review in the *Los Angeles Times*, called *September 30, 1955* "one of the most directly autobiographical movies I can remember."[93] This fact was not lost on many in the cast and crew. Kurumada remembered filming the scene by the Arkansas River in which Jimmy J. makes the mud Oscar and being struck by a curious sense of *déjà vu*. "It was very obvious that that's what we were doing," he said. "That was kind of what Jimmy was trying to recapture, his feeling about that. That one scene is a little bit of a microcosm ... for those of us who were fortunate enough to be allowed in this inner circle of what was going on, it was like that. It was like sitting around Richard Thomas and having him explain, 'This is what I'm trying to do. This is how passionately I feel about it. And this is why it's important.'"[94]

Tom Bonner, a witness to much of what was fictionalized in *September 30, 1955*, noted, "The movie took place over maybe forty-eight hours, but that was a collage of things that would have encompassed a whole school year. I would call the things that happened amongst the group in that movie caricatured ideas of what we really did. They were broadly overblown. For instance, we never would have stolen anything, like they stole some stuff out of a liquor store. Never would we have done something like that. But the idea was that we were just wild, silly, fun-loving college kids, and we just did nutty things."[95]

But as closely as Bridges hewed to specific incidents from his early life, as well as its overall sweep, the central event of *September 30, 1955* was entirely imaginary. "The only thing that didn't actually happen," he revealed, "was that the Billie Jean character didn't catch on fire from the candelabras."[96]

The film arrives at that point through a remarkable series of scenes that follow Jimmy J.'s confrontation with his mother. Jimmy J. contrives to hold a "wake" for James Dean at the splendid home of Charlotte's parents. (Her father is a Senator.) Frank and Pat will not be there, but Hanley and Eugene are to join them. It doesn't take much persuasion for Jimmy J. to convince Charlotte that there is simply no way that Billie Jean cannot attend. "Jimmy, I can't have Billie Jean in my mama's house.... Oh, all right, if she has to. I guess she has to," she says. Charlotte relents, perhaps figuring it is sometimes better to keep enemies/rivals close at hand.

When Jimmy J. calls Billie Jean to inform her of the plans for the evening, the film cuts between two silhouetted profile shots of them talking; Jimmy J. faces screen right, Billie Jean screen left. "Silhouettes are really something I enjoy doing on the screen," Gordon Willis said. "The thing is, they can strike a different chord depending how you stuff them into a film. I really have no rule about when to do it. It's about whatever feeling at that moment

Four. Going Home

I want to evoke. They can be a menace, they can be loving, sensuous, mysterious, and can be very comical."[97] In *September 30, 1955*, silhouettes are used to bring Jimmy J. and Billie Jean together in their own visual world and to separate them from the other characters; no one else is seen in silhouette in the film.

Lisa Blount recalled filming her side of the conversation: "By the time I hit my mark on the stairs and the camera comes in, my head is in full screen in profile. It's a silhouette. Looking back, I had no idea that when I see this movie it's going to be my head in silhouette on the screen. I didn't think in those terms at that time. I didn't realize. I didn't adjust my performance for size, so to speak. I'm really glad. I had no reason not to trust Jim in that the size of those moments were exactly right. I mean this honestly: This was *his* doing because I would do anything he said. If he said, 'Let's make it bigger, more dramatic' or 'More whispery' or whatever.... But I just did it the way I did it and he left it alone. A girl comes running down and she's keeping her voice down because she doesn't want her mom to hear. He set it up in such a way that it organically would occur without interference from anybody. He didn't have to direct me because he had already set the groundwork up in such a way that all I had to do was literally just go A, B, C, D, follow the plan and be this girl and say these things."[98]

Billie Jean's mother, Melba Lou, was played by Susan Tyrrell, who had been Oscar-nominated for her performance in John Huston's masterpiece *Fat City*. As a representative of the adult world in *September 30, 1955*, Melba Lou is miles away from Jimmy J.'s mother. She is single, usually seen in the company of a mysterious gentleman caller referred to as "Mr. Brown," and prone to saying things like, "Oh my God, my beans are boiling over," in the midst of an otherwise serious conversation. Whatever else she is, Melba Lou is very far from being "proper"; Tyrrell's energetic performance is a delight.

"Oh, I loved Susan so much!" Blount remembered. "I was absolutely in awe and in love with her. This is, swear to God, the truth: I knew she had come in. Jimmy thought the world of her. He was so excited to have her. I was already in my hotel room, looking down on the parking lot, and she walks out there. She has a turban on her head and she has leather boots up over her knees, thigh-high leather boots, and she screams, '*Where the fuck am I?*' Wow. She's the real deal.

"The character that she created, there's just something so manic and kind of creepy about her and just that whole energy that she brought to the movie was so wonderful. It was perfect casting. I just loved her."[99]

In the film, Frank is heard to say that Melba Lou gave birth to Billie Jean when she was thirteen years old. According to Blount, this line was added at Tyrrell's behest — another instance in which Bridges was willing to adjust his dialogue to suit a particular performer. "She hated playing someone who would have a child my age," Blount said. "I don't know how old she was at the time, but believe me, in my career I got to that point early enough where you're going, 'Wait a minute. You're going to make me have a teenage child?'"[100] (In fact, Tyrrell *was* too young for her character: In 1976, when the film was shot, she was only thirty-one.)

While on the phone with Jimmy J., Billie Jean says, "Jimmy, this has to be a very special night. I have to think and get myself up to my own imagination"—another lilting turn of phrase by Bridges. When Jimmy J. picks Billie Jean up, she is revealed to have transformed herself into Vampira (Maila Nurmi), who was well-known as a friend to James Dean, swathed in a black robe, her face made white with pancake makeup. She has transformed her room, too. Black paint has been splashed on the walls to form the shape of a spider web. She stands in a corner, at the center of the web, explaining, "I just couldn't stand my regular old room after he died."

Blount said, "I remember Jimmy gave me the paint brush and I got to paint the spider web! I decorated the room. I was so proud of that, just like she would have been! For all of the right reasons, so that [Jimmy J.] would come in and see it and be really hypnotized by this whole thing."[101] Nonetheless, Jimmy J. resists Billie Jean's "hypnotization" until much later in the evening. He rebuffs her overtures when Billie Jean suggests they do what Charlotte "suspects has happened already."

At Charlotte's house, in a rare moment alone together, he confesses to her, "I'm no good, Charlotte. I just can't help it. I'm bad." He seems to authentically care for her, calling her "so good, so fine, so sweet, just everything a girl ought to be." But Billie Jean always has a way of pulling Jimmy J. away from Charlotte and back toward her and their obsession. Pettily, Billie Jean takes the wind out of Charlotte's sails after Charlotte proudly talks of her family's brand new television set: "It's not nearly as good as the movies," Billie Jean decrees. "It's just this little old box with all this snow on it. I wouldn't have one in the house." (Actually, Billie Jean's put-down of television is rather astute, anticipating Susan Sontag's comparably eloquent denunciation of the medium in a conversation with Roger Copeland in 1981: "The first time I saw television, it just gave me a headache. I thought it was so dreadful to look at this tiny, out-of-focus image and then have everything interrupted all the time by commercials."[102])

By the time this scene was shot, Blount was completely in character. She even related to the emotions she imagined Billie Jean might have been experiencing. "I remember feeling small," she said. "I'm the only one there in all of this getup.... I just felt like I wanted things to be a lot more about me, but Deborah's character kept pulling the spotlight and it bugged me. It bugged me in a real way and it bugged me in the movie. There was sort of an authenticity to it. [Benson] was *so* great. She blew me away, just how off-the-cuff she could be with her choices because she played a character who was just that kind of girl. She never answered to anybody. For once, Billie Jean gets the floor and it's like it's not all that hot. She can't really make anything great happen. That's how I felt."[103]

The way in which Billie Jean "gets the floor" is by leading a séance, complete with Ouija board (Hanley's suggestion), to communicate with Dean. Though a guest of Charlotte's, she tries to take over, ordering that all of the furniture be removed from the living room. Charlotte is powerless to stop this action, as Jimmy J. endorses it unreservedly. "If we're going to try to communicate with him," Billie Jean insists, "we've got to simplify this room. There are just too many things in it. There should be just one chair — one chair for him." Jimmy J. exclaims, "Absolutely right, Billie Jean." "*Simplify this room*"—again, what dialogue!

"James Dean, are you in this room?" Billie Jean intones repeatedly, eventually joined by the others, the camera seeming to loom over them. As they move the planchette on the Ouija board to decipher the answer to their question, the film cuts to arresting overhead close-ups of Jimmy J., Billie Jean, Charlotte, Hanley, and Eugene. These shots suggest, in a very offhand way, that perhaps there *is* something to the "signs" Jimmy J. and Billie Jean insist they have been receiving since Dean died; the angles of the shots seem to attest to Dean's presence in the room. When Billie Jean startles the group and proclaims that she "feels" the spirit of Dean ("I felt him! He's sitting right there, right there in that chair!"), everyone but Jimmy J. scatters, disbelieving her. But she and Jimmy J. share a two-shot, again in silhouette, as she elaborates on her ghostly vision. Though only minutes earlier Jimmy J. professed his love for Charlotte, he is now back in Billie Jean's arms. In a way, Jimmy J. and Billie Jean are like the brother and sister characters in Kurt Vonnegut's great novel *Slapstick*, who, when together, gave "birth to a single genius, which died as quickly as we were parted, which was reborn the moment we got together again."[104] Jimmy J. and Billie Jean do not form a "genius," but together they do form something like the ultimate James Dean devotee.

Billie Jean lacks Jimmy J.'s periodic flashes of self-awareness. For example, when she first enters Charlotte's house and finds all the lights on, she insists upon darkness. She says, "Candles are not only okay, candles are beautiful. There should not be any electric light tonight. I think electric lights disturb the spirits. I think since the invention of electricity, we've had less communication with the other world." She may disavow electricity on a night such as this one, yet the most profound relationship she has in her life is with a deceased actor whose likeness is projected on a movie screen; well, it simply isn't apparent that Billie Jean recognizes this as a contradiction. She carries around one of Charlotte's mother's candelabras for most of the evening, a harbinger of things to come. Heretofore Billie Jean has been the only one to dress in ghoulish costume and makeup. Jimmy J. decides that everybody will follow her example in order to "shake up" some couples known to be making out in their cars at the local cemetery (among them, naturally, are Frank and Pat). Of course, Billie Jean decides that no modifications to her "getup" are needed: "I'm perfect. I'm exactly who I want to be." On their way to the cemetery, Jimmy J. is more manic than we have ever seen him—and more careless. As Hanley is driving down a darkened road, Jimmy J. reaches from the back seat to briefly cover Hanley's eyes. He also has him dim the car lights, narrowly missing an oncoming pickup truck. Does Jimmy J. have a death wish? Billie Jean is oblivious to the real danger she and the rest of them are in. "This is the darkest night of my life," she screams in ecstasy.

At the cemetery, this quintet of made-up misfits crawl past gravestones almost balletically, as Willis's camera glides with them. The film has settled into a kind of dream state by now. We experience no amusement as the kids pop up and frighten the living daylights out of the couples. As the evening descends into chaos, Billie Jean, standing atop a tombstone, begins to shriek, wildly waving two fully lit candelabras. She loses her balance, the fire engulfing her. Instantly, the catastrophic consequences of Jimmy J. and Billie Jean's recklessness are apparent.

The scene curiously recalls a flashback in Otto Preminger's *Tell Me That You Love Me, Junie Moon*, in which the titular character, played by Liza Minnelli, is driven to a cemetery by a demented date and is horribly disfigured when he pours battery acid on her. The scenes share an obvious similarity in plot and setting, though I have no way of knowing if Bridges was even familiar with Preminger's film, let alone influenced by it.

Richard Thomas was well aware of the dark side to his character: "The thing about Jimmy J. that's interesting to remember is that his obsession with Dean is just that. It is an obsession. It's not just, 'I'm moved by this and I want to become this.' He over-identifies and because they over-identify, these things happen. And at the end of the script, after her tragedy, when you think he might have learned a lesson about that, no, he's still completely caught in the grip of this obsession. He's going to carry it with him to Hollywood, presumably. So there's a shadow side to it. It isn't exactly what you'd call—that cringe-making phrase—a triumph of the human spirit!"[105]

* * *

It was during the filming of the séance scene that sound mixer Chris Newman experienced "one of the sweetest things that has ever happened to me in my entire life."[106] Newman, a legendary figure of the American New Wave, had worked with Gordon Willis on such films as *Little Murders*, *Klute*, and *The Godfather*. *September 30, 1955* was their fifth film together. Newman recalled:

> We had moved from Arkansas to Universal. We were shooting one of the scenes in the house where everybody was walking around with candelabras. At one point, all of the lights go out because the candles go out. If I remember correctly, Gordon had done something very, very unusual, rather innovative, and that is he had muslin ceilings across the top of the sets. We had electricians with lights up above them. They would pan the candelabra as the candelabra moved. The lamps would diffuse through the ceiling, through the muslin, and would track with the candelabra to give the impression that the light was truly coming from the candelabra.
>
> It was extraordinary, but it was hard to do. Today we would have done it with television assist and all kinds of other stuff. It was hard for these guys to do it. They didn't really understand what he was doing. He became more and more impatient with their performance.
>
> In the middle of this, we're doing our regular boom work. It was working pretty well for us. But we had a problem with the camera. The camera was noisy. In those days what you would do with a Mitchell BNC, which is what we were using, is, you'd open up the door and you'd change the pitch as the film was going through the gate, which often would decrease the amount of noise. However Universal, in their brilliant non-trusting of camera assistants, had removed the pitch controls from the cameras. So if you opened the door and tried to adjust the pitch, you couldn't do it. Effectively what was happening was, if we had camera noise, there was no way to minimize the camera noise, not easily, not traditionally. First of all, I didn't know that. Secondly, when I found out, all we could do was reload and hope the magazine would be quieter. And also I didn't really know then what I could get away with. When you have less experience, you're not always sure about the parameters. It's one of the hardest things for a sound person to really understand and come to grips with. What's the most noise I can admit on the track that eventually will disappear in the rerecording or processing or whatever? It makes you overprotective. It's a classic mistake that all entry-level sound people make.
>
> So we do a take, which was fine for me except that there was some camera noise. And I guess Gordon was really happy because we had done a bunch of takes and the guys on the towers who were doing the panning of the lights, who were screwing up each time, got it right this time. But of course I was not aware of that. And I asked for another take. Gordon got pissed off at me. But I got another take out of it. We did another take and it was better for camera noise. I don't know if it was better for lighting, but it was good enough because then we went home.
>
> By then, I had gotten very friendly with Bridges, who was a sweet, sweet guy. He kind of welcomed me and my enthusiasm to the set. It was the kind of job where I could do no wrong, absolutely. In any case, Gordon was pissed

off and wouldn't talk to me. Jim said, "What happened?" I said, "Well, I'm not sure what happened. But he's annoyed because I asked for another take." Jim said, "Well, I'm driving him home and I'll talk to him." So I go home and I was absolutely miserable. I felt awful. I mean, here's a guy that I have this kind of tight, respectful relationship with. In many ways, I was trying to emulate what he was doing from a sound standpoint. He's angry with me and I don't even know what the hell is going on.

I remember sitting at the hotel where I was and saying I don't want to spend the night tossing and turning and thinking about this and go back to work the next day. This is true, this is not apocryphal: I literally reached for the phone to call Gordon because I knew where he was staying and the phone rang. And it was Gordon. He said, "I'm sorry," I'm this, I'm that. I said, "Well, I'm sorry, too. And what the hell was going on?" And then he explained to me about the lighting. I said, "Well, you know, if I had known that, I would never have asked for another take even if there was camera noise. I would have crossed my fingers that they could have dealt with it."

It was all rosy after that. It was one of the few times that I ever had a fight with him anyway. It was startling to me that the phone rang literally as I put my hand on the phone.

Newman is "sure" that Bridges had indeed spoken with Willis as he drove him to his hotel room: "Bridges was that kind of guy."[107]

* * *

In the final act of *September 30, 1955*, Jimmy J. (who has been kicked out of school) visits Billie Jean as she is recovering from her burns. Three weeks have passed since the fateful night. He finds her covered in white bandages, only part of her face visible. She doesn't say a word. Privately, Melba Lou suggests to him that she might be a candidate for shock treatment unless she begins to talk again. He cares about her or he wouldn't be there to see her, but there is the discomforting thought that he cares almost as much about the death of James Dean, a person whom he never met, as his mother reminded him, as he does about the injuries suffered by Billie Jean, his closest friend. At her bedside, all he can speak of is Dean's new film, the posthumously released *Rebel Without a Cause* and the many rumors surrounding Dean's death, including the possibility that he might still be alive. In their classic book *Midnight Movies*, J. Hoberman and Jonathan Rosenbaum described the Dean cult well: "In 1956 ... as many as two thousand fan letters a week were being sent to James Dean, a full year after his fatal car accident, mostly by teenage devotees who refused to consider him dead. Rumors circulated that Dean was alive in a sanitarium, perhaps disfigured, or that he had been reincarnated in another body."[108]

Even when Jimmy J. says that he accepts responsibility for Billie Jean's accident, he does so because Dean's character in *Rebel Without a Cause* does something similar in the film. Jimmy J. "doesn't even get it," Lisa Blount said.

"That's what the scene is really about. He says, 'No, no, they're saying he's still alive!' I mean, that's some weird shit! He doesn't hear that this girl has been burned and 'scarred for life.'"[109]

Jimmy J. goes on and on in what amounts to, finally, one of the great film monologues of the seventies. Thomas was more than up to the task, though he still approached the speech with some trepidation. He observed,

> It's funny, when you do a play and you have big monologues, during the course of the rehearsal process you integrate them into the performance as a whole. You discover how they connect with what comes before and what comes after. The most obvious examples are Hamlet's soliloquies. When you prepare those, you're like, "Oh, no, I have to do these." But over the course of the rehearsal period, they're subsumed into the text as a whole and the performance as a whole. Even though they are these mountain peaks, the sense of continuity kind of protects you a little bit from them. You get to ramp up to them.
>
> But when it's a film performance and you have this script and you go, "I have this part and I've got these two scenes with these big fuckin' monologues in them," they sort of stand alone. You know you're going to go out there one day and you're going to shoot *that* scene with *that* monologue and that's what it's going to be about. How's it going to go? Am I going to be ready? You wake up in the morning and you go, "Oh, my God, I've got to do this scene now. This is the big scene." Because of the way you make movies, they tend to stand up as these heights that you have to scale on this particular day. They're fraught with a kind of anxiety, for me anyway, that don't come up when you put them into a play.
>
> There's also that feeling on the set: Okay, now, this is the scene where we're going to do this.... It's all prepared for you and they keep it very quiet and everybody knows you have a job to do, unlike in the theatre where the audience is out there and the actors are sitting around and you're going to do it and then you're going to leave and somebody else is going to come on and do the next scene. So they're highlighted even more and the pressure becomes, in a strange kind of way, a little greater than it needs to be. And at that age, I was really intensely aware of what these demands were going to be. Learning these speeches is no problem for me because of my work in the theatre and because I have a good memory for writing. But you want to fulfill them. Because you don't get to do them eight times a week and you kind of have to hit it that day, it's like, "Okay, how was it on that day? How was I on Wednesday? If I had done it on Friday, would it have been better?" It's one of the frustrating things about this particular way of acting.[110]

Jimmy J.'s talk of how he must go to California to find out more about his hero finally becomes too much for Billie Jean. She screams, "Stop it! I don't want to know any more! I don't want to hear any more!" She impulsively tells Jimmy J. to break the mirrors in her room, which he does with actorly flair. "I'm scarred," Billie Jean says, hauntingly. "I'm scarred for life."

"The truth is I did not have the acting chops to do that scene, and I knew I didn't," Blount revealed. "I didn't have a plan. I hadn't been trained. I was really terrified because I knew that that had to be right. So all I could think to do was not to talk! When in doubt, you just do what your character does. I tried to literally just not talk for days leading up to it, so that my voice would hopefully come out sounding whatever a voice sounds like when you haven't used it in several days. But it didn't work. I've always been very, very sad that that moment could have really been something extraordinary—the makeup was wonderful and the costuming and the music, oh my—but I just didn't feel that my performance really worked."[111]

Blount is mistaken. In just a few lines, she perfectly expresses the profound *disappointment* of a girl whose grandiose dreams have been, like the mirrors in her room, shattered. She is left to a life in Conway, Arkansas, not Hollywood, and a much sadder one than if she had never seen *East of Eden* or known Jimmy J.

Hearing the sudden burst of commotion, Melba Lou enters her daughter's room. Words are exchanged between the three of them. Jimmy J. exits clumsily, not having learned a thing. He tells them, "I got to go now. This whole thing is starting to feel like a movie. I mean, you know my life does that to me sometimes. Sometimes I feel like I'm moving in a big, big movie." As in the stunning moment in Norman Mailer's *Maidstone* in which Mailer and Rip Torn have a scripted/unscripted fight on camera, here Jimmy J. conflates the movies and real life to a shocking degree. Billie Jean says what we are all thinking: "This ain't no movie, Jimmy J."

So he leaves Billie Jean to her room and to her sorrow. He has a last look at his former comrades at a football game: There is Charlotte, being crowned homecoming queen during halftime; there are Frank and Pat in the stands; there is Hanley, sheepishly drinking a beer. Again we see him from behind a chain-link fence. But earlier he was inside the fence on the football field; with everything now having changed, he is on the outside looking in. He takes in the sights before him, but midway through the marching band's rendition of "The Star-Spangled Banner," he hops on his motorcycle and leaves the campus of Arkansas State Teachers College.

Willis's camera pans with Jimmy J. as he speeds down Conway's main boulevard, passing the movie house where he saw *East of Eden*, until we settle on the same composition that opened the film. As Jimmy J. disappears into the distance, late afternoon turns to twilight and finally to night. "The shot was done in the simplest possible way," Willis explained. "The camera was locked-off and I made exposures from day through night. Dissolves tied it together."[112] In his memoir *Digressions on Some Poems by Frank O'Hara*, Bridges's friend Joe LeSueur paid tribute to this remarkable shot: "[I]n the gathering dusk, there is a ravishing long shot of an old-fashioned, small-town movie theater marquee and a workman on a ladder removing the letters that spell out EAST OF EDEN and replacing them with MARILYN MONROE IN SEVEN YEAR ITCH. It is an extraordinarily privileged moment in the American cinema."[113] (Alas, LeSueur slightly misremembered the shot; MARILYN MONROE IN SEVEN YEAR ITCH is already on the marquee when Jimmy J. drives by it.) In an interview, Susan Sontag once spoke of the "sense of space" and "sense of physical grandeur in American literature," citing as an example the essays of Ralph Waldo Emerson: "There's an amazing sentence in Emerson where he talks about a dream he had and he says that he saw the world shrunk to a ball in his dream. And then he says this amazing sentence: 'And I ate the world.'"[114] At the end of *September 30, 1955*, there is the same feeling of what Sontag calls "space eating," as Jimmy J. is en route from one part of the country to another in a quest to remake his life.

But let us not get carried away with the superficial romanticism of the image. Vincent Canby couldn't have been more mistaken when he suggested that Bridges intended audiences to believe that "after Jimmy J. goes roaring off to California on his James Dean-like motorcycle, Jimmy J. will grow up to be a writer and director of movies, like Mr. Bridges."[115] Maybe Jimmy J. will go off to do great things. Or maybe Canby's own prognostication — "that Jimmy J. will land in Hollywood; work at odd jobs and, eventually, settle down as the manager of a supermarket"[116] — is closer to the truth. The point is that Bridges never allows us to forget the wreckage left in Jimmy J.'s wake. Think about the final shot more closely: The camera does not join Jimmy J. to accompany him as he "roars off" to the West Coast. It stays behind in Conway, with the pain and anguish of Billie Jean. The title *September 30, 1955* memorializes not just James Dean but also the sad fate of the girl who was his greatest fan.

* * *

Walter Thompson, Bridges's editor on *The Baby Maker* and *The Paper Chase*, died the year before *September 30, 1955* went into production. Initially, Bridges sought out another legendary editor, Dorothy Spencer. Like Thompson, she had worked with John Ford, having edited his classic *Stagecoach* in 1939. But as with Michael Preece and several other members of the crew, Spencer left the production after Richard Thomas broke his leg.

Bridges first asked Verna Fields, the seasoned editor of Peter Bogdanovich's *Paper Moon* and Steven Spielberg's *Jaws*, to cut *September 30, 1955*. Fields was by then working as an executive at Universal and declined, instead recommending the services of a young assistant editor whom she had been mentoring, Jeff Gourson. "She said, 'You know, I have a few people I would like you to meet that I think would be very good for you and for the movie,'" Gourson recalled. "She set up a meeting with Jim and me. From that point on, we just hit it off. It was my first official movie editing job. I was scared to death. I had Verna in my court to back me up. She was there when I needed her, which helped my confidence. But working with Jim was just an unbelievable experience."[117]

Though not a lot of footage had been shot before Thomas's accident, Bridges nonetheless wanted Gourson to be on location in Arkansas to assure that the new footage matched the old. "I didn't really have an editing room, per se; however they did set up a Moviola in the prop truck for me," Gourson remembered. "Whenever they needed to match something, I would be out there to run the clip for them on the Moviola....

"I really, really enjoyed it and I learned a lot. It made my job easier because I was there when Jim was shooting. Obviously, most of the time the editor can't sit there because he's got to be in the editing room editing. But this situation was unique because I was able to sit there and listen to how he spoke to the actors and directed them. He knew what he liked when he saw it. When I went back to cut it, I kind of remembered what kind of comments he made. So it made it a little bit easier for me to put it together knowing what was in his head at the time."[118]

Gordon Willis had very strong preferences when it came to how his images were cut together. The cinematographer said, "I don't believe in doing thousands of cuts, then giving it to the editor to make the movie. 'Dump truck directing' is my reference to that style of moviemaking. You have to know how to cut before you can shoot well. The lack of definition in movies today is appalling. Very few people know how to mount a narrative any more. If a scene works in one cut, you don't need ten. Or it might need ten; let's not make it twenty."[119]

Generally speaking, Bridges adhered to Willis's philosophy of filmmaking. Gourson confirmed that Bridges "knew exactly what he wanted and he was very, very prepared. He shot what he needed and, for the most part, it went together very, very easily in the cutting room."[120] Gourson considered himself "very fortunate" to have been chosen to edit Bridges's third film and to follow in the footsteps of Walter Thompson. But there were growing pains for the young editor, which Bridges handled in his typically tactful manner.

"There was a comment he made to me one day," Gourson said. "I cut a scene for him. Being my first job as an editor on a movie with raw material, an editor has a tendency of taking all of the material and just putting it together because it was shot. So we put it together and he looked at it. He said, 'Hmm, very interesting. Now what I would like you to do is, I would like you to look at the scene and think what the scene is really *about*.' Obviously, I didn't cut it the way it was supposed to be; I had just assembled the material together. That was my first really big education with him in editing. Look at the scene, read the scene in the script, what does the scene really tell you?, what is it trying to say to you?, and transfer that to the film. And when I re-did it, it was totally different. I went, 'Oh! I get it.'"[121] In time, Gourson surpassed Thompson as the editor with whom Bridges worked most often; after *September 30, 1955*, Gourson completed the editing of *Mike's Murder* (a film begun by Dede Allen) and edited the entirety of *Perfect*.

During the post-production of *September 30, 1955*, Debbie Getlin was hired as Bridges's assistant. Like Gourson and Kim Kurumada, she would work with Bridges for most of the next decade, becoming a trusted helper and friend. Early in her career, Getlin had worked for the executive vice-president in charge of production at Universal, Edward Muhl, until she took a sabbatical to have a family. Upon her return to Universal, she found that Muhl had retired. "The studio sent me out on a temporary assignment while they were waiting for a new executive to come on board," Getlin recounted. "That temporary assignment was to set up offices in a bungalow on the back lot for a production company that was returning from shooting a film in Arkansas.... I had no idea what I was going to be in for. I was just supposed to set up offices. The director, the producer, and the editing facilities were supposed to be working in this bungalow. I had like three days to get furniture, a phone system, office supplies, editing equipment, before everybody from the film crew arrived and they wanted to start cutting the film."[122]

Getlin remembered the first time she met Bridges:

> He arrived at the new office with Jack Larson. It was so fun to meet them. They walk in the door and Jack was just dressed impeccably; he always was. Perfectly pressed shirt, bowtie, jacket. And Jim looked like a comfortable unmade bed. He always wore jeans and loafers. His shirt was wrinkled and not pressed like Jack's. He always had this tweed jacket with leather-reinforced elbows that he just loved. He loved telling people that it was a Brooks Brothers jacket and Lincoln died in a Brooks Brothers suit. And his hair.... I just couldn't get over his hair when I first saw him. He had the original punk hairdo. His hair was kind of thin. It looked like he had just gotten out of the shower and kind of ruffled it up with a towel and that was all he did. And I think that is all he did! He was just precious and the minute you looked at him, you fell in love with him. To see him walk in with Jack, they were absolutely the odd couple. They were the odd couple before *The Odd Couple* was popular.[123]

Kurumada's description of Bridges meshed well with Getlin's: "Jimmy lived extremely simply. He always needed a haircut. He wore jeans and a pressed shirt. I used to try to buy him a jacket so he would have something to wear! He'd stuff all this stuff into a big leather tote bag that he'd carry around, so if we had to go out to a dinner or someplace he could just throw that on. That was his style. We'd be coming home and he'd say, 'We have to stop at McDonald's.' He'd order two beef patties with nothing else. It was so he would remember to bring something home for his dog so Jack wouldn't have to worry about what the dog had that night. And that would be right after having a La Scala dinner with Guy McElwaine. That was just Jimmy."[124]

Though she worked for him for seven and a half years, Getlin's fondest memories of Bridges are from the summer she managed the bungalow where *September 30, 1955* was being cut:

> I was running around the office trying to do three things at once and the phone started ringing off the hook. Jim just walked out of his office and he leaned against the doorway. He had his hands in his pockets. He was just watching me run around the office. I looked up at him and I asked him if he needed something. And he shook his head no; he didn't say anything. He just continued to watch me try to keep up with everything that was happening and taking care of everybody. And I was very focused on this phone call. I seem to remember it was an important phone call. I was trying to set up something with Jerry Weintraub and we were trying to determine where this meeting was going to be. And Jim just walked over to my desk with his hands in his pockets and he stood over this plastic lamp that was at the corner of my desk. Slowly, he leaned over and he just let some drool fall from his lips onto the lamp and he watched it bubble. Then he looked up at me with this real satisfied grin and I started laughing hysterically. It got so bad I could not finish the phone call and I had to ask if I could call back! I was on the floor. But that was Jim Bridges. He knew how to always keep everything in perspective. No matter how stressful it got, he found a way — without saying a word — to keep everything in perspective. I knew at that moment that that was the beginning of my time with him and that I wanted to work for that man as long as he would have me.[125]

Bridges's favorite pie shop was located near the Universal lot. "Almost every day at four o'clock, Jim would look at his watch and he would go, 'It's pie and ice cream time!' in his Southern accent," Gourson recounted. "We would go over and I would select some pie and ice cream. He loved food and loved to eat."[126] Getlin said, "He would order all of the types of pies that he just loved and order a fork for everybody. We would just sit there and eat pie. I said, 'Jim, I can't leave the phones.' And he goes, 'If it's important, they'll call back.' There was nothing more important to him than keeping everybody happy and motivated."[127]

According to Gourson, Bridges relished the editing process: "He'd lie on the couch or he'd sit behind me. I don't remember him ever really wanting to get into doing it himself, but he just enjoyed being in the cutting room. I always like to make my cutting rooms as comfortable as possible because you do spend half your life in there. I try to make it more like a living room. So he really, really enjoyed it. I think he found it very comfortable and relaxing."[128]

When *September 30, 1955* was completed, Getlin couldn't bring herself to leave. "There were two decisions that I ended up making," she recalled. "When the executive came on board at Universal, they called me and they said, 'We can take you off that project now.' And I said, 'I have to tell you something. I don't want to go.' They said, 'You know that you are going to be making less money here.' And I said, 'I know, and I don't want to go.' So I stayed with Jim and I think that he really appreciated the dedication. We discovered that we really worked well together. When we were between films, Jim paid me personally. Then he would move to another studio to do a project and, in his negotiation, I believe he negotiated my salary at the same time. Possibly not; that's what my understanding is. Thinking back on it now, I wouldn't be a bit surprised if Jim just paid me right out of his pocket."[129]

* * *

From the beginning, *September 30, 1955* was misunderstood, including by the studio that produced it. "Universal did not understand the film at all," Richard Thomas said. "They didn't get it the way nobody got *The Waltons*, until it was a hit. But they did not sell that picture. That picture was not marketed at all. We were right in the middle of that auteur period. It would have been perfectly acceptable to market a small, personal American film. If it had been in French, it would have been a whole other story. I think they thought they were getting *American Graffiti*, which they weren't getting."[130]

Willis referred to the film as "not something that Universal wanted to make."[131] It is equally accurate to say that it was not something Universal wanted to *release*. One of the few critics to champion *September 30, 1955*, Janet Maslin, wrote three feature articles about the film in *The New York Times*, one of which puzzled openly over Universal's lack of support. After praising Thomas's "bravura performance" and Bridges's "sparkling direction and his funny and imaginative screenplay," Maslin noted that the studio "has had a terrible time marketing the movie, which has been ready for almost a year."[132] Five ad campaigns had been tried, she wrote, and "the film's title ... used to be *9/30/55* until audiences proved slow to recognize the numerals as a date."[133] (The film is identified as *September 30, 1955*, not *9/30/55*, on the print that was finally released, though many cast and crew members still refer to it as *9/30/55*.) Maslin's was a lone voice; the reviews by Canby, Haskell, and Sarris were not pans as such — they just misperceived the film's tone, misunderstood its meaning.

On some level, though, that didn't matter to those who worked on *September 30, 1955*. For them, the reward was in making a movie with James Bridges. Thomas said, "It is what you long to have with a colleague, which is a collaboration that is intense, personal, unguarded, that is professional, but that also involves a relationship with the whole person. I think most people who worked with Jim could say that they not only worked for Jim Bridges, they had a relationship with Jim Bridges and that that relationship finds its way onto the screen, in terms of what he gets out of you and in terms of what you deliver for him. So it was a kind of whole person collaboration, always."[134]

Much like *The Paper Chase* did for its cast, *September 30, 1955* made the careers of those making their screen debuts. Less than a decade later, Tom Hulce starred in Milos Forman's *Amadeus*. Dennis Quaid eventually became one of Hollywood's biggest stars. Deborah Benson called the film "a wonderful way to come into town."[135] The following year, she starred opposite Quaid and Scott Jacoby in *Our Winning Season*. She recalled, "*September 30, 1955* was an amazing credit to have, especially with Jim's reputation out here. It helped a lot. It was a huge stepping-stone. It probably kept me from having to wait tables for years, trying to come in from a different direction. It was an amazing gift."[136]

Lisa Blount roomed with Benson when they went to Hollywood for the first time. She briefly moved back to Arkansas before deciding, "No, I really want to give it a shot."[137] Some decent roles came her way and then a highly coveted one: In *An Officer and a Gentleman*, starring Richard Gere and Debra Winger, Blount again played "the girl from the wrong side of the tracks." She felt this typecasting was due to the impression she made in *September 30, 1955*. "An actor can hopefully have a range, but when you're breaking in, you need kind of a hook," she said. "You need something that they'll remember you by. So I became very good at those characters. It was absolutely because of this film."[138]

Blount said that Bridges had a part in her being cast in *An Officer and a Gentleman*. After she read for the film, "Debra Winger went and called Jim up, right there, while I was there, and asked him would he vouch for me. They put him on the line with everyone and he said, 'Of course.' And that was that. He did that for me. He just stepped into that role without any hesitation. None at all. I think he did that for a lot of people. You can be friends, but not really willing to stand up for someone. I mean, how was he to know if I could play this role in *An Officer and a Gentleman* or not? Every gal in town wanted that role. Who was I to have it? But Debra had a lot of power at that time and she really liked me. He was a mentor always. Always there. He would always take your phone calls."[139]

Four. Going Home 103

* * *

When it comes to James Bridges, in the end all roads lead to Tennessee Williams. Blount doesn't shy from comparing the two: "They understood women. They could write roles for women like hardly anyone else ever could, especially Southern women. They loved Southern women."[140] From Charlotte and Billie Jean to Melba Lou and Jimmy J.'s mother, *September 30, 1955* is full of memorable Southern women. It would be some years before Bridges wrote a film with a female protagonist (*Mike's Murder*), but he always had an ear for female dialogue. And actresses, from Benson and Blount to Jane Fonda and Debra Winger, invariably did their best work in his films.

Some years after *September 30, 1955*, Blount was up for the part of Stella in a television version of *A Streetcar Named Desire*. "I was determined to play Stella," she recalled. "Tennessee Williams died before they were able to actually shoot the show. On his desk was a memo that they found that had some number of names of women to play Stella and a number to play Blanche. And he had a red circle around my name. I got that piece of paper. My manager found out about it and he got that for me. If I wasn't going to get to meet Tennessee Williams, then what was I living for? For him to die on me was just like, 'This can't happen!' And then I didn't get the part. My life was off track and then I find out he knew who I was, he had seen my work. This is after I'd done *An Officer and a Gentleman*, so he knew me enough to know that I could definitely play this role for him. It was like from the grave, I get this message from him."[141] Not unlike James Dean communicating from "the other world" with Jimmy J. and Billie Jean....

Williams undoubtedly knew of Blount — and not just from *An Officer and Gentleman*. He probably remembered her from his friend James Bridges's film, too.

Five

Going Nuclear (and Commercial): The China Syndrome *and* Urban Cowboy

How to top a masterpiece? This is what James Bridges confronted after making *September 30, 1955,* and the most perceptive observers of his work knew it. Reviewing his next film, *The China Syndrome, Chicago Reader* critic Dave Kehr wrote that it "looks like a hack job, particularly after the personal anguish of *9/30/55,* but it's a very good hack job: strong, simple, and perfectly paced, until the last reel flounders in a bit of overkill."[1]

Bridges could do better than "a very good hack job," but it would be difficult for any director to sustain the heights of a film like *September 30, 1955.* Even John Ford couldn't do it. According to Peter Bogdanovich, Ford "always used to say that he tried to alternate his pictures by doing 'one for them' and then 'one for myself,' meaning he would accept an assignment to satisfy the studios and the box office, and this would often enable him to get the backing for his more risky, personal projects."[2]

Bridges did exactly this. "When Jim would have a hit, he would want to make a personal film," Jack Larson explained. "When he was the goose that laid the golden egg with a hugely successful film like *The China Syndrome* or *Urban Cowboy* or *The Paper Chase,* he would then want to do a personal film and they were basically about what he knew and were *romans à clef.*"[3]

At first, Bridges didn't want to direct *The China Syndrome.* The film was a union of two separate projects about nuclear power that were being developed by Michael Douglas and Jane Fonda, who became the film's eventual stars and co-producers. Douglas explained, "An unsolicited script came through the transom called *The China Syndrome.* It was written by a gentleman named Mike Gray.... And I read *The China Syndrome* and thought, 'Wow, this is a really good monster movie,' and by that I meant it was a real thriller. There was this machine, this nuclear power plant, that was out of control that had a sort of monster-type feeling to it."⁴ Meanwhile, Fonda and her producing partner, Bruce Gilbert, "were inspired by what happened to Karen Silkwood" and were "developing our own movie about nuclear power. We were particularly interested in me playing a television reporter."⁵

Coincidentally, both projects were at Columbia Pictures, Fonda explained, "so this very smart woman at Columbia, the vice-president in charge of production, Roz Heller, said, 'Hmm. We're only going to do one nuclear film. Maybe the two of you could kind of like pool resources.'"⁶ Bridges was recruited to "pool" the screenplays. Gilbert said, "It was a testimony to a real kind of brilliant idea about structure that Jim Bridges ... brought to a melding of these two stories to create the movie that we call *The China Syndrome*."⁷ Bridges, who had worked so well with unknown actors on his previous two films, was reticent about making a film with stars of the caliber of Fonda and Douglas. He discovered, however, that "Jane and Jack [Lemmon] and Michael were as easy to work with as if they were anonymous."⁸ (Douglas had, in fact, worked with Bridges before; he had a supporting role in *When Michael Calls*, a TV movie written by Bridges.) But there was another reason for Bridges's hesitation in agreeing to direct *The China Syndrome*. According to Larson, he thought that the film's subject matter — the dangers of nuclear power — "was a huge responsibility. He would get up every morning and pray that he didn't betray this responsibility on this film and what the film had to say. He wanted to be objective and fair.... Jim felt that it was a big responsibility on his shoulders that sent him back to his Assemblies of God prayerfulness. He would pray every day."⁹

The China Syndrome was released on March 16, 1979; on March 28, the Three Mile Island nuclear power plant accident occurred. But even before this infamous coincidence, opposition to nuclear power had been growing across the country. "In Seabrook, New Hampshire," wrote historian Howard Zinn in his essential *A People's History of the United States*, "there were years of persistent protest against a nuclear power plant which residents considered a danger to themselves and their families. Between 1977 and 1989, over 3500 people were arrested in these protests."¹⁰ Bridges, described by Larson as "a Democrat from Arkansas"¹¹ who enthusiastically attended the peace marches his friend "dragged" him to during the Vietnam War, undoubtedly was aware of the breadth and gravity of the anti-nuclear movement, and wanted to do right by it.

He took the assignment.

* * *

Kim Kurumada was impressed. He considered the set of *September 30, 1955* to have been "run much more professionally than most Hollywood sets were run."[12] In the course of working on the film, he had also developed a friendship with Bridges. Kurumada recalled that, on location in Conway, Arkansas,

> it was hot and it was humid and we were staying in kind of a lousy Ramada Inn-kind of motel. Well, Jimmy used to take Gordon and myself and Fred [Gallo] and Richard Thomas and a couple of people out to dinner. He would choose the most expensive restaurant that he could find and he would always pay the bill. That was Jimmy's way of thanking us. That was Jimmy's way of keeping us in his inner circle appreciative. I don't think he had to do it, but the fact that he did do it certainly is what further endeared all of us to him. It wasn't about the fact that he was picking up the tab, it was the fact that he *thought* enough to extend himself to do that. He could have just said, "I'm tired," and gone to his hotel room. He didn't do that. He was always making the extra effort, whether you were an actor or a part of the crew, to try to do what he could do so that you could perform your best. Most people say, "Hey, you're getting paid for this, aren't you? So be professional about it." Jimmy used to remind people that he was a simple boy from a simple Arkansas town and that everybody likes to be patted on the back once in a while.[13]

After *September 30, 1955* wrapped, Kurumada ran into Bridges and Larson on a beach in California. "They asked me what I was doing," Kurumada said. "I told them I wasn't doing anything. Jim said he had this script and he wanted me to read it. It was *The China Syndrome*. I wasn't sure if this was just a chance encounter and that's how I wound up working on it or if he had had me in mind."[14] Fred Gallo, the first assistant director on *September 30, 1955*, had started producing films and was not available to do that job on *The China Syndrome*. The question came: Would Kurumada, the second assistant on *September 30, 1955*, be Bridges's first assistant on *The China Syndrome*? According to Kurumada,

> Jimmy knew from *9/30* that I could work with him in a very specific way, but also in a developmental way. Just like I would tell Gordon, "How are we doing, Gordy? Is it going to be very long?" he knew that I could kind of roll with the punches on this one when we didn't know what was going to happen. "Who's in charge of this show? Is it Michael Douglas or is it Jane Fonda?" At the time, Michael had just won the Academy Award for [producing *One Flew Over the*] *Cuckoo's Nest*. Jane was back from a lot of public recognition and her relationship with Tom Hayden was high in the public profile and the politics and things like that. She'd just done *Coming Home*.
> So Jimmy asked me to come in and look at it principally because there were a lot of problems with *The China Syndrome*. The Jane character wasn't totally fleshed out and he rewrote it. Jack Lemmon, who was already signed to the picture, had a show date. He had to go back to New York to do a play—I think it was *Tribute*—and he had to make that date.... How are we going to put all of these pieces together? I was flattered that Jimmy had asked me to try

to help him with this, but at the same time I was a little bit overwhelmed. I wasn't that experienced myself in doing this kind of stuff.[15]

As the first assistant director, it was Kurumada's responsibility to devise a shooting schedule. His first breakdown came out to over seventy shooting days, "which was a real lot in that time. Most features were shot in sixty days.... I went over the schedule of what we needed to do with Michael Douglas and with Bridges. I had to do it with Michael because he was my producer. I went over the schedule and it was still seventy-some odd days."[16]

What happened next was, in Kurumada's words, "a masterful Bridges chess play." While still haggling over the schedule, the director had a meeting with the president of Columbia, Frank Price. Kurumada recalled,

> For some reason, Jimmy wanted me to go with him to this meeting. I didn't know why he was asking me. I was only the first assistant. I wasn't the producer, I wasn't the production manager. But he wanted me to go to this meeting with Frank Price. We sat in Frank's office. Frank basically said, "What are you trying to do with this property?" Jimmy said, "Well, Frank, there is such a thing as the Nuclear Regulatory Commission. There are such things as nuclear power plants and they work. I need to be very sure that the film that I make is not a mockery of any of this. I need to make sure that it's an accurate portrayal whenever possible." Frank looked at Jimmy and said, "I completely agree." Frank stood up and Jimmy stood up. I looked around and then I stood up. I thought, "That's the end of the meeting!" And we walked out of there and I just kept thinking and thinking. Then I understood, "I know how to break this movie down. I know how to organize this movie. From the head of the studio, I know what exactly we can do." So that produced the seventy-some odd day schedule. People looked at it and said, "It's way too much." I said, "I think it's what we need."
>
> Then we get called for another meeting. This time, the meeting is back to Columbia and it's with Johnny Veitch. Johnny Veitch was probably one of the best senior executive heads of production that Columbia has ever had. He was a first assistant on *The Manchurian Candidate*. He was a very strong personality. So now we had to go in front of Johnny Veitch and explain what we were trying to do and why this picture was going to cost what it was going to cost.... Johnny said, "I want to see the schedule." I explained to him the schedule. I said, "This is what we plan on doing. This is what we're shooting on this day. When we do this scene, these are the things I'm trying to allow for." We went through the whole schedule. Johnny looked at it and looked at it and looked at it. He said, "Yeah, okay. Okay. Okay." After he said his last "Okay," I said, "Well, that's the last day of the schedule and that's seventy-six days." So Johnny looked at me and he said, "Well ... guys, we've got to find an answer to this. I mean, come on. We've all made a lot of pictures!" And Jimmy said, "I haven't. I've only made three!" And, again, that was the end of the meeting! So I thought, "God, Bridges, you set this whole thing up so you could deliver that line!"
>
> We walked out of there and I thought, "Well, I'm going to get a call tomor-

row morning from Johnny Veitch saying, "I don't care what the director says, you'd better fix this." But that call never came. I then knew — without Jimmy telling me — what I had to do. I knew I had to make sure that everything was right on this picture. I had to get everything organized so we could make it work. I knew that I could do it, but I also knew that this was kind of what Jimmy had in mind all along. This was how he was going to make all of these pieces work. He was going to have me set a very strict pattern.... All I had to do was get a solid plan and start executing that plan, start making that thing work.[17]

* * *

The final screenplay of *The China Syndrome* was credited to Mike Gray, T.S. Cook, and Bridges. In it, Jane Fonda played Kimberly Wells, a Los Angeles television news reporter with red hair similar to the comic strip character Brenda Starr, "one of my childhood heroines," she said.[18] Michael Douglas played freelance cameraman Richard Adams, who draws the assignment of filming Wells's story about the nearby Ventana nuclear power plant. Jack Lemmon played Jack Godell, the plant supervisor. A potentially catastrophic accident occurs, which is witnessed by Kimberly and Richard.

Jane Fonda. Michael Douglas. Jack Lemmon. Not one star, but three. Bridges was a long way from *The Paper Chase* and *September 30, 1955*, with their low-wattage casts. But a bit of "serendipitous luck" occurred, thanks to Kurumada's much-debated schedule. "Because Jack had to be in this Broadway play, I tweaked the schedule so that we shot all of Jack's stuff first," he explained. "So the schedule was totally wacko. We shot all of Jack's stuff first, and sometimes it didn't make sense to be shooting his stuff first. Then I would feed in Jane's stuff just so that we could get Jack out of the way. I would feed into the shooting schedule the things that we had to do with Jane only in a supporting way. I then left the back end of the schedule where we could just concentrate on Jane. All of her stuff with Michael Douglas, all of her stuff with the news, all of her scenes with James Karen, that was all at the end."[19] Ultimately, Kurumada felt that Bridges benefited from this "wacko" schedule because "he really *didn't* have to work with three stars all at once."[20]

It was a good thing, too, because each of his stars worked differently. Kurumada compared Fonda to Muhammad Ali. He said, "When Ali was doing his comeback, some sports writers said to Muhammad, 'You used to say you were going to take a guy down in three rounds. How come it took you fifteen rounds to get rid of this guy that wasn't anything near the level of a Floyd Patterson?' And the sports writers started to say, 'Well, you know, Muhammad saves himself. He just expends the amount of energy that he needs to win and no more because he's now concerned with his comeback and longevity.' Well, somehow, that's exactly what Jane's MO was."[21]

Lemmon was an actor constantly seeking to refine his craft, Kurumada recalled: "Part of the reason that Jack liked to go back and do Broadway shows was, it sharpened his skills. It sharpened the way he thought an actor should be. It was the discipline of doing seven shows in a week. He felt that was important in maintaining your craft as an actor. So getting the physical things for production for Jack were not a problem. Saying, 'Jack, you have to be here at six o'clock in the morning and you're probably not going home until five or six o'clock at night,' that was not a problem....

"We were watching dailies with Jack once. We looked at it and we said, 'Wow.' Jimmy said, 'That is so good that I'm not sure which version of your performance I want to use.' And Jack turned to him in the screening room and said, 'Think of me as a grocery store. Go up and down the aisles and pick out what you want.'"[22]

Script supervisor Marshall Schlom said that Lemmon "just adored" Bridges. "I don't know if it was contractual or not, but they brought a small upright piano in on the set," Schlom remembered. "Jack sat and noodled on the piano all day long. That was our atmosphere on the set. That's very rare. Then he would sit and do crossword puzzles. It was just incredible because he could be sitting in a chair and somebody would call him and say, 'It's time for you, Jack.' And his favorite expression was, 'Magic time,' so he would just put down everything and go in front of the camera, cry or do whatever he had to. When they said, 'Cut,' he went back to the chair and picked up the crossword puzzle. It was phenomenal.

"He loved Jim, as we all did. There are all kinds of people in this world and Jim was just the most wonderful guy that you could ever meet. You would want to be next to him for the rest of your life. He was more like a brother than an employer, if you will."[23]

Bridges's assistant, Debbie Getlin, joined *September 30, 1955* only as post-production was getting underway. But on *The China Syndrome*, she was on board from the very beginning of his involvement in the project:

> Jim was a writer-producer-director, so based on what was happening in his life, my responsibilities changed. When he was writing and when he was developing the script for *The China Syndrome*, I would go to his house. He had this magnificent Frank Lloyd Wright house in Brentwood. Amazing. It was so funny, the first day that I went there to meet him, I'm driving down this typical Los Angeles neighborhood and all of a sudden I look to the left and there is this house that is totally out of context with whatever else is in the neighborhood! It's like a tree house. I started laughing hysterically and I go, "That has got to be it!"
>
> A lot of times, Jim would wake up at five o'clock in the morning and go downstairs to his basement. It was a house in California that actually had a basement. That's where his office was. He would type on his old Underwood

typewriter — not electric. That's what he was comfortable with, typing up scripts. Then he would pull the page out and he would look at it and he would make notes with a pen. Then he would leave a pile of pages for me. When I would arrive at his house in the morning, I would be upstairs at the dining room table with my *electric* typewriter — thank you very much — and I would re-type the script with the changes.

We were always talking about the storyline. "Read this to me, Debbie, and tell me what your reaction is." We would kind of bump things off of each other. Sometimes he would give me a project to do, like, "Debbie, I need to write some dialogue for Jane Fonda. She's standing in front of a nuclear power plant and she's a reporter and she's describing how a nuclear power plant works. Could you write that dialogue for me?" So I would have to go do research....

When he was interviewing actors and crew, I was there scheduling appointments. I was basically doing everything on the personal side of his life so that he wouldn't have to think about anything except working on the movie.[24]

* * *

For the first time since *The Baby Maker*, Bridges didn't have Gordon Willis with him behind the camera. Filling in was the talented and versatile James Crabe, who shot many films for director John G. Avildsen, including *Rocky*. Shortly after *The China Syndrome* was completed, he was nominated for an Academy Award for Avildsen's *The Formula*.

But Crabe only worked with Bridges on this one occasion, and the results are mixed. In a generally scathing *Film Comment* review, Richard T. Jameson lamented Willis's absence from the picture. If Willis had shot *The China Syndrome*, it "would have had a better chance at developing the cinematic resonances the subject deserved.... Crabe got the job, and the result is a TV movie on the theater screens."[25] Jameson conceded the presence of only "a single interesting image: the concentric rings on the surface of Jack Godell's coffee registering the otherwise undetected secondary vibration from the turbine trip, bespeaking subtler, more dangerous disturbances in the works."[26]

Jameson selected an eye-catching image, but it isn't the only one. What about the graceful way in which Bridges and Crabe take us in and out of the visitor's gallery above the control room as Kimberly, Richard, Richard's assistant Hector (Daniel Valdez), and plant public relations representative Bill Gibson (James Hampton) witness the accident unfolding before their eyes? In one shot, the camera starts on the outside of the gallery's window and cranes down to reveal the inside of the control room below, signaling a change in perspective; up until this point, we have only been privy to what Kimberly and Richard have seen as they have toured the plant with Gibson. Now we are taken into Jack Godell's world.

A bit later in the same scene, Bridges indicates without any dialogue that Richard has begun to film the scrambling plant workers he sees through the window. In a profile close-up, Richard is in the foreground of the shot, with Kimberly beside him, and Gibson and Hector in the far background past her. Forbidden by Gibson to photograph this part of the plant, Richard covertly begins to do just that after it becomes clear that something frightening is taking place. Kimberly mouths to Richard, "Are you filming?" He discreetly nods his head. We pan down from the close-up of Richard to the camera in his arms.

Thought and planning have gone into shots such as these. At the same time, it is impossible to deny that *The China Syndrome* is an ugly film. It is ugly in a way that no Bridges film was before or after. After all, what is appealing about a nuclear power plant? Consider the fact that Bridges's directorial credit appears over a wide shot of the Ventana plant as Richard, Kimberly, and Hector drive up to it on a dirt road. Obscured by a thick haze, the plant mars the landscape, blotting out most of the mountain range which stands behind it. There is no way to prettify such a scene, and Bridges and Crabe evidently chose not to even try.

The production was designed by George Jenkins, who had previously worked on *The Paper Chase*. "Jim knew how to assemble talented people and it was just a matter of trying to manage them to make the thing work," Kurumada remembered. "I had worked with George on *President's Men*, so replicating the inside of a nuclear control room wasn't *that* difficult. He could do that. What was tricky was making the bells and whistles and the action authentic. Even though the average audience didn't understand it, we knew that there would be some guy who really works in a nuclear power plant and if they say, 'Oh, that isn't how it happens at all,' Jimmy said we can't have that happen."[27]

Jenkins's set is masterful, but it is also monstrous. (Lest we forget, Douglas originally thought of *The China Syndrome* as a "monster movie."[28]) Watching the film, it's hard not to think of the question Major Amberson plaintively poses to Eugene Morgan about the rise of the automobile in Orson Welles's *The Magnificent Ambersons*: "Do you really think they're going to change the face of the land?" The Ventana plant doesn't just change the land—it *defaces* the land. It is appropriate that Bridges and Crabe eschewed too much visual elegance in photographing it. Barbara Hershey was correct when she observed that "[t]here's not a bad person" in *The Baby Maker*.[29] The same, more or less, was true of Bridges's subsequent films *The Paper Chase* and *September 30, 1955*. But that began to change with *The China Syndrome*. The film doesn't have a villain *per se* (only numerous figures of cowardice and greed), but the Ventana plant itself is as menacing as any conventional movie heavy.

Like the dialogue in one of Jack Larson's plays, Bridges's filmography is full of rhymes. Two of his films (*The Paper Chase* and *September 30, 1955*) take place on college campuses during the fall. Two (*The China Syndrome* and *Perfect*) have journalists as leading characters. Two (*September 30, 1955* and *Urban Cowboy*) are set in the South. Though it was the most impersonal film of his career, *The China Syndrome* nonetheless reflects aspects of Bridges's other films, usually in surprising ways. One of the most striking is Douglas's portrayal of Richard Adams, who spends most of the film in a state of agitation and outrage at the perceived "cover-up" that stems from the refusal of Kimberly's station to air the footage he shot at the plant.

Kurumada observed, "Michael's character was in some ways one of the more difficult because he was the kind of young radical. I wondered sometimes, and Jimmy and I used to talk about it, 'God, every time Michael Douglas is talking, he's *yelling*. Aren't they going to get tired of him yelling all of the time?' But I think that Jimmy felt, no, that's kind of the point. When people are like that, you *do* get tired of them. His point kind of was, political activists who are yelling all of the time, even though they're telling the truth and they have a message worth listening to, you get tired of hearing them yelling. Sometimes we are our own worst enemies in that we destroy the listener we're trying to reach the most. Those kinds of thoughts ... that was a lot of Jim Bridges."[30]

The way that Kimberly relates to Richard (and his melodramatic outbursts) is remarkably similar to the way Jimmy J.'s mother relates to her son (and his melodramatic outbursts) in *September 30, 1955*. After Richard makes a scene at a meeting with station management, Kimberly confronts him outside in the hallway. Though Richard is ultimately vindicated, and Kimberly won over to his perspective, she, like Jimmy J.'s mother, sounds like the voice of reason as she tries to persuade him that his petulant behavior is not helping anything and that she is "not ashamed that I've got a good job, and I have every intention of keeping it, and getting a better one!" Even the staging and framing of this exchange recalls a shot that occurs in the scene with Jimmy J.'s mother in *September 30, 1955*: a medium two-shot with Jimmy J./Richard to the left and Jimmy J.'s mother/Kimberly to the right.

Similarly, aspects of Jack Godell are not unlike Professor Kingsfield in *The Paper Chase*. Certainly Richard's incessant yelling compares unfavorably with the cool, composed demeanor that Godell shares with Kingsfield. A navy veteran who admits to "loving" the Ventana plant, Godell comes to have reservations about its safety, but those reservations are based on his knowledge and experience. He is not basing his doubts on a roll of film depicting events he doesn't fully understand, as Richard is.

Godell also uncovers the facts surrounding Ventana's safety more doggedly than Kimberly, who, prior to the Ventana accident, does not seem inordinately unhappy about doing stories on such things as singing telegrams.

Five. Going Nuclear (and Commercial)   113

And when Godell discovers that the plant's welding X-rays are really a single X-ray duplicated again and again (one of the film's most visually thrilling scenes), he hasn't just *happened* upon his discovery, as Richard and Kimberly have; he was *looking*, carefully, for signs of something amiss. Though Godell finally has a kind of nervous breakdown, taking over the control room by force in order to expose the plant's dangers, this only occurs after threats are made against his life by shadowy forces connected with the plant.

Could it be that Bridges used up all of his energy in working with Fonda, Douglas, and Lemmon? In its lack of interesting supporting performances, *The China Syndrome* is unique among all of his films. James Karen, Peter Donat, and Scott Brady had done fine work before, and would certainly do fine work again, but their talents are not well utilized here. The performances lack texture and depth; they are cardboard constructions, something that could not be said of the supporting performances in any other Bridges film, certainly not *September 30, 1955*. The sole exception is Wilford Brimley, playing Ted Spindler, a worker at the plant.

According to Thomas, the casting of Brimley was typical Bridges:

> I was on the set of *The Waltons* one day shooting and the phone rang. I had a call and it was Jim. He said, "Richard, you need to help me. I'm about to do something and I don't know if it's the right decision or the wrong decision. I'm about to hire an actor and I know that you've worked with him and I really need to know what you think." Now, I'm not taking responsibility for this, but I think it's very cool.... I said, "Well, who is it?" He said, "Wilford Brimley." Well, Wilford Brimley had a very, very small recurring part on *The Waltons* as one of Will Geer's cronies, hanging out at the general store, so I knew Wil for a few years as an ex-horse wrangler and just a terrific character guy in this very small part. He'd gone in to read for Jim and knocked his socks off. Jim said, "I think I'm going to do this. Tell me if I should." I said, "You couldn't be picking anybody better because he's going to give you a completely authentic performance from beginning to end. He's the real thing." Now that's not why Wil got the job, but if I had said, "Oh, God, no, don't do that," he might have thought twice. But it made me once again understand how Jim was willing to go out on a limb for an actor in a casting situation that would have gone counter to the establishment every time.[31]

Debbie Getlin said, "When I saw that last scene, I went to Wil and I said, 'I know it's taken you a long time to get here, but what are you going to do with all of the success?' And he goes, 'You're kidding.' And I said, 'No, no, no, no!' Oh, he was just magnificent."[32]

* * *

Jeff Gourson wanted to join Bridges on *The China Syndrome*, but he was forced to sit out both it and Bridges's next film, *Urban Cowboy*. "I wasn't a seasoned enough editor for the studios," he explained. "As much as I wanted to do those, I guess the studios felt they needed somebody a little bit more experienced."[33] To edit *The China Syndrome*, Bridges turned to David Rawlins, who had recently completed a pair of John Badham films, *The Bingo Long Traveling All-Stars & Motor Kings* and, somewhat more famously, *Saturday Night Fever*. The project appealed to Rawlins because of "the script. It was a marvelous script."[34]

Assistant editor Francesca Emerson, who had worked with Rawlins on *Bingo Long*, recalled, "David is the best as far as an editor. He was like a young hippie and very handsome.... David was a trip. David is a fine editor, so he really had a lot of say as to how that film was put together."[35]

Emerson reiterated Gourson's contention that Bridges "knew exactly what he wanted"[36] in the cutting room. "Jim, being a writer-director, when you write something, you also visually see how it should be," she said. "You already know almost how it's going to look. It's just a matter of having a good editor who gives you that pace, who knows the pace, and also who comes in with no baggage."[37]

Notably, *The China Syndrome* has no musical score, but it didn't start out that way. Rawlins said that the decision to eliminate the score was reached during post-production: "The composer had done a score for it. In fact, it cost them $150,000. Little by little, we took it out. To begin with, it was apparent that it wasn't necessary to have one. It took away the realism. You notice that *Schindler's List* doesn't have very much of a score to it. It really gives you that theatrical feeling and you don't want that theatrical feeling."[38] A song by Stephen Bishop, "Somewhere in Between," is heard over the opening credit sequence, which shows Kimberly, Richard, and Hector driving on the freeway on their way to the plant. But Rawlins justified the song's inclusion because "it was on a car radio. We took dramatic license; it was a very *loud* car radio!"[39] "I love David," Emerson said. "We were like fire and water in that editing room, but we got the job done."[40]

Four years after *The China Syndrome*, Mike Nichols's *Silkwood* was released. Coincidentally, script supervisor Marshall Schlom also worked on that film. He noted, "Two different kinds of productions completely and two different kinds of directors in that the subject material was handled differently. Oddly enough, Mike Nichols and Jim Bridges have a similar personality and a respect for the actor and a respect for the people on the set."[41] Nichols considered his film to be "about an awakening,"[42] which is also a good way to describe Jack Godell's journey in *The China Syndrome*. In the end, *Silkwood* is the greater film; more character-driven, less didactic in its sloganeering, it is in many respects Nichols's best work. But *The China Syndrome* paved the way.

* * *

Richard T. Jameson's pan notwithstanding, *The China Syndrome* was received enthusiastically by the critics. Roger Ebert called the film a "terrific thriller," praising Bridges's "exquisite sense of timing and character development to bring us to the cliffhanger conclusion."[43] In *The New York Times*, Vincent Canby, who found *September 30, 1955* and its protagonist so problematic, proclaimed the film "smashingly effective" and "very stylish." Canby suddenly sounded like a James Bridges aficionado, calling him "a gifted and witty melodramaticist.... He has an ear for the way people talk, an eye for the pressed-plastic look of our transistorized world and sympathy for minor dishonesties that can suddenly shape the way people behave when faced with major problems."[44]

At the 1979 Cannes Film Festival, Jack Lemmon deservedly won Best Actor for what was perhaps his finest performance since director Billy Wilder's *Avanti!* (1972). Bridges received his first and only nomination from the Directors Guild of America. With Mike Gray and T.S. Cook, he was also nominated for an Academy Award for the screenplay. Lemmon, Fonda, and production designer George Jenkins received Oscar nominations, too, though none won. Twenty years after its release, it was the only Bridges film selected for inclusion in *The New York Times Guide to the Best 1,000 Movies Ever Made*.

Such accolades ring a little hollow when given to a film, however estimable, that fundamentally lacks the richness and depth of its predecessor. Just before he began making *The China Syndrome*, Bridges affirmed the unique place *September 30, 1955* held in his career: "I think it's probably the best movie I'll ever make."[45]

Very little got by James Bridges.

* * *

Entirely independent of one another, several people who were to become intimately involved in Bridges's next film, *Urban Cowboy*, read the article upon which it was based long before they knew it was going to make it to the big screen. "The Ballad of the Urban Cowboy: America's Search for True Grit," by Aaron Latham, appeared in the September 1978 issue of *Esquire* magazine.

One was Debra Winger, then an up-and-coming actress with only a few film and television roles to her credit. She had an instantaneous understanding of one of the story's leading characters, Sissy. "I read it and felt like something had gone wrong with the grand plan of the universe!" she remembered. "I mean, this was my character to play. Without a doubt I could get inside the head of this girl—I was shocked to learn it was going to be a major film."[46]

Meanwhile, David Rawlins encountered Latham's article while flipping through *Esquire* on a plane ride:

I was doing a color session with the cameraman, Jim Crabe, who lived in New York. I was flying back and on the plane I read Aaron Latham's article. I showed it to Jim Bridges when I got back to California. I said, "This would make a hell of a movie." Francesca Emerson, who was my assistant on *The China Syndrome*, agreed with me. He looked at it and threw it in the corner and never looked at it again, never read it! And about a month later, we were dubbing *The China Syndrome*, and he came waltzing into the room and said, "I've got another movie to do! I'm doing *Urban Cowboy* at Paramount!" And Francesca said, "Isn't that the story that came back from New York?" I was the first one to bring it to his attention![47]

At *Esquire*, Latham had been assigned the story by Clay Felker. "He told me he wanted me to write a story about a bar in Texas," Latham later recalled.[48] The bar in question was Gilley's, which, Latham reported, "had a mechanical bull and a mechanical punching bag and four and a half acres under one roof and several thousand city kids dressed up as cowboys."[49]

Bridges explained his interest in the material: "Here are all these men who've never seen a horse or been near a cow but who dress up every night and come into town and act just like cowboys. And risk their necks riding the wild bull.... However, I said I wouldn't commit until I'd spent several weekends at Gilley's with Aaron Latham."[50] So, in the midst of finishing *The China Syndrome*, Bridges agreed to adapt and direct "The Ballad of the Urban Cowboy." "The last time I knew what I was going to do was while I was cutting *China Syndrome*," he said much later. "I knew I would do *Urban Cowboy*."[51]

Bridges collaborated with Latham on the screenplay. "When I showed Jim my initial attempt at a script for *Urban Cowboy*, he politely informed me that most screenplays are not written in the past tense," Latham reflected. "Then we moved into an office on the Paramount lot, a big room with one desk and two typewriters.... Sometimes I would wake up in the middle of the night and write a scene. The next morning, I would show Jim my pages. Then he would show me the pages *he'd* written in the middle of the night. And the dialogue would always be the same. Only his typing was better."[52]

According to Latham's wife, television journalist Lesley Stahl, even after Bridges and Latham completed the screenplay, her husband "glued himself to ... Bridges, managing to become his right hand during the making of the movie."[53] Much as John Jay Osborn, Jr., did during the filming of *The Paper Chase*, Latham served as a guide to the world Bridges was going to depict on the screen.

* * *

Over the course of the making of two films, *September, 30, 1955* and *The China Syndrome*, Bridges had formed a close partnership with Kim Kurumada. He recalled,

I was naturally expected to do the jobs of the first assistant director, with running the set and organizing the crew and things like that, but I was very fortunate because he asked for my opinions on certain things about crafting the movie. That's usually something that directors don't do, but Jim was unique in that he would sometimes ask people what they thought about a certain aspect of how the movie should be made. Most directors don't do that. They usually have their own idea of how they want it to be made. But Jim's approach was that he felt he might hear an approach or an idea that he hadn't thought of if he would be open to listening. By the same token, you don't have time to listen to everybody. A lot of the people don't understand what it is you're trying to accomplish. So if you were fortunate enough to be in a position to work closely with Jim, either as the first assistant director, which I was, or as the cinematographer or in some cases the editor, he would try to bounce ideas off of you and see if an idea was worthwhile.[54]

An example of this occurred early in the making of *Urban Cowboy*, on which Kurumada was again the first assistant director:

There is a scene where John Travolta and Debra Winger, as part of their honeymoon, go to a prison rodeo. Jim had asked me what I thought about that. I said to him, "Well, I have worked in a prison before on a prison movie. Ideally, if you could somehow shoot the real thing, that would be a gigantic headache for me as the first assistant director to go out and try to organize that, but as far as the film goes, it could be really interesting. Even if I have all of the money and all of the resources, I won't be able to replicate with Hollywood extras or background people what real prison people look like. Having worked in a prison, it's like prison people have a different attitude and they carry themselves differently. There's just an atmosphere, there's a feeling."

Jim said that what I had said to him wasn't new, that he had actually thought of that and in fact he had done some research on his own and the Huntsville prison was having its actual rodeo sometime in February. He said, "How do you think we could do that?" I said, "Well, number one, that's kind of a pipe dream, but it would be possible for us if we went down there. I could help organize, along with the cameraman, if we could take a small film crew and maybe we could just go down and shoot part of it." He said, "What would we need?" I said, "Well, what is it you want to shoot?" He said, "I want to get the flavor of what Texas is. I think we shoot some stuff at the rodeo and then maybe we could shoot the parade." I thought, "Wow, shooting a parade is kind of a tall order depending on what you do."

But in the end, we wound up doing it. Jim wound up selling the idea to Paramount and getting the approval of Bob Evans.[55]

Initially, Kurumada said, the idea was to film the rodeo and parade with a small unit that would build into a bigger unit "and start making the rest of the movie. As it turned out, we couldn't do that for a number of reasons. But Jim didn't want to give up on that, so we wound up going down to Texas in January or February for about a week or two, shooting the prison, shooting

John, shooting those things, and then coming back to Los Angeles and continuing to prep the movie for two or three months before we went back to Texas in July to start the main part of the movie. That was a very unusual way of making the movie. Very few directors are given that opportunity.[56]

Travolta played Bud, a young farm boy who moves to Houston, staying with his Uncle Bob (Barry Corbin) and Aunt Corene (Brooke Alderson). He finds work at an oil refinery that also employs his uncle. "Working with John was the best experience I've ever had in films," Bridges reflected.[57] He enhanced the role of Bud after Travolta was cast: "I didn't make the part any bigger once we had John, though; just better."[58] The actor was up to the challenge; Travolta had never been finer than he was in *Urban Cowboy*. But, Kurumada explained, "other than in John's case, the casting was a problem. So we started this casting process. Bob Evans had his own idea of who should be playing the female lead."[59]

That would be Sissy, the woman Bud meets one night at Gilley's, marries, separates from, and eventually reconciles with. Sissy Spacek was initially considered for the role. Kurumada said, "I was a fan of Sissy Spacek's, but Jim wasn't. Jim said, 'No, I'm just not convinced that she's the right person.' We tested dozens of women. We tested Michelle Pfeiffer when she wasn't known. We tested Kim Basinger when she wasn't known. We tested Annette O'Toole, who I thought was a strong runner-up if we didn't pick Sissy Spacek. Annette looked like she could do it."[60]

Lesley Stahl remembered, "I thought Sissy Spacek would be perfect, but Aaron said that when Debra Winger auditioned, he came face-to-face with the Sissy he had created and talked Bridges into hiring her."[61] Kurumada said, "Once Jim tested Debra, he was *convinced* that she was the right person. But nobody else was convinced. She hadn't done anything. Bob Evans mocked her, saying, 'The only footage we have of her is standing next to Lynda Carter as Wonder Woman's little sister.'"[62] Bridges finally succeeded in casting Winger, she recounted in her fascinating memoir *Undiscovered*, "with a loyalty I had not witnessed in my life."[63]

Winger said, "I think there were more beautiful girls and more exotic-looking girls than I — maybe some were more experienced than I was, but somewhere in that small crunch of time I let Jim know that I could *be* this girl for him. No holds barred. And that I wanted it more than anything, at the time. He included me in the screen test, which was all I asked for, and when there was opposition he basically stood up and said, 'I won't make the film without her.'"[64]

It was the beginning of the most intense collaboration Bridges ever had with an actor. Years later, he told *The New York Times*, "When you lock horns with Debra, you never feel it's anything personal. We had a horrendous fight on *Urban Cowboy*. She refused to play a scene, and I had to shut down the set for a whole day. I was furious with her, but then I looked at the scene and realized that there was something wrong with the dialogue. Her instinct had been right."[65] But this "locking of horns" was a rare occurrence.

Winger commented, "He was always easy with an actor making it his or her own as long as the sentiment, direction, and subtext didn't change. But for me there were only a few times his words were not better than anything I could ever come up with and usually that meant I just didn't want to be audible there. I improvised a bit and he allowed it. Liked it."[66]

Unexpectedly, and somewhat inexplicably, Bridges took the actress under his wing during the making of the film. She recalled, "All through the shoot, really, with no logical reason (except that we felt an immediate love for each other that defied description) he told me about everything as it was going on. The production was fraught with energies from many directions wanting to push things here and there."[67]

Kurumada made a similar point about the pressures Bridges came up against on the film:

> What people didn't know was that Jim was juggling some very, very powerful forces to make *Urban Cowboy* work. On the one hand, you had a producer who is very dynamic, Bob Evans. Bob had a studio deal and he was well known for doing pictures like *Love Story*. He was at one time the president of Paramount Pictures. He was now producing, so he had a lot of clout with the studio. But he had his own ideas of what *Urban Cowboy* should be and they were not the same ideas as Jim's at all.
>
> Then you had another co-producer named Irving Azoff. He came in because he was going to be co-producer and he was going to provide the music. Irving was an executive who had very strong ties with the record industry. This was a time when studios were kind of courting music companies because they had figured out that oftentimes the soundtracks were extremely useful in promoting the movies. It was at a time when soundtracks were released before the movie opened and the songs of a movie were being played on the radio. They served as a tremendous promotional tool for the movies. By the same token, they helped the sale of records because of the tie-in with the movie and the tie-in with movie stars....
>
> So you had the whole record industry and their interest. At that time, it was possible to get money from record companies to help finance your movie. You can't do that now, but then you could. And you wonder, "Why is a record company investing in a movie?" It was because they were controlling the music royalty parts of it.
>
> You wanted the contribution of the record industry, but you certainly couldn't let them take over the movie. This wasn't, after all, a musical. So that was a very strong force that Jim had to deal with.[68]

His leading actors settled upon, Bridges next addressed the supporting cast, which was typically eclectic. As Wes, an ex-con whom Sissy has an affair with, Bridges cast Scott Glenn, so memorable in a very different role in *The Baby Maker*. "Nobody wanted Scott Glenn," Kurumada remembered. "In fact, unbeknownst to me and to several other people, while we were down in Houston prepping the movie, Scott Glenn went down to Houston on his own and just hung out waiting. I think it was almost like by default. We got so late and I said, 'We have to have this part cast in the next day or so,' and finally the studio just gave in and said, 'Well, do you have somebody?' And Jimmy said, 'Yeah, of course I have somebody! He's ready right now.' 'Well, can he be down there?' 'Yeah, he can be down here.' Well, of course he was already there. That was kind of how Jim did things sometimes, when he ran into resistance."[69]

Brooke Alderson, who is delightful as Aunt Corene, was new to feature films, though not to filmmaking: "I had done some art films — not the nudie kind, the art kind — with Rudy Burckhardt. I had done three films with him. I'm in the New York art world by marriage. My husband is Peter Schjeldahl and he's the art critic for *The New Yorker* magazine."[70] Alderson had also been active doing stand-up comedy and was regularly appearing in television commercials, including one "that paid me quite a bit of money and so I decided to parlay that and go out to the West Coast and see if I couldn't make a dent there."[71]

In California, she met Bridges and Jack Larson through mutual friends. "I had knocked around and did a lot of clubs," she recalled. "Jim came to see me and wrote the part for me. I had been doing a Texas character. And then I never did another stand-up in my life!"[72] Alderson had her choice of parts: "He said, 'Is there anything that appeals to you?' I said, 'Well, the aunt sounds like something I could do.' It also sounded like it wasn't a major part and it was something I could get my feet wet with.

"My part kept growing. He was amazing to me. He kept adding scenes for me to be in. I was there through pretty much the whole shoot. He kept me on for the one final shot. I think he was just being very generous because I was collecting a paycheck without doing very much but sitting around. I remember it as just being a very happy set."[73]

Bridges's generosity extended to his selection of a cinematographer. On *The China Syndrome*, the second camera operator was Reynaldo Villalobos, whose credits by that point included Martin Scorsese's *Alice Doesn't Live Here Anymore* and Michael Ritchie's *The Bad News Bears*. In *The China Syndrome*, there was a scene "where the X-rays are supposed to be delivered and the henchman heads a car off the road and the car goes over a cliff," Kurumada remembered. "Rey shot that. And when you saw the wide shot, you could see that the car came off a little bit too fast and it came very close to the camera. But you could see in the film Rey Villalobos shooting, then running away because he thinks the car is going to hit him, and when he sees that it doesn't, Rey runs back and starts operating the camera. Well, when Jimmy saw that, he felt Rey had a sense of dedication and loyalty that was very important."[74]

Bridges took note of the young cameraman, as did *The China Syndrome*'s co-producer and co-star. As Villalobos recalled: "Michael Douglas came up to me and said, 'I think I'm making everybody mad in dailies.' I said, 'Why?' He said, 'When your stuff comes on, I go, "Oh, that's great! Look at that, look at this!"' In essence, Michael kind of helped me out with Jim because he liked the work."[75] So when it came time to decide who was to photograph *Urban Cowboy*, Bridges's choice was easy. According to Kuramada,

> Rey was an unknown and Rey was untested, but I think the thing that Jim saw in Rey Villalobos was a bit of an artist. He saw a person who was willing to try to experiment and try different things, but by the same token would listen to what Jim wanted, would listen to what Jim was trying to do. In a lot of ways, I think what Jim wanted was an inexperienced cameraman, somebody who wasn't going to embellish or emphasize or put something up on screen that was an enhancement. Part of the thing that Jim felt was, "Make it real and I'll deal with the enhancements." So for that, I think he did not want to get into a dialogue with his cameraman about nuance or subtleties or certain things. But by the same token, he wanted somebody who understood that and would from time to time make a suggestion. And Rey did at a particular point, which really verified that Jim's instincts were right.
>
> The shot that Rey put into the film was the shot of Debra and John sitting face to face. It's a profile shot of the two of them and there's smoke in the background and they're sitting at a table inside Gilley's, just looking at each other. It's the night they met. That shot was never in the script, that shot was never designed. It was when we were in Gilley's and we were lighting for another shot. The stand-ins were in. And Jim looked over and saw Debra and John sitting across from each other at this table and they were just talking. Jim quickly told Rey to pan the camera over and start shooting them.... Rey looked at it and said, "Yeah, that's a great shot. Let's get it." He just turned the camera on.[76]

Like Scott Glenn, Villalobos more or less fell into being hired by the studio on *Urban Cowboy*. He remembered,

> I had worked with Bob Evans on *Players*, so I knew Bob Evans. I was sitting on the set, reading that they were going to do *Urban Cowboy*. I was thinking, "I'd like to move up. I'd like to start shooting." So I went to Paramount and walked into Bob Evans's office and said, "Hey, I want to shoot your movie!" One thing led to another and he said, "Well, you can shoot the test. We'll see

how that turns out." We shot the test. Actually, I never really got hired! Bob Evans never said anything.... I remember C.O. Erickson, the production manager, called me and said, "Well, we've got to figure out your deal and figure out what we're going to do." I said, "I need a crane. I'm going to shoot anamorphic." I just started asking for things that I wanted! He said, "Oh, okay. You better go to the head of Paramount." I went to the head of Paramount and walked in. Dick Kline was a cameraman I worked with before on other movies and he's sitting there. I walk in and the guy says, "It's your first movie and we're going to pay you scale." I said, "Great, great." I walked out a cameraman. It was funny — to this day, Bob Evans never really hired me![77]

Villalobos's decision to shoot *Urban Cowboy* anamorphically was indicative of his ambitious visual conception of the film. As editor David Rawlins observed, "Paramount didn't realize what they had. They didn't realize that Jim was going to shoot ten billion feet of film! They didn't realize that Rey was going to make an epic out of it and light it the way he did and shoot eight cameras with playback and so on."[78]

Villalobos said, "I wanted to shoot anamorphic because it was Texas and wide. Gilley's was five acres. The production designer [Stephen Grimes] was an Englishman. He was quite good. He said, 'I don't think it's going to work. It's hard with the lighting...' I said, 'No, I think we need that negative space.' We did it and after the first dailies, he came up to me and said, 'Rey, you're absolutely right. This is great.'"[79]

Villalobos's rationale for selecting the 2.35:1 aspect ratio was not dissimilar from Gordon Willis's on *The Paper Chase* (the last Bridges film to be shot in that ratio). "It's a great ratio for dealing with people in a given space," Willis said. "It's also great framing close-ups with a lot of negative space on the screen — close-up right, lots of space left."[80] Though Willis was already a legend in the industry, and Villalobos was only just embarking on his career, they shared similar instincts, which Bridges recognized.

Villalobos did all he could to persuade Bridges to look through the camera, but the director usually declined. "Between you and Gordon Willis, I don't have to look through the camera," Bridges told him.[81] Villalobos reflected,

> Maybe it should have been daunting, when I look back, but it wasn't because you're just in the moment. And I think it wasn't daunting because of Jim. He just was very calming. You went in, you did the work the best you could day by day. So I give it to him; he didn't make it daunting. I remember the very first day of shooting. It's when Travolta is leaving the house at dawn. We had all of these shots in the field and of him leaving. It was eleven or twelve o'clock. I'm up on the crane and he's coming out of the house. I looked around and there was just too much light. It was like noon. It was noon. It didn't fit. And this is the very first day of shooting. I thought to myself, "Well, I'm either going to be a great cameraman or I'm not going to be a

cameraman." So I'm on the crane and I motion for it to come down. I come down on the crane. I get off and I walk up to Bob Evans and Jim and the production manager. I said, "We can't shoot any more. It really doesn't look like dawn. There's really too much light." There was a quiet pause for two seconds. Everybody looked at me. Then Jim looked at me and said, "Okay, fine. We'll come back tomorrow." It was the start of my career with him. He was really a great person.[82]

* * *

"It was one of the very few movies I've ever done where day one of shooting is scene one in the movie," Kurumada said. He continued:

> And that again was a design that helped Jim get his cast together and it was a design that Jim used to try to make the transformation of the character. That was what was really remarkable about Jim. You didn't know that he had all of these other plans and agendas working in the background, but *he* knew. Part of the thing was, "Well, how do I transform John Travolta from the discotheque *Saturday Night Fever* into the urban cowboy?" Part of the way to do it was to begin the movie and to begin John's work in continuity.
>
> So we start off with him coming down the stairs and he's got this beard. He's driving off to Houston to get a job. Now in the story he goes to Gilley's and he has the beard and he's not the urban cowboy, then he comes back and shaves the beard, and then the first night you see him without his beard, Jim had designed this reveal. It's a classic reveal. You know, you start on the boots and you slowly pan up. He knew exactly how he was going to shoot it, way before we ever did.[83]

Winger has an equally memorable entrance later in the film (though it occurs long after we have been introduced to her character). As Sissy walks into Gilley's to ride the mechanical bull herself for the first time, she is first seen backlit and in silhouette. Bridges films Travolta and Winger not as actors, but as movie stars, despite the fact that Winger wasn't one yet.

The film's style echoes the moods of its leading characters. Dissolves punctuate many scenes. Fade-outs are not uncommon. That Bud's nightly trips to Gilley's are the highlight of his life is reflected in the perfunctory way that scenes of him at work are presented; often we only get a few shots of Bud on the job before Bridges and Rawlins cut to a lengthy scene at Gilley's, usually filled with high-spirited music and dancing. We are as relieved as Bud is to be in such an environment.

Another important supporting character was Pam, a wealthy Gilley's patron whom Bud begins seeing after his marriage to Sissy disintegrates. Pam is essentially a 1970s-era, Houston-based reincarnation of Charlotte in *September 30, 1955*. Her patrician elegance was embodied by Madolyn Smith, yet another actress to make her screen debut in a Bridges film. Bridges isn't critical of Pam, just as he isn't of Charlotte. "I didn't want to do a cliché rich bitch from Texas," Smith said.[84] Even so, the audience is all the time rooting for Bud and Sissy to get back together.

In Leo McCarey's screwball comedy classic *The Awful Truth*, "the awful truth is that they need each other," Dave Kehr wrote, referring to the recently divorced couple played in the film by Cary Grant and Irene Dunne.[85] So do Bud and Sissy, who, like Grant and Dunne, take up with people *we* know from the first they shouldn't be with. If anything, the irredeemably loutish and ultimately violent Wes is even *less* appealing than Ralph Bellamy's provincial Oklahoman in McCarey's film.

Yet Bridges, like McCarey, is ultimately magnanimous toward most of his characters. If there is little redeeming about Wes, Bridges imbues Pam with an aristocratic graciousness that finally defeats her other impulses. In fact, she is the one who ultimately leads Bud back to Sissy (even though she previously stood in the way of that happening). She is a "shit," she tells him in a climactic scene, "but not that big a shit" to conceal from him Sissy's longing to be with him again. "You don't love me, Bud, and I don't even love you," Pam tells him. "Not like that. So you shouldn't let her get away."

Earlier, after Bud and Sissy are married, and he is driving her (blindfolded, naturally) to the trailer he has bought as a wedding present, we cut to shots of matching miniature personalized license plates in the rear window of his pick-up truck. They read BUD and SISSY. When they break up, Bud takes Sissy's plate down and tosses it in the glove compartment. At the end of the film, when Bud and Sissy have reconciled, he reinstates her plate in its place of prominence, and all seems right with the world. It's not hard to see why *Urban Cowboy* was the most audience-pleasing film James Bridges ever made.

When Latham wrote his *Esquire* article, he later admitted, "I was viewing those urban cowboys from above and smiling to myself. When we started working on the movie *Urban Cowboy*, I stopped laughing. I stopped because a work of fiction — unlike a work of journalism — must embrace its characters.... So I started to identify with the cowboys and cowgirls in Gilley's, in part because I had moved from writing journalism to writing fiction."[86]

Indeed, no character is condescended to in *Urban Cowboy* or any Bridges film, whatever their station in life. Vincent Canby, in his negative *New York Times* review of *Mike's Murder*, missed Bridges's intentions and sensibility badly when he wrote that "for perhaps the first 15 minutes ... it seems that Mr. Bridges might possibly pull off the trick of making a first-class movie about second-rate people."[87] There are no "second-rate people" in Bridges's films, but instead something akin to what the great Marxist critic Fredric Jameson wrote of the characters in Robert Altman's *Popeye*, "who, no longer fettered by the constraints of a now oppressive sociality, blossom into the neu-

Five. Going Nuclear (and Commercial) 125

rotics, compulsives, obsessives, paranoids, and schizophrenics whom our society considers sick but who, in a world of true freedom, may make up the flora and the fauna of 'human nature' itself."[88]

In his films, Bridges is never reluctant to depict class distinctions (e.g., Charlotte and Billie Jean in *September 30, 1955* and Sissy and Pam in *Urban Cowboy*), but he does so without malice. As Richard Thomas astutely observed, Bridges "could appreciate it when it was buttoned-up and very proper and he could appreciate it when it was crazy and wild and out of control."[89] Frankly, Canby expressed nothing but the kind of snobbery Bridges would have abhorred when he wrote of "people with names like Bud and Sissy and Wes and Pam" in his review of *Urban Cowboy*.[90] Bridges loved these characters (excepting Wes) in all of their diversity and eccentricity, good taste and bad taste. Even Melba Lou in *September 30, 1955* is not just an object of humor; she is also the only adult character in the film to speak with sensitivity and comprehension about James Dean's death: "Jimmy J. and Billie Jean are just exactly alike. All they do is talk about movies and movie stars. You'd think there was nothing else. They go off to the movies, then come back and act out the movies. Life imitates art around here, let me tell you! And today—this Jimmy Dean, sweet little thing you just wanted to hold and cuddle, dying so tragic like that...."

Audiences embraced *Urban Cowboy* unreservedly when it was released in the summer of 1980. Grossing $53 million domestically at the box office, it edged out *The China Syndrome* as Bridges's most commercially successful film.[91]

Six

What Became of Jimmy J.: Mike's Murder

It is surprising — even a little startling at first — to realize how well directed *Mike's Murder* is. This sounds unfair, and it probably is. The films that preceded *Mike's Murder* (*The China Syndrome* and *Urban Cowboy*) both triumphed with the critics and the public, and they are effective, accomplished films, as the previous chapter, I hope, demonstrates. But they lacked the directorial distinction that marked earlier films like *The Paper Chase* and, especially, *September 30, 1955*, not to mention the personal qualities those films contained to varying degrees. By the time *Mike's Murder* was belatedly released in March 1984, it had been six years since *September 30, 1955* came out — a long time and time enough to forget that Bridges was much more than a maker of polished Hollywood product. The film's artistry thus took some critics aback. In *The Boston Globe*, Michael Blowen wrote, "*Mike's Murder* is so unlike Bridges' previous work that moviegoers might be surprised at its audacity. Don't be. James Bridges, with this fully formed work, has become more than a first-rate filmmaker, he's an artist."[1] Pauline Kael expressed similar sentiments, writing in an impassioned review in *The New Yorker* that the film was "probably the most original and daring effort" of Bridges's career.[2]

One is tempted to shout, *Don't forget about* September 30, 1955! But the effusiveness of Blowen, Kael, and other critics is understandable. *Mike's Murder* is a great film, equal to the very best American movies of its period, including Peter Bogdanovich's *They All Laughed*, John Cassavetes's *Love Streams*, and Blake Edwards's *Victor/Victoria*. It is also the best directed of Bridges's films of the eighties. He is unburdened by the silliness that sometimes mars *Perfect* or the challenging production circumstances of *Bright Lights, Big City*. That isn't to say that *Mike's Murder* didn't have its own arduous history before it finally reached screens. But it is clear that Bridges felt during the making of *Mike's Murder* much as Hitchcock did as he was directing *Rear Window*: "I was feeling very creative at the time. The batteries were well charged."[3]

Six. What Became of Jimmy J.

* * *

Death is never far from Bridges's films, whether it's the death of James Dean in *September 30, 1955*, the killing of Jack Godell at the end of *The China Syndrome*, or the loss of Jamie Conway's mother in *Bright Lights, Big City*. Death is referred to in the very titles of *September 30, 1955* and *Mike's Murder*.

But it isn't death itself that interests Bridges so much as our reactions to it. As Dean's death was responsible for Bridges making his way to Hollywood in the first place, the death of a friend motivated him to write *Mike's Murder*. Actor Paul Winfield, the magisterial African-American actor best known for *Sounder*, "had an affair many years ago with a guy he met on a film shoot named Mark Bernaleck," Jack Larson told David Ehrenstein in *The Advocate*. "After the affair they stayed friends. [Bernaleck] had a little apartment in ... Brentwood, taught the local girls tennis, and drove a cab. He was the handsomest person I've ever seen."[4] Through their friend Winfield, Larson and Bridges got to know Bernaleck. But his life didn't have a happy ending. Larson explained to Ehrenstein that "some guys ... said he'd burned them in a drug deal. After things cooled down, we were supposed to meet for dinner. But then he was savagely murdered."[5]

Bridges was, according to Larson, "incensed about it.... Jim was haunted by it. In Jim's mind, he wanted to do a film about one of these girls who has a date — it's exactly what's in the film — with this very hot, convincing young tennis player, and how she, who is also haunted by what happened to this guy, goes into this world of things she remembered him talking about and tries to find out about him. She knew nothing about him except that he was a good tennis player and a hot guy. That was the genesis and Jim wrote the script."[6]

"*Mike's Murder* was made on a shoestring budget," Kim Kurumada remembered. "It came about because one day Jim and Alan Ladd, Jr., were having a conversation. Laddie said to Jim, 'Do you have any ideas for a movie?' Jim said, 'Yeah, I do, but it's not your mainstream kind of film and it can only work if I have control and I can put it together.' And Laddie was one of the few people in Hollywood that would do those kinds of things. He had the Ladd Company, so he would back a Philip Kaufman movie when nobody else would, for example. He really recognized when somebody was a real filmmaker.... Laddie's approach was, if there's a good story here, and if I can trust the people that are making it, I'll see if I can support it."[7]

Larson said, "Then the Ladd Company, instantly on one Saturday, made a deal to do it. Jim said he would bring it in for a certain amount of money, a very small amount of money. I was going to be one of the producers of it. We met at Alan Ladd, Jr.'s house with Jay Cantor. Jim had the title, *Mike's*

Murder, which Jay liked very much. Jim was impassioned to do it. The film is a real *roman à clef*."[8]

In his review of *September 30, 1955*, Vincent Canby announced his "conviction" that, after Jimmy J. arrived in Hollywood from Arkansas, he would "work at odd jobs and, eventually, settle down as the manager of a supermarket."[9] Canby, no admirer of the film, was trying for humor with this imaginary scenario. But *Mike's Murder* provided an answer to the critic's sarcastic speculation. Mike Chuhutsky (Bridges's stand-in for Bernaleck, played in the film by Mark Keyloun) is "fresh from Ohio," according to a line heard in the film's trailer (but absent from the film). "What did he know about the city?" Well, Ohio is not Arkansas, but for Bridges's purposes, they are equivalent. Both Jimmy J. and Mike are dreamers, enticed to come to Hollywood from a place between the two coasts. Is it too much of a stretch to imagine that Jimmy J. could have ended up like Mike, with a few mistakes and a bit of bad luck? *Mike's Murder* posits what might have become of Jimmy J., and it is all we have to go on since Bridges never followed through on his proposal to make a sequel to *September 30, 1955*.[10]

"[F]inally and unequivocally innocent" is how Leslie A. Fiedler described Henry James's Daisy Miller.[11] It's also not a bad description of Betty Parrish in *Mike's Murder*, the most Daisy Miller-like of all of Bridges's characters. A bank teller, she isn't quite Mike's girlfriend; they have a sporadic romance, but she loves him sincerely and is shattered when he is murdered. She is unprepared for the rude awakening she receives in the way the world works. "In this case, ignorance is true bliss," Mike's friend, Philip (Winfield), the record producer who brought him to California, warns Betty. But she isn't ignorant (or innocent) for very long.

The creation of Betty Parrish sprang from Bridges's *other* motivation in making *Mike's Murder*: to lure his friend and protégée Debra Winger out of a premature retirement. "Debra periodically decides to quit acting," Larson explained. "She did *Urban Cowboy*, which made her a major star, and then she did a film with Richard Gere, *An Officer and a Gentleman*, which both she and Richard hated. I lectured them both one night at Paul Jasmin's house. I said, 'You're both absolutely dumb. You don't talk against the film. It's a wonderful film. I enjoyed it, you're lucky to be in it. Quit badmouthing the film!' She gave up and left Hollywood. Jim wasn't having it. He wrote *Mike's Murder* for her and he insisted she come and do it. All during the making of it, she was darling, she was wonderful."[12]

"I had made one of my first left turns out of show business. He wrote this specifically for me to bring me back in and show me how this new 'independent' approach was the wave of the future," Winger said. "I believe I had moved back to Ohio [where Winger was born]. It was based on a real story that had been gnawing at him, although Betty Parrish was a totally made-up character. Oh, her last name was my invention. Otherwise it's pretty much vintage Jim."[13]

Mike's Murder was shot in 1982, the same year that Winger starred in James L. Brooks's *Terms of Endearment*, but she seems far younger in Bridges's film, her character more inexperienced in life, certainly too immature to be a wife or mother, making her propulsion into Mike's world all the more suspenseful. It's a demanding role, Bridges said, because "[i]t wasn't filled with a lot of things for an actress to grab on to. I needed someone who had that rare relationship with a camera that allows an audience to see her think. I knew Winger could do it."[14] Kael compared her performance to "Jeanne Moreau in *La Notte*, only it really works with Winger — maybe because there's nothing sullen or closed about her. We feel the play of the girl's intelligence, and her openness and curiosity are part of her earthiness, her sanity."[15] To reformulate François Truffaut's famous assertion that *Bonjour Tristesse* constituted Otto Preminger's "love poem" to its star Jean Seberg,[16] *Mike's Murder* is Bridges's "love poem" to Winger. The similarities don't end there. Just as Seberg blossomed in *Bonjour Tristesse* after giving a flawed performance in her first film with Preminger, *Saint Joan*, in *Mike's Murder* Winger surpasses her work in *Urban Cowboy* to such an extent that it is difficult to know what Bridges saw in her in their first film together to know that she was capable of a performance of such subtlety, beauty, and humanity, one around which his entire film is built.

Winger is simply magnificent. She would not do better work until she played Joy Gresham to Anthony Hopkins's C.S. Lewis in Richard Attenborough's *Shadowlands* (1993).

In an impressionistic fashion, the first shots in *Mike's Murder* establish the basis of Mike and Betty's relationship: casual, offhand, uncommitted. We see Mike giving Betty tennis lessons, playfully helping her improve her serve. We soon dissolve to images of the two of them in bed together, as John Barry's lush score overwhelms the soundtrack.

But this is a film of juxtapositions, and the very next scene is a world away from Mike and Betty's idyll: In the middle of the night, we see Mike and his friend Pete (Darrell Larson) at a rundown restaurant called Big Tomy's Famous Chili Burgers and Famous Chili Dogs. They order some food (which is memorably seen being prepared in the kitchen underneath the opening credits), but something else is clearly on their minds. After exchanging glances with a man who enters Big Tomy's, orders a Pepsi, and then quickly leaves the restaurant, Mike and Pete head outside to the near-vacant parking lot, where, in a wide shot, they execute a drug deal. The action is viewed from afar, as two men in a car are revealed to be watching all of this as it has unfolded. After the deal is done, the men drive up to Mike and Pete, bellowing something about how this is their "territory." A melee breaks out and Mike dashes off on foot. A wide shot of Mike running down a cavernous Los Angeles street, backlit by streetlights and completely alone, evocatively expresses his desperation.

Another juxtaposition occurs when Mike hails Betty down in her car and tells her, in vague but worrying detail, some of this saga. After she drops him off at an acquaintance's house — actually, Philip's imposing mansion — we cut to a series of shots of Betty at work, manning the bank's drive-up window. The dreary routine of her job lacks the manifest excitement of Mike's life on the edge (echoes of the shots of Bud at work in *Urban Cowboy*), but its very plainness and safety makes it seem appealing by comparison.

Bridges nimbly establishes the emotional and erotic connection that exists between Mike and Betty. When she is driving him to Philip's mansion in the scene described above, it is, remarkably, only the second time the two are seen together in the film. As he is talking, anxiously looking behind to see if anyone is following them, she shoots him a quick, concerned look — not unlike the look Charlotte gives Jimmy J. in the radio station as he listens to the news of James Dean's death — that quietly conveys how deeply she cares for him, even though we have hardly seen them together. The film's sense of time is purposefully vague; it's unclear how long it has been between this scene and the scene at the tennis court — six months "at least," they decide while talking. Critic Dan Sallitt praised these "isolated romantic meetings" and the way they "are neatly compressed, conveying a sense of wasted time and emotion that depends, paradoxically, on the characters' anonymity."[17] The fleeting nature of Mike and Betty's romance anticipates Richard Linklater's *Before Sunrise* and *Before Sunset*, the theme of which is summarized in the lyrics to the song Julie Delpy sings in the latter film, "A Waltz for a Night."

The role of Mike proved vexing to cast. Larson remembered, "We were down to the wire, the film was going to shoot, and we didn't have a boy to play the part. There'd been several people who weren't right. Kevin Costner might have done it, but was too old. There was a young man who was British and that was the problem. He was very handsome and later did the sequel of *Grease*. But he was British and it needed to be absolutely an American."[18]

As it happened, Larson's longtime friend, Paul Morrissey, the director of such films as *Trash*, *Heat*, and *Flesh*, had recently completed his latest film, *Forty Deuce*, which featured a supporting performance by a young actor named Mark Keyloun. Larson persuaded Bridges to attend a late night screening of the film. "Paul Morrissey was extravagant in his praise of him and very right, so Mark did it," Larson said.[19]

In *September 30, 1955*, not even Billie Jean's accident, her being "scarred for life," awakens Jimmy J. to the foolishness of some of his actions. Likewise, Mike doesn't emerge chastened from his early run-in with rival drug dealers. Mike joins Jimmy J. and Richard Adams in *The China Syndrome* as another male protagonist in a Bridges film who is at once sympathetic and maddening. Your heart sinks when Mike makes a date with Betty, and she waits and waits and waits until the inevitable phone call comes that he can't make it. "The minute I get home, I'll come over and I'll make it up to you, okay?" he pleads. But he never makes it home.

Phone conversations are very important in *Mike's Murder*, as David Thomson observed. "Debra Winger has an affair with a 'Mike,' but she spends more screen time on the phone to him than actually with him," he wrote in his brilliant *Film Comment* essay "Telephones." "The film turns on missed phone connections, answering machines and even one of those bags into which we throw all the torn envelopes and match folders with numbers, urgent as a turn-on once, but now the blunt reminders that we are known, and forgotten, as numbers."[20] Indeed, Betty learns over the phone that Mike has been killed. A photographer friend of Mike's, Sam (Robert Crosson), who has taken snapshots of Mike and Betty on the tennis court, calls to tell her, a moment not unlike Jimmy J. hearing of the death of Dean over the radio. (A 1972 made-for-television movie adapted by Bridges from a John Farris novel prefigures the omnipresence of telephones in *Mike's Murder*: *When Michael Calls* concerns a woman [Elizabeth Ashley] who receives menacing phone calls from someone purporting to be a deceased relative.)

Mike misses his date with Betty because he and Pete have arranged to sell some cocaine to a slick drug kingpin and his wife, imagined by Bridges in the most sleazy manner possible (silk shirts, gold jewelry). Though he is ostensibly dealing drugs, in this context Mike seems downright clean-cut. Indeed, Mike's involvement in this transaction feels peripheral. He is there, he is a participant, but it is Pete who is running the show and it is Pete who commits the fatal error: stealing some coke for themselves when no one is looking. Mike shakes his head "no," deep down knowing better, but he doesn't stand up to his cocky, obnoxious cohort, finally nodding his head in acquiescence. They both pay the price for Mike's reticence. When Pete drops Mike off at his apartment building, he is accosted and taken inside, where he is murdered. In the first version of the film, edited by Dede Allen, Mike's murder was seen in graphic detail. After Allen left the project, Bridges worked with his editor from *September 30, 1955*, Jeff Gourson, on a major reimagining of the film, including the removal of the murder scene. "One of the first things that we did was the scene that was very, very graphic, we ended up re-editing to make it not as visually graphic," Gourson explained.[21]

Along with Wes in *Urban Cowboy*, Pete is Bridges's most unlikable creation. When Betty visits Sam as she is beginning to learn more about Mike, he calls Pete "that awful kid Mike started bringing around about a year ago. Little son of a bitch. He had no respect for anybody or anything. First night he was here, ripped off every prescription drug from the medicine chest and then denied it." This much is obvious from the photo Sam shows Betty of Pete, in which he is seen giving the camera the finger. We have no reason to believe that Bridges disagrees with Sam's assessment; there is nothing about Pete — impulsive where Mike is innocent, wild where Mike is merely playful — to disprove it. Darrell Larson's performance is a masterpiece of nervous energy. On the lam and suffering from cocaine withdrawal, his increasingly frenzied behavior is something to behold.

Mike's murder draws Betty into Mike's world, just as Dean's death draws Jimmy J. to Hollywood. When Betty is in a scene, Bridges films things from her perspective. A good example is when she goes to see Sam. As she walks through the hallways leading to his apartment, the film intercuts shots of Betty with point-of-view shots of the dark, twisting corridors. Bridges stays with Betty even after Sam has invited her inside. Before they get to talking, Sam briefly resumes a phone conversation and Betty is left by herself to wander the apartment. She stops to look at a photo of Mike featured prominently on a wall. His face hovers over a brightly lit birthday cake.

After she converses with Sam for a few moments, Betty retreats to the deck, walking into a close-up. There is then a cut to a shot from Betty's point of view: Across the way, she sees the tennis court where she and Mike met. Cut to a slow zoom to Betty's face. Cut back to a zoom to the courts. In the next shot, Sam emerges behind Betty, her face now in tight close-up, his in soft focus in the background. This is Sam's apartment, his world, but Bridges makes the scene all about Betty. Sam says, "I used to watch him play from here. He was a hell of a tennis player." The melancholy in Sam's voice is matched by the grief on Betty's face.

When Robert Crosson was cast as Sam, he hadn't acted in more than twenty years. "Bob Crosson had been a very good actor," Jack Larson said. "We had worked together in the deep past."[22] Throughout the 1950s, Crosson made regular appearances on such television programs as *Whirlybirds*, *Dragnet*, and *The Ford Television Theatre*; in 1954, he appeared in an episode of *The Adventures of Superman*, which Larson, of course, starred in. Crosson began writing poetry and "quit acting," Larson explained. "He managed to keep a roof over his head. He painted houses for a living. He remained close to a great friend of mine, who is really Cherry in the play *Cherry, Larry, Sandy*, Nellie Carrol, and she was always trying to help him. He was certainly an alcoholic and had the bad habit of suddenly calling you at two o'clock in the morning and needing to talk. But he was a very good actor. Because Bob and

I had acted together, I suggested him and Jim leapt on it. He's very good in the film.... We hoped that he would get agents again and work because he was painting houses, such as he could! He was a bit of a mess. But going on writing poetry and having it published."[23] Unfortunately, he never acted in another film.

* * *

In a 1999 *Los Angeles Times* appreciation of *Mike's Murder*, critic Kevin Thomas put it well: It isn't that Betty "is desperate in her single state (she has a boyfriend), but that she has never been so thrilled — or, ultimately, so touched — by a man as she has by Mike, who has retained an innocence at his core and is indeed fatally naïve."[24] Betty loved Mike, as did Sam, but no one loved him more than Philip.

Paul Winfield "had always loved Mark Bernaleck," Jack Larson said, referring to the real-life inspiration for Mike. When it came time to cast the role based on Winfield, the actor "wanted to play himself in the film, and he did, brilliantly."[25] And "play himself" really is the right way to put it; the most Bridges changed was Winfield's profession, "from an actor to a record producer," Larson said.[26]

Appropriately, the sequence in which Betty calls on Philip is in many ways the centerpiece of the film. The curving, tree-lined driveway to his mansion echoes those earlier shots of the winding hallways in Sam's apartment building, as Bridges expertly visualizes Betty's journey into Mike's world. "To Philip, in his caftan on his Brentwood terrace," critic Sheila Benson noted in her favorable *Los Angeles Times* review, "the faintly doughy, cherubic-faced Mike was a love he will never forget."[27] "I adored Paul," Winger recalled. "He played the hell out of that small role."[28] Winfield was never better — not even in *Sounder* or Samuel Fuller's *White Dog*— than he was in *Mike's Murder*. The first openly gay character in a Bridges film was given life by one of the finest actors the director would ever work with.

At Philip's mansion, Betty is first greeted by one of his assistants, Randy (William Ostrander). As she waits for Philip, Randy says, "It's been a weird week. I've known two people personally that got murdered this week. They were both drug-related." Vincent Canby quoted this line admiringly in his *New York Times* review, but he seemed to take it as comic, calling Randy "wide-eyed and naïve."[29] Well, Bridges said something very similar in an interview with Janet Maslin in the *Times*— and he wasn't kidding: "I had known five people who had been murdered dealing drugs, people who had touched my life very casually, the way Mike touches Betty's life in the movie."[30] More than any of his other films, long stretches of *Mike's Murder* are infused with a soulful solemnity, not to be mistaken for the *outrage* of

The China Syndrome. Reviewing *Bright Lights, Big City* in *New York* magazine, critic David Denby scoffed at the film's serious tone: "James Bridges ... who seems to be warming up for a remake of *Camille*, is much too flat-footed." Referring to a deathbed scene near the film's end, Denby wrote, "Suddenly, we're in a Bergman film, where anguish is inescapable and unending."[31] I think Denby is mistaken about *Bright Lights, Big City*, but this actually describes the tenor of *Mike's Murder* well — and it is not to be made fun of.

Even so, Bridges always finds moments of humor. Betty's Daisy Miller-like innocence is revealed again when she demurely says, "No thanks," to Randy's invitation for her to join him in snorting some coke. During their conversation, Randy also speaks of Pete: "I like Pete. He's a little out-of-control, but I like him. Philip doesn't like Pete." He pulls out a tape he made of Pete, Mike, and himself carousing in Philip's living room, with Philip eventually exploding at Pete after several bottles of wine from his cellar have been opened. In the video, Philip says to Mike (in Pete's presence), "I told you to keep that asshole out of my house." This escalates into a shouting match between Philip and Mike. The reaction on Betty's face as she watches tells us that she has likely never before seen Mike get angry, truly angry. We don't know what the final outcome is, as Philip suddenly appears, ordering Randy to turn the tape off. He invites Betty to join him outside, where Paul Winfield delivers a monologue comparable in every way to Richard Thomas's at the close of *September 30, 1955*.

Betty and Philip are in a two-shot as they first walk around his spacious patio, overlooking a hazy Los Angeles skyline, but Bridges then divides them: The camera pans with Philip as he mills about. As they continue talking, the film cuts between reverse shots of Betty and Philip. Eventually, Betty is standing in front of the ledge. After he asks, "Are you the girl with the C scale out of tune?" he joins her, walking into a two-shot. "I thought so. Oh, God, he loved that." Seen mostly in separate frames so far, they are now joined in the same image, as we are about to learn how much these two very different people — a bank teller and a music industry mogul — have in common.

Philip asks Betty, "Were you in love with him?" She answers, softly, "Yes." Cut to an over-the-shoulder shot of Philip, who says, "So was I." Cut to an over-the-shoulder shot of Betty, who looks surprised that another could love Mike as much as she. Cut to an over-the-shoulder shot of Philip, continuing: "And in the beginning, I mean, just desperately. You see, I was the one that brought him here. Contrary to what he may have told you, because he had all kinds of stories that he used on different people.... He was always preparing a face for the faces that he met. But the truth is, I was driving through ... well, driving cross-country on a promotional tour and I picked him up, picked him up hitchhiking."

As the scene goes on, Philip continues to talk, both about his relationship with Mike — the lines spoken heartrendingly by Winfield — and about the circumstances of Mike's murder. "I'm very happy that I know so little," he says. "I don't want to get involved. You don't want to get involved." As he warns Betty, "In this instance, ignorance is true bliss."

It's a warning that goes unheeded. Just two scenes later, Betty is again driving through Bridges's Los Angeles, "with its labyrinthian highways traveled by isolated cars," as Michael Blowen described it.³² Perhaps Betty does not even know where she is precisely going, but she has not left her visits with Sam and Philip satisfied; she must know more. "She can't let go of him so quickly — not without understanding more about him — and she tries to find out anything she can," Pauline Kael wrote.³³ She finds herself at 1020 Granville — Mike's apartment building — which she had passed earlier. This time, however, she stops and goes inside.

Voices are heard as she approaches his apartment; police detectives are still there. As she peers through the doorway, she gasps as Bridges — in a moment reminiscent of Hitchcock's use of red in *Marnie* to signify Tippi Hedren's aversion to the color — cuts to a fast zoom-in to a blood-soaked section of carpeting. Betty focuses on it before looking up, her hand covering her mouth in horror. She sees blood spattered everywhere, as the investigators casually process the scene. Intercut with Betty's horrified face are brief shots of Mike's phone, the walls of his apartment, and a photo of a smiling Mike, all covered with blood.

Since Bridges and Jeff Gourson removed the footage depicting Mike's murder, the crime scene Betty views, grisly as it is, provides but a glimpse of what was actually done to Mike. Originally, Bridges said, "[w]e had knives and a cut throat and blood spurting onto the wall."³⁴ In the film as it was released, these acts are only indicated. This doesn't diminish their power. When Betty comes home, she is seen wailing in her bed, overcome not only by her sadness, but also the horrifying particulars of Mike's death. It is one of the few moments in which she loses control of her emotions. In this respect, she is nothing like Jimmy J., who often seems to be at the mercy of his. For most of the film, as if in a state of mourning, Betty calmly observes. Winger realized this: "Two days before shooting started, I realized that I didn't know what a person's face was supposed to look like when they're listening.... Betty has an internal dialogue going on...."³⁵

* * *

Mike's Murder was Bridges's second collaboration with Reynaldo Villalobos. Since photographing *Urban Cowboy*, Villalobos's career had taken off: He shot the smash hit *Nine to Five*, with Jane Fonda, Dolly Parton, and

Lily Tomlin, Paul Brickman's *Risky Business*, and Stanley Donen's penultimate film *Blame It on Rio*. Kim Kurumada remembered, "Jim and I talked and he said, 'What do you think about Rey?' I said, 'Well, Jimmy, you gave Rey a career. If you think that he is the guy you want — and he will remember that you're the one that gave him a career — I think it can work. But because this is a low-, low-budget movie, we have to have somebody who can understand that and at the same time satisfy what you want.'"[36] Though *Mike's Murder* is far richer visually than *Urban Cowboy*, the director and cinematographer worked together in much the same way as before. "We just looked at the locations and the story and I just shot it," Villalobos recalled. "I'd worked with him before so it just continued like we had never stopped. I guess he liked what I was doing and he just let me do it. Working with Jim was very natural and very easy."[37]

As the film goes along, Betty's anguished searching is paralleled with Pete's ever more desperate attempts to avoid Mike's fate, as he pitiably flees his would-be assassins. Betty and Pete finally converge in the film's climactic sequence, which depicts Pete holding Betty hostage in her house on a dark and stormy night. Much as he did in the denouement of *The China Syndrome*, when Jack Godell takes over the Ventana control room, Bridges builds unbearable tension in a single, enclosed location, aided this time by the shadows coming through the windows of a small, unlit house. This scene — the most intense in the film and also the most prodigious work of Villalobos's career — summons memories of Bridges's classic episode of *The Alfred Hitchcock Hour*, "An Unlocked Window."

Earlier in the evening, Betty had dinner with her friend Patty (Brooke Alderson, another *Urban Cowboy* alumna) at a Mexican restaurant. The lighting inside the restaurant gives everything a red cast, echoing the crime scene. Villalobos uses a neutral palette most of the time — as Michael Blowen noted, "Winger is pale — her sensuality disguised by bland costumes and lighting that washes out her facial features"[38] — making the periodic intrusions of red all the more jarring. Patty's admonition to her friend — "My advice is to stay out of it. You don't know what he was up to. You don't know *what* he was doin.' Stay out of it!" — falls on deaf ears. What's more, Betty is already "involved." As she has paid visits to Sam and Philip, Pete is about to pay *her* a visit.

On Betty's quiet suburban street, the camera gracefully cranes down from the tops of trees blowing in the summer night to reveal Patty driving up to Betty's house. Other than the rustle of the wind, there is little noise, no sound effects. Patty suggests that Betty stay with her for the night, but she declines. Patty waits in the driveway as Betty approaches the front door, but she doesn't see Betty go inside. Betty struggles to find her keys in her purse. We cut from shots of her concerned face to POV shots of Patty slowly driving away; it's too late if Betty has any second thoughts about her suggestion. Betty locates her keys and begins to open the door. Then, out of nowhere, a voice: "*Betty!*"

Pete emerges from behind the bushes and grabs Betty, covering her mouth with his hand. The two burst into her house. More deranged and unhinged than ever, he turns off what light there is in the house. "No light," he insists. "I can see out. They can't see in!" Rare for a Bridges film, most of the scene is shot with a handheld camera, intensifying our identification with Betty. Pete holding onto Betty as if for dear life, they move together to the kitchen, where he wants something to drink. "Don't move fast!" he repeatedly cautions her as they walk as one. He takes her coat off, saying, "Mike always said you had a great ass. From what I can see in the moonlight, Mike wasn't bullshitting." Even in a moment of abject desperation, Pete is still, as Sam put it, "a little son of a bitch," a completely lurid, offensive personality. The phone rings; of course, Pete doesn't allow Betty to answer it. It is Sam, who leaves a message, warning her that "if this kid Pete shows up at your place, for God's sake don't let him in. He came here already acting like a crazy man." But there is nothing he can do to help Betty now. In the kitchen, she spots (but Pete does not) a knife on the countertop. He begins insisting "they" are outside. "They" are "the enforcers" out to avenge Pete's petty thievery. ("It was a mistake. So simple. I had done it a dozen times before.") He drags her to the living room window. "They're out there. Do you hear them? Do you hear them?" he asks. "No, it's just the wind," she reassures him. She is, as ever, remarkably cool-headed.

As in "An Unlocked Window," Pete is convinced that the danger is outside, in the rain and shadows and night. But the danger to Betty is *inside* in the form of Pete. They crouch by the window as Pete rants and raves and tries to explain himself. Reminding him of the drink he wanted, Betty manages to get up by herself and head for the kitchen. Before she gets there, the phone rings again. This time it is Patty, who begins to leave a message. In an unthinking moment, Betty reaches for the phone but Pete leaps to his feet and knocks it away. He then spots the knife. He grabs it and shoves her to the floor. "You went for the knife! You were going to stick me like a pig!" he says in the same bizarrely whispering tone he has used throughout the scene. As he brings the knife closer to her, continuing to ramble, Betty begins shaking the refrigerator. Unbelievably, she manages to briefly persuade him that an earthquake is occurring. In his stupor, he is caught off guard and she wrests herself from his grip.

Betty darts to the music room, where she slides the piano against one door and then locks the door of the connecting bathroom. Pete forces it open as Betty shuts the second piano room door. They struggle furiously until, through the doorway, a pair of hands is seen to suddenly envelop Pete's stunned face. The door is slammed shut and Betty walks to the back of the room. Pete's moans are heard in the adjacent room, followed by screeching tires, and then silence. Betty cautiously walks toward the door blocked by the piano, sliding it out of the way. She walks out and finds the screen door ajar, blowing ominously in the wind. Pete is gone and so is whoever was after him. In a grim irony, the enforcers who have so heartlessly murdered Pete have inadvertently saved Betty's life.

* * *

The beautiful coda of *Mike's Murder* returns us to daylight. As Betty walks in from getting the mail, she receives a call from her parents, who, naturally, express their concerns. She tries to reassure them, saying she refuses to get a gun. She explains to her father that the thugs who killed Pete were not after her. While she is talking, she spots a package in the mail. It is from Sam. After she hangs up, she tears it open. Sam has sent photographs. The note inside reads: "Betty — Thought you might like these — Sam." We are transported back to the film's opening shots as Betty looks through Sam's photos of Mike, and of Mike and Betty together on the tennis court. In receiving this gift from Sam, Betty demonstrates how much she has grown. She has become less proprietary about Mike, able to share his memory with others who loved him — the message of the final episode in Jean Renoir's last film, *Le Petit Théâtre de Jean Renoir*. As Ronald Bergan recounts in his biography of Renoir, a husband accepts it when his wife "falls in love with a vet who had come to attend to their dog.... But he learns the virtue of tolerance, and decides that it is better to share his wife than lose her."[39]

Betty sighs and walks into the music room, where she sits at the piano, perhaps for the first time in a long time. She plays a few notes. In this space, she is engulfed by memories of Mike: the out-of-tune C scale, the piano that is partly responsible for her survival that horrible night. When she turns and looks to her bedroom, more memories: the bed she shared with Mike, the mirror she sat in front of when he called her very late at night one time. The film ends on a profile close-up of Betty, held for just a tad longer than we expect. It's one of the most resplendent moments in all of Bridges's films. Betty's simultaneous sadness over and acceptance of Mike's death recalls not only the final shot of *The Baby Maker* (a close-up of Tish as she watches her child driven off to his new home), but also exemplifies what Cornel West has written of Chekhov: "His magisterial depiction of the cold Cosmos, indifferent Nature, crushing Fate and the cruel histories that circumscribe desperate, bored, confused and anxiety-ridden yet love-hungry people, who try to endure against all odds...."[40]

* * *

After beginning as a production assistant on *The China Syndrome* and *Urban Cowboy*, Marty Ewing was the second assistant director on *Mike's Murder*. He remembered Bridges being guided by his instincts during the filming:

> Because it was personal to Jim, he had instincts that we hadn't seen before. We would go on location scouts. In my new role, I was involved in that aspect of it. I remember one time going to a location that was going to be one of the drug deals. We scouted it at night. Jim wanted to be there at night and see the quality of the light that existed, but he also wanted to spend a little time there. It's maybe ten o'clock. We drive up and it's brightly lit. I'm not certain what led us there in the first place, but immediately Jim thought to himself, "They would never do a drug deal here. This is the wrong place." So we didn't spend more than two minutes there.... He knew that area and that side of town because he lived in Brentwood. Some of the places that we filmed were near him. Like great directors, he was constantly observing things. That movie was really close to home to him in many ways.[41]

Script supervisor Marshall Schlom, who had worked on *The China Syndrome*, remembered that most of the sets were built with four walls, meaning that he had to sit atop a ladder to perform his job. "Twice, as I was sitting on this ten-foot ladder, teetering precariously in the air, I felt somebody climbing up the ladder behind me," Schlom said. "One time it was Steven Spielberg and the other time it was Warren Beatty. Warren I had known because I had done a couple of films with him, including one in Europe, and he knew me. He was coming up to say hello. Steven and I had never met and he was very much interested in Jim's work. Apparently, Jim had invited him to come, so he wanted a vantage point as well. So he climbed up! The two of us were on this ladder. He was standing behind me and I was sitting on the platform."[42]

From the start of post-production, however, there were problems. Dede Allen had cut many of the great films of the sixties and seventies — Arthur Penn's *Bonnie and Clyde*, George Roy Hill's *Slaughterhouse-Five*, Sidney Lumet's *Dog Day Afternoon*— but, according to Jack Larson, her approach to *Mike's Murder* was, in one respect, flawed. "She is a great editor and she is a wonderful woman," Larson said. "She had a daughter the same age as Debra's character, a very pretty girl who was on the verge of getting married. Dede identified Debra's character with her daughter. I felt, and then Jim later felt, that Dede's cut — and it's the only thing negative I would say — was too close. She was in all the time on Debra, more on Debra than on the boy. That was the major problem with the film, which is very unfortunate because he's a wonderful kid, Mark Keyloun."[43]

But the real trouble came when the film was finally shown to audiences. "It had one of the most disastrous previews of all time up in Larkspur Landing," Larson remembered. "Nobody was prepared for it."[44] Bridges said, "They started screaming at the screen.... They hated it. They booed, they hissed. Because the violence was so real. I had two black men cutting up a white boy and cutting his throat and the knife entering the heart and the blood spurting all over the wall.... Girls were heard crying in the lavatory after the screening ... saying, 'How can they expect us to go on with our lives after we've seen this film?'"[45]

Kim Kurumada said, "I remember looking at preview cards when we did *Mike's Murder* and people would say, 'Where's the guy in the navy suit coming in at the end to sweep her off her feet?' They literally said, 'I want to see Debra Winger repeat her performance in *An Officer and a Gentleman.*'"[46]

"We came back and something had to be done," Larson explained. "Warners was threatening not to release it. They were humiliated. They thought they had a gold mine with Jim and Debra. Jim didn't want Debra, who he talked into coming back from Cleveland, to have an unreleasable film. So he then asked Laddie to re-edit the film and do some shooting. [Jim] restructured it, he enlarged Darrell's part, and he re-edited it with Jeff [Gourson]. Dede went on to *The Breakfast Club*. She was already committed."[47]

Gourson said, "Jim called me. He said that he had this movie, it's very bizarre and very gory, and it was previewed. He said that Dede Allen had originally cut it with him and she moved on to another project. He asked me to come in and work with him on it."[48] In addition to addressing the violence in the film, Bridges and Gourson also "gave it more of a linear approach,"[49] removing many of the flashbacks (some of which can be glimpsed in the trailer) that Bridges had originally included. Nonetheless, much of Allen's editing was kept "intact," Gourson said. "The scenes that were really in question were the flashbacks and the murder scene. On those, we did a completely different approach."[50]

During the three days of additional photography, Marty Ewing served as the first assistant director:

> We went back to a house in Venice and we shot some footage at Darrell Larson's house. On the last of the three days, Kim had an appointment somewhere and had to be out of town. So he kind of left me to manage it. On that day, we didn't do very well and didn't get what we needed to get. So Jim called me the next morning and said, "You know, I feel terrible about not getting this stuff. Is there any way we can go get these few establishing shots that we didn't get?" We talked and I said, "Well, let me give Rey a call and see if I can find the equipment and maybe we can go out and grab these shots." They were fairly simple shots, but Jim took it personally that things didn't go that well on that last day. It was a trying time for him. Any time your film doesn't

test well.... Rey and I went out with Jim and the location manager and essentially grabbed these shots before the police showed up or the homeowners really knew what we were doing! It was a home under construction. Fortunately, the workers weren't there. Everything just worked out beautifully. We got the shots and then I got yelled at by Kim for doing that ... because we hadn't planned it and we didn't have permits. All that stuff we're supposed to have, I was able to forgo in my mind's eye because Jim wanted it so badly and I so wanted him to feel good about getting it and not having to worry about it. He had so many other things on his mind.[51]

Originally, the film's entire soundtrack was made up of songs by Joe Jackson; this, too, didn't survive Bridges and Gourson's re-editing. "It was a terrible mistake and Jim is culpable on that one," Larson said. "Every time they got in a car and turned on the radio, any place you were, you had a Joe Jackson song. It ruined the integrity of the atmosphere. It was like a Joe Jackson concert.... It was an absolute mistake. That's what previewed. So then John Barry came in and did a beautiful score. I'm an old-fashioned person; the scores of films need to tell the audience what to feel. This film, of all films, needed exactly that: to underline the emotion of the film."[52]

Among the admirers of *Mike's Murder*, such as *Hollywood Elsewhere* blogger Jeffrey Wells, there has been a clamoring for a release of "the original Bridges cut."[53] But Bridges staunchly defended the changes he and Gourson made: "I think this is a better picture than it was, and I never would have allowed it to be released otherwise."[54] Fascinating as it would be to compare the two versions, it is hard to imagine a greater *Mike's Murder* than the one we have before us. Unfortunately, the film's release was as mishandled by Warner Bros. as *September 30, 1955*'s release was by Universal. Pauline Kael speculated that Warners "probably breathed a few sighs of relief as they buried it" in March 1984.[55] But this only spurred the critics who appreciated the film, like Kael, to speak up on its behalf. "*Mike's Murder* reaffirmed why people have the kind of respect they have for Jim, why they have the kind of respect they have for Alan Ladd, Jr.," Kurumada said. "These are people who really do have a different take a lot of times. Their Hollywood is a different kind of Hollywood."[56]

* * *

Mike's Murder was Debbie Getlin's last film with Bridges. "I didn't even finish that project with them," she said. "I left before it was completely edited. I remember going to the screening, but I had just stopped working for Jim at that time. And the only reason I did that was, it was at a time with my children ... I had been working for Jim for seven and a half years, and now I had an eleven-year-old and a seven-year-old."[57] She remembered those years as "the most amazing chapter of my life. It was so incredible to be with Jim as he was going through these experiences. It was fun to see him in the very beginning of his career. Hollywood can be devastating to people. Hollywood can change a personality in a heartbeat, and I don't think that Jim ever lost the ability to keep things in perspective, like that day that he spit on my lamp!"[58]

One time, when Bridges was preparing *The Verdict* (which, before Sidney Lumet and Paul Newman made it, he was going to direct as a vehicle for Robert Redford), Getlin was with Bridges in their office when an actor friend stopped by. "On this particular day, he had three little golden retriever puppies with him," she said. "He knew that Jim loved dogs, so he brought them in. These little puppies were just kind of running around our office. I got down on the floor and I was playing with these little puppies. Jim came out of his office; he had just gotten out of a conference call. And he sat down on the floor and we were both playing with these puppies. He just looked at me, having such a good time with these puppies, and he stuck his hand in his pocket, he pulled out $500, gave it to the actor, and he said, 'Debbie, pick out which one you want. It's your puppy. Happy birthday.' I said, 'Jim, it's not my birthday!' 'Pick out which one you want.' I took that puppy home and that was the best dog I ever had."[59]

Mike's Murder was also the last time Villalobos was the DP of a Bridges film (though he did do some pick-up shots on *Perfect*, which was photographed by Gordon Willis). "I considered him one of my best friends," Villalobos recalled. "If you needed help, he would help you. If you needed financial help, he would go, 'Oh, yeah, fine.' I found out later that he helped a lot of people. He was a great friend."[60]

"The thing that Jim taught me, because we were close, was more the ability to not take yourself so seriously because the more you do that, the more it clouds your ability to see things clearly," Kurumada observed. He continued:

> If you can kind of see through the maze of everything that's going on, and you can be patient, you'll know what the right thing to do is. A lot of times, he would come into my office and he would be totally frustrated because of something that wasn't happening or something that someone had promised him they would do and now they wouldn't. But he knew how to balance that in his life. He knew when to have his bulldog Mike Ovitz go after somebody and when not to, and then go on the next day.
>
> He knew he never was going to be in a position where he had to work for money. He was never going to be in a position where, "Oh, I have to take this movie because I have to pay off this or that or whatever." From the very beginning, he had sorted all of that out. It was never about being invited to the right parties or this, that, or the other. Jim had a very fulfilling and private personal life with Jack and their artist friends. One day I went over to see him

and he had this David Hockney [painting]. It was just leaning up against the wall! I said, "I've seen this. This is an incredible thing and you just have it leaning up against the wall." And he said, "Yeah, I should find a place to hang this, but it's okay for right now." That's kind of the way Jim was. He had this Frank Lloyd Wright house, but you never knew it. And unless you were ever invited there, you never saw what was inside.[61]

* * *

After years of advising Bridges on aspects of his films incognito, Jack Larson finally took a screen credit on *Mike's Murder*. "During *Urban Cowboy*, Bob LeMond, who was John Travolta's manager, said, 'You know, it would make everything much easier if you would take a title. Unless you take a title, the studio doesn't want to deal with you,'" Larson remembered. "So with that, Jim and I decided I should take a title. And they would deal with me because Jim wouldn't deal with them. He did not want to talk with what's called 'the suits.'"[62] On *Mike's Murder*, Larson is credited as associate producer, an overdue recognition of the multifaceted contributions he made to all of Bridges's films, not just those that his name appears on.[63]

For Bridges and Winger, the greatest sorrow was that they never worked together again. Other opportunities arose in the years following *Mike's Murder*, but none came to fruition. Winger remembered, "There was a script he dreamt of doing called *Bee Season* (not the one that was made and nothing to do with spelling bees!), there was [Wendy Wasserstein's] *The Object of My Affection*, which I believe got made, and there was the Libby Holman project [a biopic of the torch singer] which was probably closest to our collective heart."[64]

Bridges and Winger should have made all of these films (and more). After all, George Cukor directed Katharine Hepburn ten times. And how many ballets did George Balanchine choreograph with Suzanne Farrell in mind? *Twenty-three*, according to Farrell.[65] But Winger felt that what she learned from working with Bridges on even two films was enough to last a lifetime: "Suffice to say, Jim was and will always be my mentor. He taught me to trust myself and without that, I would not have been able to work with any of the great directors I have had the good fortune to make a film with."[66]

Seven

Perfecting Perfect

In its initial conception, James Bridges's next film, *Perfect*, was very different from the one he ended up making.

In 1983, *Rolling Stone* published an article by Aaron Latham, who had written the story upon which *Urban Cowboy* was based. Entitled "Looking for Mr. Goodbody: Perfect!," the piece, as sociologically insightful as Latham's best work, was about a Los Angeles health club called the Sports Connection. Latham sent it to Bridges, who "agreed to help bring *Perfect* to the screen."[1] Executive producer Kim Kurumada attributed Bridges's willingness to jump into the project to the frustrations he experienced while making *Mike's Murder*:

> There were obviously some things that bothered Jim about trying to finish *Mike's Murder*. Jim and I talked about it several times. One of the things that he said was, "When you make a small, handcrafted, low-budget movie, you get some of the benefits but there's also some things that you give up in contrast to a high-budgeted, big-marketed project." He said, "This next one that we're going to do"—and I don't know if we'd even finished shooting *Mike's Murder*, maybe we had and we were in the middle of editing it, but we certainly hadn't previewed it—"I don't want to have these same kinds of issues." There were issues such as, "Can we spend a little more money to do this or do that?"
>
> He told me that Aaron had this article that he had written for *Rolling Stone* and he wanted to make this movie *Perfect*. He said, "It has a lot of the things in it that studios support. They'll feel commercially confident in it because it'll have a lot of sex in it, it'll have a lot of girls. We won't have any problem getting the studios to support this kind of a movie from a commercial standpoint. We just have to make sure that it's a good movie."[2]

Kurumada accompanied Bridges to several clubs similar to the Sports Connection. He remembered, "We went to look at it and saw that people were dressing up and buying expensive, sexy, bright-colored clothes. It was as much about what you were wearing and to be seen to come to some of these places. It was a far cry from the old YMCA, gray socks, gray sweatshirt gym."³ Bridges had sympathy for the workout addicts who frequented clubs like the Sports Connection. "Jimmy always was concerned about his own weight," Kurumada said. "Jimmy always felt that he didn't discipline himself enough in his eating and stuff like that, but he really enjoyed life. So he kind of had a personal feeling about people who starve themselves to look better, etc., etc., and all of this cultural pressure that's imposed. He felt that this was an interesting phenomenon. Working out, staying in shape, having good sex — this was now the new culture, the new hip craze to do."⁴

Part of making the project into "a good movie," however, entailed shifting the focus away from the club in the story (also called the Sports Connection). Instead, the film would be about "a reporter who is writing a story much like the one that I had actually written," as Latham explained.⁵ In his view, "[j]ust as a B-western was embedded in *Urban Cowboy*, embedded in this is a '40s newspaper drama."⁶

Kurumada said that Bridges regarded Latham's article as a commentary on "vanity, especially Southern California vanity, and people pursuing false values. But the irony was that Jim often felt the people who criticized those people for having false values had even *worse* false values, were even worse themselves."⁷

Perfect became about the moral education of Adam Lawrence (John Travolta), a *Rolling Stone* reporter who writes about the Sports Connection, and who goes from mocking the subjects of his article to empathizing with them. At one point in the film, Jessie Wilson (Jamie Lee Curtis), an aerobics instructor at the club with whom Adam has an affair, poses a rhetorical question to him: "What is so wrong with wanting to be perfect?" For Kurumada, this line goes back to what he called Bridges's "hometown roots.... 'What's wrong with dreaming? What's wrong with trying to make yourself like the Barbie doll you want to look like? What's wrong with that?' And that was a central issue that Jim really believed in. He said, 'If I hadn't thought like that, I never would have been able to get out of Arkansas.'"⁸ Adam's initial condescension toward Jessie and all of the others who seek to improve, to "perfect," their bodies couldn't be further from Bridges's own position.

Latham said that Travolta had "spent so many hours being interviewed that he had great insight into how reporters work."⁹ The actor himself admitted, "I'm really surprised that they thought of me. I mean, I'm not the first actor you think of when you think of an investigative reporter."¹⁰ But the truth is that he is completely credible in the role. The qualities of Adam — his intelligence and belligerent determination to get to the bottom of something — were precisely those that Travolta exhibited so brilliantly three years earlier in Brian De Palma's *Blow Out* (certainly his best performance).

Bridges was careful, though, to establish Travolta's character — which was so different than the one audiences remembered from the last Bridges-Latham-Travolta collaboration—early in the film. Kurumada remembered that Bridges said:

> "You know, nobody's ever seen somebody throw a glass of tomato juice in John Travolta's face." Both of us kind of laughed. I said, "Are you thinking about Jimmy Cagney and the grapefruit?" And he said, "No, when you're dealing with Travolta, you've got to tell the audience *right* away what's going on, what to expect." Again, this was maybe a throwback to *Mike's Murder* when the people said, "I wanted Debra Winger to go off with the guy in the white suit." He said, "You know, we can't have that happen to us again."[11]

So the fourth scene in the film has singer Carly Simon, indignant at Adam for a story he has written about her, tossing a glass of tomato juice at him. The scene makes clear that Adam is not being played by a "movie star."

"Of course, the reporter would need a boss, so we wrote in an editor who was similar to Jann Wenner, the actual editor and publisher of *Rolling Stone*," Latham recalled.[12] There followed one of the casting coups of *Perfect*: Wenner himself played his on-screen counterpart, Mark Roth. "[Jann] had approval of who played that character," Jack Larson said. "And nobody would do except Robert Redford! It was John Travolta's idea that Jann do it.... But suddenly it came up that Jann should play it himself."[13] Bridges remembered, "We had to beg him to take the part. He was very nervous about it. But he was perfect for the part."[14]

As the film begins, Adam and Mark are simpatico. When Adam first pitches his idea about writing about a health club in Los Angeles ("the singles bars of the eighties"), he corrects Mark about "what" he is going to go after, not "who"; people, as such, are of no great concern to him. They are casualties of his war on "hot tubs and alfalfa sprouts," as Mark gleefully notes. "We haven't done L.A. in a *long* time. I mean, it would be *wonderful*." After Adam has flown from New York to Los Angeles to begin writing his story, and he meets Jessie, Mark advises him by phone, "Just remember, get close to her while you're doing the research, but when you sit down to write..." Adam finishes his boss's sentence: "...forget she has a mother. Right, right. Don't I always?" After he hangs up, Mark's date asks, "So who's going to get the Lawrence treatment this time?" He callously replies, "Some girl he met."

Adam's method of "getting close" to Jessie is taking her to lunch and regaling her with tales of a fictitious version of his article, one he has no intention of ever writing, let alone filing with *Rolling Stone*. "The baby boomers are leading a physical Great Awakening comparable to the spiritual Great Awakenings that have gripped America about every hundred years," he says to her. "See, I think people want to take responsibility for themselves instead of leaning on institutions. For instance, the government. I mean, do you think anyone believes that the government will take care of us any more? Not since Vietnam or Watergate, no. Or big corporations or even doctors. So you have to take care of yourself. A hell of a lot of people are out there trying to get in shape, as you well know. I think I feel we've come full circle, almost back to Emersonian America, *Self-Reliance*."

Jessie is no dummy; she smiles and says, "Pretty good," as Adam describes the "hook" to his story, which sounds more plausibly like a doctoral thesis than a cover story in a popular music magazine. She almost can't believe it when he actually recites a quote *by* Ralph Waldo Emerson! But she certainly has no clue how profoundly Adam intends to betray her and her compatriots at the Sports Connection.

* * *

The fluid nature of the project (which had outgrown its modest origins as a literal translation of Latham's original *Rolling Stone* article) posed challenges for Kurumada, who was organizing the production:

> I was very, very lucky because at the time the head of [Columbia Pictures, the distributor] was Guy McElwaine and the head of production was Sheldon Schrager. I had known Sheldon before because he was an executive producer-production manager while I was a first assistant on a picture with Jerome Hellman. Jerome Hellman's biggest claim to fame was producing *Coming Home*. So Shel knew me from working with Jerome. Sheldon said, "Well, Kim, I know how you are going to do this and I know how you are going to work with Bridges. So I'm willing to give you a little leeway in trying to get this thing put together and organized. Just keep me informed of what you have in mind." That made it much easier. Sometimes a few essential cards have to fall into place in order for things to move in a certain direction. And that, for me, was certainly one of them. It totally removed a lot of the problems that we'd had because of money or size of project or actually studio resources. They were all now more available to us because of this project and because I had the confidence of the head of production.[15]

By 1984, when Bridges was slated to begin filming *Perfect*, it had been eight years since he last worked with Gordon Willis on *September 30, 1955*. It was high time for them to get together again. "I remember the incident like it was yesterday," Kurumada said,

> Jimmy and I were talking about who the cameraman should be. We started to walk across to go get some lunch. Jim knew my apprehensions about Gordon. He's a perfectionist and he's sometimes very difficult to convince. Sometimes he can be very stubborn. Sometimes Gordon's moods can be very mercurial. Sometimes he can be very difficult to get along with in his demands. And he had a reputation for being very difficult....
>
> So Jimmy and I talked about that. As we were walking to lunch, Jimmy

stopped and he looked across. I had said, "This was not cinematography-wise a really challenging project. It's not period or any of this stuff." So we stopped at the lot and Jimmy looked around and you could see across the lot. It was the typical Hollywood picture with people running around like a beehive, moving sets, people pushing racks of costumes one direction, carpenters pushing scenic walls another direction, etc. And Jimmy said, "Now you see, Kim, if you and I were standing here with Gordon right now and he had a camera, and we were trying to shoot this little thing of Hollywood, Gordon could make it look interesting." I said, "Yeah?" And he said, "Now imagine what it would look like with fifty buxom, stripped-down, gorgeous women and a hundred mirrors." And I said, "Okay, we'll try to get Gordon."[16]

Regrettably, Willis wasn't pleased with the final result. "*Perfect* is indulgent, and I can't say I like it very much," he said. "This is no one's fault. It's the way the cookie crumbles."[17] It's true that the *mise-en-scene* in *Perfect* does not reflect the characters' relations to one another, as it does in *The Paper Chase*, nor is the film as beautifully photographed as *September 30, 1955*. But it is indisputably the work of a master; Willis's taste in composition and facility in blocking are as commanding as ever. What's more, his approach to representing Los Angeles on screen (which he had previously done in *Annie Hall*) mirrored that of Bridges, who refused to satirize his adopted hometown, despite the opportunities the material offered him. "The L.A. light in *Perfect* actually looks like L.A., where the L.A. light in *Annie Hall* is a parody," Willis explained.[18]

"In the morning, we would spend anywhere from a half an hour to up to two hours rehearsing the scene, staging the scene, and making certain every aspect of that scene was fleshed out," second assistant director Marty Ewing recalled.

> Then the actors would leave and Gordon would come in and light for whatever time he needed. That process was ... very deliberate. Jim really liked it because any issues that the cast had were worked out without a hundred people standing around watching. It was a closed set during rehearsals. There were four or five people there plus the actors. Then they would bring in just those who absolutely needed to see the rehearsal, which wasn't me, and then they would let the actors go to finish their makeup, hair, and wardrobe while Gordon lit. They would very deliberately block out the shots. There would be little tape marks on the floor after each rehearsal that would have the camera height and the camera lens. And they would list the shots out. So we all knew in this very deliberate fashion, "Okay, there are ten shots to this sequence. We're going to shoot the side looking to the left first and then we'll relight after shot five and do the other five shots after the relight." It wouldn't necessarily be in order for the actors. It would be in lighting order, which some directors like, some directors don't like. Some directors don't care what the lighting order is. They just want to make certain that their actors are ready for

the close-ups when the actors are ready. For Jim, by rehearsing as much as he did in the morning, that aspect of it was taken care of. It wasn't like, "Oh gee, I didn't think we were not going to shoot my close-up until 6:30 or 7:30 at night."[19]

* * *

Mike Nichols has spoken of his belief in "statement of theme," citing as an example the first line spoken in *The Graduate* when Dustin Hoffman is on the airplane: "Ladies and gentlemen, we are about to begin our descent into Los Angeles."[20] In *Perfect*, Bridges follows the Nichols model when he treats us to a brief prologue of a pre–*Rolling Stone* Adam working the obituary desk at the *Jersey Journal*. Frustrated by his station, he complains to his editor, who sagely counsels him, "Think of it this way: This is your last chance in journalism to write anything nice about anybody."

The *Jersey Journal* editor is prescient; Adam meets a multitude of good people at the Sports Connection, but he doesn't even consider writing anything nice about them. Early in the film, as he is being given a tour of the club, he is introduced to a couple who met there, Sally (Marilu Henner) and Roger (Mathew Reed). "They are nice people," Adam is told. So is Linda (Laraine Newman), of whom it is said, "She was a mess. I've never seen anybody work so hard to get into shape." Linda has something of Betty Parrish's innocence. She is not mistrustful of the press as Jessie is. She is honest to a fault with Adam, answering his questions about singles bars (which he equates the Sports Connection to), and even giving him the eventual title of his piece, "Looking for Mr. Goodbody." She says, "It's a lot safer looking for Mr. Goodbody than looking for Mr. Goodbar." Newman, who proved herself a brilliant comedienne in the early seasons of *Saturday Night Live*, delivers the film's best and most touching performance. Jamie Lee Curtis correctly observed that *Perfect* "was Laraine's movie. There's always one performance in every movie that stands out — and it was hers."[21] After Curtis read Linda's lines at a rehearsal before production began, she revealed to Latham that "she really understood that girl. She said that if she weren't playing Jessie she would like to play Linda."[22] As good as Curtis might have been, the role was Newman's. Along with Swoosie Kurtz in *Bright Lights, Big City*, this would be the best supporting performance in all of the later Bridges films.

While in L.A. writing about the Sports Connection, Adam is simultaneously working on another story, a much more serious piece about a disgraced computer tycoon named Joseph McKenzie who is facing a criminal trial. That story is gradually falling apart for a variety of reasons and Mark is bearing down on him to wrap up his Sports Connection piece. So it is under duress that Adam pulls out his notebook late one night and flips to a page with his notes on Linda. We see he has scribbled down a vulgar quote someone has said about her, that she is "the most used piece of equipment in the gym." He circles Linda's name and underlines the quote. Adam will not write about Jessie, but he will, if forced, write about Linda, which is worse because she is more vulnerable. (When Roger proposes to Sally at her birthday party, Adam sees how crushed and envious Linda is.) Adam can't play favorites this way; no less than Jessie, Linda is deserving of respect and privacy, even if she is guilty of opening up to a reporter from *Rolling Stone* and even if she, like others at the club, are guilty of leading what Adam considers tacky or superficial lives. He wastes no time, fooling Linda into thinking he is "seducing" her and that he wants to make her the "focus" of his piece. She talks too much, revealing her plans to have plastic surgery on her face, as well as her romantic frustrations. All the while Adam is brandishing his tape recorder and notepad.

Jessie discovers this draft of his article during one of their trysts in his hotel room. As Adam is talking on the phone, she scrolls down the screen of his word processor and is horrified by what she finds, as are we. She is not, of course, mentioned, but Linda is, and so are Sally and others. Jessie begins deleting the text on the screen. When Adam comes in, she confronts him, furious not only by his decision to write such a vicious story, but also by his hypocrisy: "You talked to me about Emerson and baby boomers and the physical Great Awakening, and all you do is write a fucking little piece about people getting into each other's pants."

Adam protests, "Hey, everything I wrote in that story is true."

"Everything the other reporter wrote about me was true, too, but it stills hurts," Jessie replies, referring to a newspaper story written about her when she was a teenager that damaged her career and reputation. "It's not the truth I'm worried about, it's the tone and hurting people and using them. You're so disgusting. How can you be nice to somebody like McKenzie and then shit on Linda? What did she ever do to you or anybody else, for that matter? Nothing. What's wrong with wanting to be the best that you can be? What is so wrong with wanting to be perfect? What's wrong with wanting to be loved?"

Chastened, he says, "Nothing."

As she leaves the room, she tells him flatly, "You're going to ruin her life."

Curtis is devastating in this scene. In *Perfect*, the actress validated the promise she showed in John Landis's comic tour de force *Trading Places*. Kurumada remembered a dinner he and Bridges had with Guy McElwaine before Curtis had officially been cast:

> It was a fancy Italian restaurant in Beverly Hills. We got there and I thought we were just going to be sitting in the regular part of this fancy restaurant, but

then we get ushered into this private room. We're sitting there about to have dinner and Jamie Lee Curtis shows up. I had no idea — what the hell is she doing here? I don't know if she found out we were having dinner with Guy and so she just conveniently made herself known. She wasn't assigned to do the picture. She was obviously trying to position herself to get the movie. I thought, "Well, this is either going to make you or break you as far as Bridges is concerned." Because I knew that sometimes he did not respond very well to that, although he always admired somebody's moxie. He always admired their guts for showing up at something like that. Oftentimes he wouldn't approve because sometimes something would happen there that would set the project back a little bit.

So Jamie shows up. She looks like a knockout. She just is gorgeous.... She sits by and, wisely, just stays for a cocktail, doesn't stay for the dinner. But she's made her presence known and, of course, Guy is kind of smitten with her. He's the head of the studio.[23]

Curtis proved to be the ideal choice for Jessie Wilson. Latham recalled the first reading of the script after Travolta and Curtis were cast: "It was really exciting when he asked her if he could interview her and she said no. The words worked, or seemed to. The chemistry worked for sure."[24]

The film was poorly reviewed. *Boston Globe* critic Jay Carr praised Curtis as "the film's most interesting presence. Even when she's set up to look silly, doing pelvic grinds in a leotard, she suggests an art deco hood ornament come to life. There's something appealingly fierce in her physicality."[25] The actress loved working with Bridges: "He's amazing. I've never seen anyone who takes as much time and cares so much for the details. Unless he thought a scene was great, he wouldn't let it go."[26]

After Jessie's jeremiad, Adam has a change of heart. Though Jessie, Sally, and Linda may be seeking physical perfection, the real story in *Perfect* is of Adam perfecting his moral self, which is very much in peril throughout most of the film. But he comes around, helped by Jessie. He writes the story he said he was going to write in the first place. He even calls it "Looking for Mr. Emerson."

Of course, this will not do for Mark, who, in Adam's absence, demands that his original notes be used to revert the story to its "Looking for Mr. Goodbody" origins (and to include details about Jessie that Adam intended to leave out). This is the version that goes to press. Following a series of shots of the magazine coming freshly off the printers, we cut to Linda and Sally driving up to a newsstand to buy a copy. When Linda flips eagerly to Adam's article to see what it says about her, she is shattered. They bring the magazine to Jessie, who is preparing for a class by herself in her usual room at the Sports Connection. Sally stays by the door, looking on as Linda hands the magazine to Jessie. In a long shot, Linda sits down, soon joined by Jessie. No dialogue is spoken between them and Linda looks away from Jessie, staring off into the distance; in her humiliation, she can't bear to make eye contact. Willis's camera stays at a stately distance, removed from the devastation, in effect showing Linda the consideration Adam denied her.

Meanwhile, Adam is in a restaurant in Morocco waiting for the arrival of the writer Paul Bowles, whom he is going to interview for *Rolling Stone*. When he learns of Mark's betrayal from Jessie (whom he has innocently called to ask how she liked "Looking for Mr. Emerson"), he immediately ditches the meeting with Bowles to fly back to the States to do damage control. It is yet another sign of this pilgrim's progress that Jessie and her views of him have become more important to him than the author of *The Sheltering Sky* (who was in real life a friend of Bridges and Larson; he composed "an extraordinary evening of incidental music" for the Los Angeles production of *Bachelor Furnished*, Larson said[27]). When he later insists to her that he didn't write the story, he is of course being a little disingenuous; the version Mark ran is derived from his original "Looking for Mr. Goodbody" pitch. It would be more accurate to say that he didn't mean for the piece to be published in that form, that she persuaded him of how wrong it would be. By the end of the film, Adam has become an almost admirable character.

Make no mistake: Guilt is what motivates Adam to alter his thinking. It is also part of what motivates Betty Parrish's obsession in *Mike's Murder*. The last time she sees Mike, she plays hard to get — spurned by his elusiveness from their relationship. After he has been killed, how could she not feel remorse that she let her disappointment in his unpredictability stand in the way of saving him? Could she have saved him? If she had inserted herself into his life more brashly, would he have spent so much time with the likes of Pete?

One of the most striking aspects of *Perfect* is its economy. Adam's hounding of Jessie for an interview is shown in a series of short scenes from over the course of a whole workday at the Sports Connection. The Moroccan sequence is dispatched with just as quickly: There is Adam, waiting for Bowles, talking to Jessie, calling the *Rolling Stone* office to confirm what has happened, and then, a few shots later, his plane is seen landing in Los Angeles to explain to Jessie what has happened. (In the *Chicago Reader*, Dave Kehr was bemused by the film's "demonstrations of Lawrence's truly breathtaking expense account."[28]) There is a snappiness to *Perfect* reflected not just in the storytelling but also in the dialogue. (Characters habitually say things like "Sounds perfect" in response to something or other.) Perhaps it was this quality Latham was referring to when he told *The New York Times* that he considered the film to be in the vein of Frank Capra's *Mr. Deeds Goes to Town*.[29]

But for all of the zing in individual sequences (in contrast to *Urban Cowboy* and *Mike's Murder*, which were filled with dissolves, *Perfect* has no opticals of note), the film as a whole is long — longer by sixteen minutes than the far more ambitious *Mike's Murder*. There is a lot of peripheral silliness in *Perfect*: single-scene cameos by Carly Simon and Lauren Hutton, a hotel courtyard overrun by Boy George fans, and so on. Much of this is amusing, particularly a beautifully staged "chase" scene in which Adam is pursued through the Sports Connection by the management after his article has appeared, set to the "William Tell Overture." The central drama of the film, however, could have been sharpened through the shortening of some of these incidental asides. The same could be said for much of the McKenzie subplot, which leads eventually to Adam being jailed after he refuses to hand over the audiotapes of his interview with McKenzie to the government. This episode, too, does little to clarify Adam's evolution *vis-à-vis* his attitude toward the Sports Connection.

After the thankless job he did in reconfiguring *Mike's Murder*, Jeff Gourson was invited back to edit *Perfect*. "I was on that film from the beginning, which made me a little bit nervous because I'd never done anything musically," Gourson said. "But it all worked out. Once I got into editing the material, it again all fell into place. The way he shot the aerobics numbers, were ... I shouldn't say 'simple' to put together, but it was easy.... I knew what I thought was the beat, so I always tried to cut on a beat. For the most part, I did pretty well, but one day he and I were working on one of the scenes. I can't remember which one it was, but Jamie was in there dancing. I guess she came by the cutting room one day and he wanted to show her one of the sequences. So we played one of the dance numbers and she was just thrilled and excited. She said, 'This is really great, but, guys, you're on the wrong beat.'"[30]

* * *

Several years before *Perfect* went into production, Coca-Cola purchased Columbia Pictures. Larson described the marketing of the film as "an absolute nightmare. It was Coca-Cola. They amassed all of these little green books of research. They were all overseen by the man at Coca-Cola in Atlanta, who they were all beholden to because he researched for them New Coke, which was going to triumph over Pepsi."[31] Of course, New Coke did *not* triumph and neither did *Perfect*. Even though the film was playing well when it was first released on June 7, 1985, the decision had already been made to pull the plug on advertising. As Larson explained, "There was a phone call at six o'clock L.A. time and, with the exits after the opening of the film, Columbia had decided not to support the film with second week television buys. And, of course, the audience doesn't read newspapers. So it's what Bob Dingilian [Columbia's head of publicity] said: They're supporting you with window dressing. Bob was very straightforward. But you're lost if they won't do second week television buys."[32]

It isn't surprising that audiences initially supported *Perfect*. Mark reveals to Jessie Adam's good intentions, after which the film speeds to a triumphantly happy ending. Indeed, the finale is a virtual repeat of *Urban Cowboy*: Travolta and his leading lady seen in silhouette through the back of a car window, as they prepare to drive off happily ever after. But there is also the same note of ambiguity that informed the last shot of *September 30, 1955*: Adam and Jessie may be destined for happiness, but what about Linda? Isn't Jessie correct that Linda's life has, in some way, been "ruined" by the heartless exposé?

When it came to the critics, *Perfect* was panned. Dave Kehr wrote that Bridges's "excellent work in the '70s seems long behind him here."[33] Despite his support for Curtis, Jay Carr considered the film itself to be "muddled."[34] In his *New York Times* review, Vincent Canby said that it "may mark the absolute, idiotic end" of the "new kind of journalism film" that had been inaugurated by *All the President's Men*.[35]

But Canby's assertion that "*Rolling Stone* receives more reverent treatment in *Perfect* than *The Washington Post* did" in *President's Men*[36] is simply untrue. Bridges was committed to making the film believable and authentic, and if that meant immersing the audience in the details of the magazine Adam writes for, down to the casting of its actual editor, so be it. As Kurumada observed, "It was always essential to Jim that if you did not start with truth, that anywhere, as you went along the way, if you made some mistakes or you were misunderstood or you were misinterpreted, if you couldn't go back and fall on the truth, that that was what was wrong. This was an issue we used to have constant fights with the studio about. You get the argument, 'Well, that's not commercial. That's not funny. That's not entertaining.' Jim always thought that there was a way to make sure that you were truthful to it, and if you were truthful to what the subject was, that how the audience took it, you wouldn't have to worry about it."[37] Marty Ewing said, "With Jim, it was never about making something fake real. It was about making real as real as one could get."[38]

Furthermore, the omnipresent *Rolling Stone* logo and graphics in *Perfect* is strikingly reminiscent of Jerry Lewis's witty use of Dunkin' Donuts, 7 Up, Kellogg's Raisin Bran, and other brand names in his great film *Hardly Working*. As film scholar Chris Fujiwara noted in his critical study of Lewis, "The commercial advertisements that saturate the social space of *Hardly Working* ... subvert the logic of 'product placement' to reveal the advertising nature of an entire society."[39] Similarly, the "product placement" of *Rolling Stone* in *Perfect* serves to level the playing field of the film. Jessie, Linda, and Sally may be obsessed with appearances, but so is the glossy, world inhabited by Adam and Mark. Thought of this way, Adam and Jessie could be right for each other after all.

Seven. *Perfecting* Perfect

With the benefit of hindsight, it is obvious that *Perfect* is the greatest of Bridges's films that didn't originate with him. It equals Robert Altman's all but forgotten *HealtH*, which was ostensibly about a health food convention. In his friendly review of that film, Canby intuited that Altman had other things on his mind, noting in his review that the film had "a lot of random fun at the expense of the rituals and rhetoric of our political processes."[40] Just as in *HealtH*, the concerns of Bridges in *Perfect* go beyond its noisy, sexy, and colorful setting. For a director who so often used real people as the template for his films (though always disguising and fictionalizing them), the question of how to represent such people fairly must have been a pressing one.

Bridges's two masterpieces, *September 30, 1955* and *Mike's Murder*, are included in the book *Produced and Abandoned: The Best Films You've Never Seen*, a collection of reviews by members of the National Society of Film Critics, edited by Michael Sragow. Wonderful. But there is a case to be made that the Bridges film most in need of such support is *Perfect*, which continues to suffer indignities even on home video. The DVD presents the film in "pan and scan" format, disfiguring the images Bridges and Willis so carefully composed for the 2.35:1 aspect ratio. (The Region 2 DVD released in Great Britain is in letterboxed format.) What a profound, baffling dishonor to the film that marked the resumption of one of the great collaborations between a director and a cinematographer.

Eight

Bright Lights, Big City, *Big Legacy*

Asked by an interlocutor in 1989 about "American youth today," Kurt Vonnegut reflected, "I think they're deeply discouraged. The yuppies, these supposed materialists, I think, are worried about themselves and the shallowness of their happiness."[1]

In his final film, *Bright Lights, Big City*, James Bridges portrayed one such yuppie, Jamie Conway (Michael J. Fox), fully possessing of the self-consciousness Vonnegut spoke of. In the film's opening scene, Jamie sits at the bar of a Manhattan nightclub just before closing and stares at a reflection of himself after he has accepted "another drink." He says in a voice-over, "You are not the kind of guy who would be at a place like this at this time in the morning, but here you are."

If Bridges wanted to portray the plight of the yuppie, he couldn't have selected better source material. The film was based upon the 1984 novel of the same title by first-time author Jay McInerney; in *The New York Times*, Michiko Kakutani argued that "the high-gloss success of Jay McInerney's *Bright Lights, Big City* and Bret Easton Ellis's *Less Than Zero* has spawned a whole new category of yuppie fiction — stories and novels by young writers about young, alienated people strung out on drugs or alcohol or simple spiritual malaise."[2] Like *The Paper Chase* before it, *Bright Lights, Big City* was an autobiographical novel. As McInerney noted, "I worked as a fact-checker at *The New Yorker*. I was fired from that job, just as the protagonist is. I was spending too much time at nightclubs. I was doing too many drugs. I was married to a model who went off to Italy one day for the fashion shows there and never came back."[3]

But Bridges didn't "select" *Bright Lights, Big City* as his next film after *Perfect* at all. As Bridges was busy preparing other projects, *Bright Lights, Big City* was being filmed by director Joyce Chopra. Her previous film was the acclaimed *Smooth Talk*, based upon the classic Joyce Carol Oates short story,

Eight. Bright Lights, Big City, *Big Legacy* 157

"Where Are You Going? Where Have You Been?" Editor John Bloom, who was on the picture from the beginning, recalled,

> It had been a pretty unhappy four weeks during Joyce Chopra's reign and a very sad one in many ways. I think there was dissatisfaction with her work from the first day's dailies. It would have been much, much better if the differences between director and producers had been recognized immediately and Joyce had been asked to step down very early on. As it was, it was somewhat cruel. It was well intentioned, but cruel, to keep her on for four weeks and then get rid of her. It was intended to be kind, particularly from [producer] Sydney Pollack, who as a director himself was very loath to step in and fire a fellow director. He was reluctant to act upon what his instincts told him. And then after a rather long time — which was not far short of half the shooting schedule — he and his colleagues came to the conclusion that things were not working and decided to replace Joyce with James Bridges.[4]

But Bridges wouldn't even consider taking on the project until the decision had been made to remove Chopra. Jack Larson explained, "[Executives] Tony Thomopoulos and Bob Lawrence ... started talking to Jim. Jim said he wouldn't discuss anything with another director on the thing. He wouldn't come in and replace a director, but if they closed it down, he would discuss it with them. And they did close it down. Then he decided to do it."[5]

Bridges remembered, "So I said, 'I will do this film. But I can't use a frame of the other film, because I want to make my own film.'"[6] (He did inherit most of the cast, including Fox.) John Houseman, who ended up having a small role in the film (the first time he and Bridges had worked together since *The Paper Chase*), wryly observed, "It was good this came along so quickly. Jim didn't have any time to shilly-shally."[7] The director himself conceded, "The rapid decision-making was real good for me, I do believe."[8]

Bridges made the film without his usual group of collaborators, many of whom had been working with him for the better part of a decade. Kim Kurumada didn't join the production and neither did Marty Ewing. Jeff Gourson wasn't brought back as the editor, as Bridges elected to retain John Bloom (who a few years earlier had won an Academy Award for cutting Richard Attenborough's *Gandhi*). Bridges did insist that Gordon Willis shoot *Bright Lights, Big City*. "Jim and I met on weekends and every morning as we drove to the set, we'd work things out," Willis remembered. "There was no motion confused with accomplishment. What didn't work, we threw out. I camera block very quickly, and there was no excess in set-ups. The movie was basically cut in the camera."[9]

"Gordon Willis was amazing," Swoosie Kurtz, who played the important supporting role of Megan, said. "He was and is such a legend. I was so excited to be working with the 'prince of darkness,' as they call him. In all the movies I've been on in my life, I have never seen the way the crew comported themselves on a set when he was working. He demanded/required — or everyone just knew — complete quiet. And it was so wonderful. I *loved* that. I never knew how DPs or anybody could work in the chaos of everybody talking, walkie-talkies going off, and everything. It was just understood that when he was lighting and talking to his guys, it was done in hushed tones and he was doing his work. And he let everyone else do their work."[10]

As he did on *Perfect*, Willis brought a rare visual sophistication to *Bright Lights, Big City*. There are several sequences in which his images alone tell the story — most notably a confrontation between Jamie and his estranged wife, Amanda (Phoebe Cates), at an Oscar de la Renta fashion show which ends with Jamie being thrown out of the building — that are impossible to imagine in the films Bridges made with other cinematographers.

Production designer Santo Loquasto was retained and it was much to his relief that Bridges and Willis assumed control, the cinematographer said. "We took over what sets worked and trashed what was cumbersome or unworkable. Santo was very good about reworking what we asked for; in fact, was delighted we brought definition to everything quickly."[11] And "quickly" is the operative word: speaking of what passed for preproduction on the film, Bridges boasted, "All the stuff that takes months usually, we did in less than a week."[12] Bloom recalled that the film was shot "in something like six or eight weeks, a ridiculously short amount of time."[13]

If anything, the compressed schedule seemed to invigorate Bridges. "One of the main things I remember about him was his unbounded enthusiasm and energy for the project," Kurtz said. "There was always a sense of wonder, never a sense of jadedness or 'Oh, God, what time can we get out of here?' It was always a wonderful, curious, 'What adventures are we going to have today?' kind of feeling."[14]

* * *

"What I wanted to do was to be very faithful to the book," Bridges said, in one sentence summing up his approach to literary adaptation.[15] "Bridges didn't like the script which we had been working from," Bloom said. "Remarkably, he produced a completely new script in just one week. He kept very closely to the novel and used chunks virtually verbatim and produced a completely new script in this amazingly short amount of time."[16] Bridges explained that he used the first draft written by McInerney "and the novel and put them together into a 104-page script."[17]

And just as he found surprising personal resonances in *The Paper Chase*, Bridges discovered that he was able to relate to McInerney's novel, too: "The reason I really did the book was that I had lost a grandmother the year before. It's really about a boy who does not understand and recognize his grief."[18]

Jamie's "grief" is over the death of his mother (Dianne Wiest), which he has not reconciled himself to as the film opens. According to Caryn James's definitive account of the making of the film in *The New York Times*, the new draft of the screenplay, which Bridges assembled in a single week, "looked to the mother's death as the emotional center of the story."[19] And that it is. He is haunted by flashbacks of her, and the littlest things prompt them. "I think the only thing I didn't agree with Jim on," Willis recalled, "was the use of the first flashback on the mother, Dianne. The first flashback we shot was of her further away, as she stood in the door waving. On second thought, Jim wanted to be closer, so we ended up with two sizes. He picked the closer one. I felt this was a mistake. The first one, the wider one, you can't quite hold onto. It's mythic, more dreamlike. I think he was afraid he wouldn't recognize Dianne, but ... would have been better."[20]

There are also flashbacks of Amanda, who has left him to pursue a modeling career in Europe, inventively folded into the film. But, as McInerney explained, "at first, reading the book, you think that it's his wife's disappearance which has really screwed him up. In fact, it's something even deeper than that. Eventually he realizes that, as much as it hurt losing this wife ... that in fact there was somebody more important in his life, and that's who he's mourning."[21] But in sharp contrast to Jimmy J. in *September 30, 1955*, Jamie's heartache is repressed, concealed just under the surface. Hence, the initial flashbacks to his mother are brief, shard-like images (such as the one described above by Willis).

It is only when Jamie is confronted by his younger brother (Charlie Schlatter) on the pending first anniversary of her death that we are shown an extended flashback of their mother on her deathbed. Jamie sits beside her as she playfully inquires about his love life. He comforts her as she writhes in pain. It's a haunting scene, beautifully played by Fox and Wiest. A bit later, Jamie, beginning to come to terms with his pain, confesses, "I tried to block her out of my mind." Bridges masterfully conveys Jamie's intense denial by only gradually building to this longer deathbed flashback. Jamie adds, in the same conversation, "But I think I owe it to her to remember her." Though the line originates with McInerney's novel,[22] it describes Bridges's own attitude in such films as *September 30, 1955*, *Mike's Murder*, and *Bright Lights, Big City*. The living owe remembrance to the dead in Bridges's films; Jimmy J. owes it to James Dean, Betty owes it to Mike, and Jamie owes it to his mother.

As the film begins, however, Amanda is the one who is foremost on his mind. After Jamie arrives home from work at *Gotham* magazine one evening, he sits down at his desk and reads some of a short story he has been working on. He pulls the page out of the typewriter and rips it up. On a fresh page, he then types the words, "Dead Amanda." We cut to a close-up of Jamie's reflection in a mirror above his desk; a snapshot photo of Amanda is posted on it. In the same shot, Jamie suddenly turns around and looks to us, as the camera racks focus to his head. Who he sees is Amanda, bathed in effervescent light, emerging from the bathroom in her pajamas. Jamie walks into frame and they embrace in the doorway in this flashback. They then race to their bed, continuing to make out. Cates, with her Jean Seberg-like short hairdo, is an enchanting, mature screen presence; we're a long way from *Fast Times at Ridgemont High*. When we cut back to Jamie in the present, he is still looking to the distance, but he is now seen in a long shot rather than a close-up, an expression of how very far away these happier times seem to him and to us.

A rude rapping on the door interrupts Jamie's reverie. It is Tad Allagash (Kiefer Sutherland), a friend who functions as "the alter ego of Jamie," as McInerney explained. "I think we all have a friend who's cooler than we are, who's more glib, who's basically the devil whispering in our ear and saying, 'Go ahead and throw that rock,' 'Go ahead and snort that coke.'"[23] As played by Sutherland, Allagash has some of the same qualities as the preppy lothario Rick Von Sloneker in Whit Stillman's *Metropolitan*. Allagash, as McInerney suggests, encourages Jamie's worst instincts. In this way, he functions much as Pete does for Mike in *Mike's Murder*.

Jamie's cocaine abuse is seemingly what makes it impossible for him to see the most elementary responsibilities of his job through to completion. Setting aside Allagash's "bad influence," in the end Jamie has no one to blame but himself for snorting coke when he is supposed to be fact-checking an article; or for leaving the office before his work is *really*, *truly* done, hoping more than knowing that the piece is error-free as he places it on the desk of his editor, Clara (Frances Sternhagen), before going out to party with Allagash. This is all the sadder because, like Hart in *The Paper Chase*, Jamie is smart enough to be aware of the hallowed space that surrounds him. He is deferential toward *Gotham*'s crotchety editor-in-chief, Mr. Vogel (Houseman), and when he bumps into a great writer of the magazine's past (Jason Robards, in what Janet Maslin called "a scene-stealing appearance"[24]), he ends up going to lunch with him, his admiration only slightly lessened by the older writer's unmitigated drunkenness.

As Vogel, Houseman is a fleeting presence who drifts in and out of the corridors of *Gotham* magazine. ("The ephemeral is eternal," says a character in *Mike's Murder*.) When he first appears in the doorway to the fact-checking department, Jamie, at his desk, catches a glimpse of him out of the corner of his eye. He stands and says, "Mr. Vogel, may I help you?" Vogel curtly replies, "No, thank you," and turns away. In a reaction shot, Jamie looks as though he can't quite believe he has seen Vogel, let alone conversed with him. Fifteen

Eight. Bright Lights, Big City, *Big Legacy*   161

years may have passed since *The Paper Chase*, but Professor Kingsfield has not gotten any more approachable. "John was not that well on *Bright Lights*," Willis remembered. "His persona was what was left from *Paper Chase*. He was a dynamic human being, very smart."[25] In fact, some of the visual concepts from *The Paper Chase* are repeated in *Bright Lights, Big City*. In one scene, Jamie is summoned to Clara's office to meet with her and Vogel. As Vogel confronts Jamie about the difference between the words "precipitate" and "precipitous," we might as well be back in Kingsfield's classroom: Imposing close-ups of Vogel are intercut with looser medium shots of his "student," Jamie.

Around this same time, Norman Lloyd sent Houseman the manuscript of his autobiography, which was published in 1993 as *Stages of Life in Theatre, Film, and Television*. Because of their long friendship going back to Orson Welles's Mercury Theatre, Lloyd asked Houseman to write the foreword to the book. "John was in the last stages of his illness," Lloyd said. "He said he couldn't do it, he's too ill, he just couldn't write anything."[26] (In fact, Houseman died a little less than six months after the release of *Bright Lights, Big City*.) He then went to Bridges, who ended up writing "a lovely, beautiful piece" to open Lloyd's engaging book. "I can't thank him enough."[27] The tragic irony was that Bridges himself would succumb to cancer just five years later.

Jamie's only friend in the fact-checking department (and all of *Gotham*, for that matter) is Megan (Kurtz). None of his other co-workers offer sympathy, let alone assistance, when he has fallen behind on the vetting of a piece. But Megan is solicitous in this instance and in others, too; like a concerned parent, she repeatedly reminds him that his brother has been calling the office while he is out and leaving messages for him. She even calls to make sure he is awake one morning so that he doesn't arrive late for work. The film rarely strays from Jamie's perspective, but when it does, it is often to show things from Megan's point of view, such as when we see her casting her caring eyes from her own work to watch Jamie overwhelmed by a particular assignment.

According to Caryn James, Kurtz was among the actors cast by Bridges when he came on board the film.[28] He was familiar with her work, having previously offered her the role of Frankie in *Perfect*. "I went over to meet with him," she remembered of the earlier film. "They said, 'Oh, come and have lunch, we're shooting over on East 54th Street. Just come over and talk to us.' I was debating whether or not there was enough there for me to do.... I had such a great time with him and Travolta. We had lunch and chatted. I ultimately decided not to do it for whatever reason or something else came up. So we kind of knew each other a little bit from that."[29]

When it came to *Bright Lights, Big City*, "it happened so out of the blue and so fast," Kurtz said. "I just suddenly was offered it and they explained that there was this big shakeup and change in directors and a change in certain roles. I never really heard of such a thing. I felt sort of vaguely guilty taking over a role from another actress."[30] Because the screenplay was still in a state of flux, Kurtz was instead sent a copy of the novel.

The same night, Kurtz was obligated to attend a fundraising event with playwright John Guare. (She won a Tony Award in 1986 for the revival of Guare's *The House of Blue Leaves* and later followed Stockard Channing in the role of Ouisa in Guare's masterpiece *Six Degrees of Separation*.) "Of course, normally I would have cancelled everything and stayed home and read the book and given them an answer ASAP, but I had to go to this thing," she said. "I was telling John about it that night and he's always advised me on so many things. He talked me into doing *Dangerous Liaisons* when I was all against it. He's sort of very in on my life and my decisions! He said, 'Oh, my God, that's a *wonderful* part in the book.' Of course, he knew the book; he's read everything ever written. So I when I got home late, I looked at it really closely. There was a really lovely note from Jim in the book when they sent it over. He was always so gracious that way, in the way he presented things.... The next day I got back to them and said I'd love to do it."[31]

Guare had it right: Megan is the novel's most striking character and Kurtz-as-Megan gives the film's most memorable performance. Her best scene comes relatively late, after Jamie has been fired by Clara for particularly egregious errors he allowed to slip into a piece. Following his dismissal, Megan asks him to lunch. Inevitably, he misses that date (shades of Mike Chuhutsky?). They end up having dinner at her downtown apartment for "linguini and sympathy," as Jamie puts it.

The scene starts at the kitchen table. Megan begins, "Tell me about Amanda. I get the feeling something bad happened." He tells her about his marital history (and marital woes), and doesn't stop talking. Fox's monologue is delivered well, but the blocking devised by Bridges and Willis is what is special. Jamie gets up from the table and walks to the kitchen to uncork a second bottle of red wine. Megan moves from the table to a stool by the countertop. Jamie then proceeds to the living room. Megan remains at her perch, swiveling around to follow him there. Jamie moves about the space restlessly, sitting down and then getting up from the sofa, pacing from one corner of the room to the other. He never stops talking; she listens with seemingly infinite patience.

"Behind him," Jonathan Rosenbaum wrote in his review in the *Chicago Reader*, "is a spectacular view of the bright lights of the big city seen through the windows — an apotheosis of all the fake big-city skyline backdrops that have graced thousands of other Hollywood movies, only slightly less impressive than the one seen in Hitchcock's *Rope*."[32]

The backdrop is indeed arresting. Originally the scene was to be shot on location, and Kurtz's own apartment was considered by Santo Loquasto. "I had a few years before moved into this beautiful apartment on Central Park West," she said. "They asked, 'Can we come over and see it?' I think Santo came over and saw it. I remember thinking, 'What am I doing? *What am I doing?*' For some reason, he decided it wasn't right."[33] According to Willis, this was "too much of a scene" to be shot on location, so a set was built. "Santo had to slap this set together," Willis recalled. "He did a very good job. The backing was fun to look at, however, it was a bit much. I would have preferred one a little less fired up, but we had very little time to put one into place or for that matter shoot a new one, so we had to use what was available at the moment. This was a big scene, a lot to shoot. We did it in one long day."[34] Rosenbaum argued that the backdrop's very artificiality was intentional on Bridges's part, contending that he was "smart enough as a director to know that it's fake, and to use this backdrop to counterpoint Fox's confession of his own self-deceptions."[35]

So far, Bridges has cut between angles of Jamie in the warmly lit living room and Megan seated in the darkened kitchen. Not since the beginning of the scene have they shared the same frame. Jamie excuses himself to the bathroom. When he returns, Megan moves to the sofa. Sensing that it may be her turn to speak, she begins peppering him with questions and suggestions about his writing and his next job move. Uninterested in her offers of help, he joins her on the sofa and begins saying what a "rare woman" she is; he is not thinking of her career guidance. "I just loved the part where he just desperately tries to start making out with me and puts his hand up my skirt and all of that," Kurtz said. "It's just so sad and so wrong. And she knows that. He's just going for what he knows and what's comforting for him."[36] Megan deflects Jamie's romantic overtures gracefully; she truly is, as Elizabeth Wurtzel wrote in *The Harvard Crimson*, "the only decent woman in New York City."[37] As McInerney noted, Jamie has "sort of vaguely sexual feelings for Megan, but she's more of a mother figure."[38]

In McInerney's novel, Megan is much less passive in this scene, revealing details of her own life as Jamie does of his. She tells him she used to be an actress, is divorced, has a young son, and has suffered from manic depression. Bridges elected to cut this material from the film, which Kurtz has always slightly regretted. "I felt that part of my character's job in the story was to bring out in him a kinder, more compassionate side, a less egocentric, self-absorbed side," she observed. "The lead character in the film was immensely self-absorbed, taking drugs and doing all of this stuff. And if he could for a moment or two just stop and look at someone else's pain and take the focus off himself for a minute, I think it would have enhanced his character. Now maybe that's just an actress saying, 'Where did my lines go?' But it would have been a nice other side."[39]

It could be argued that Bridges's opaque approach made Megan more mysterious and kept the focus on what was most important about Megan story-wise: her gestures of kindness. Kurtz agreed that "to go into her whole backstory is lovely in the book, not necessary in the film. We have to keep moving forward with the story. But I do feel that there was a *little* something that could have been mine there that would have enhanced his character."[40]

The only remnant of Megan's past is the bottle of lithium that Jamie notices in the bathroom. Unfortunately, it's a detail that seems inexplicable in the film as presently constituted; since we know so little about Megan, we are left confused. "When he found all of those pills, it was like, 'What? What is she doing with all of those pills?'" Kurtz said.[41]

These reservations aside, Kurtz loved Bridges's directorial methods, which included positive reinforcement:

> He would praise you for the things that you were doing right, which is always a good place to start! We're all so fragile. And then he would sort of build on that and say, "I think we could use even more of that toward the end of the scene," instead of telling you what you're doing wrong, which is a sort of horrible thing to do. He never did that. He would go, "I loved that thing you did in the last take. I felt a sense of almost like you were going to cry or almost going to talk back to him, but you decided not to. I actually think you can go further than that...."
>
> When you work with a great director, it's like taking a master class in acting. I just learn so much from a wonderful director, and I think I did from Jim in how to sort of modulate a performance—a little more here, a little less there. I would rank him right up there not only because of the way he worked with us actors but because of the results.[42]

According to Kim Kurumada, "Certain directors have a persona of what a director is or what one should be":

> I did a film, just before he died, with Herb Ross, and he was almost the epitome of what some people think a Hollywood director is. The way he walks and speaks and carries himself and things like that. Jimmy wasn't like that at all. But he never let people forget who was in charge and that he was the director. One story he told me, which I just thought was hilarious, was, he in his early days had directed a play—I think it was at Cherry Lane in New York—and it was reviewed by *The New York Times*. The review gave the name of the play and that it was directed by James Bridges. At opportune moments, when something would happen, Jimmy would say, "Wait a minute. I'm the director. Make no doubt about it. I'm the director. It says so right here in *The*

Eight. Bright Lights, Big City, *Big Legacy* 165

New York Times!" And if I was present, he'd turn to me and say, "Isn't that true, Kim?" I'd say, "Yes, it is true, Jim. It does say that in *The New York Times.*"[43]

By all accounts, Michael J. Fox, famous for the TV sitcom *Family Ties* and the *Back to the Future* movie trilogy, devoted himself tirelessly to the film and to his performance. "God knows nobody in this world has thrown themselves more into a part and worked harder, both himself and with his fellow actors, than Michael," John Bloom recalled. "It was just amazing. He was astonishing. He always came to the rushes, he always was there trying to analyze what he needed to do in his character and how he could help his fellow actors. It was marvelous. That was one of the most enriching things of the whole experience."[44]

"He was fiendish," Kurtz said. "He worked like a fiend. I loved, loved, loved working with him so much. I remember him clutching those new pages of script that would come to him and just devouring them. Again, the pressure of time.... Sometimes I think we work best under a deadline. That adrenalin starts kicking in. He was so adrenalized anyway; he's kind of an adrenalized performer, he's got that wonderful energy. After his image on *Family Ties*, this was a different role for him to play, this drug-taking, coked-up, obsessive guy.... I think he nailed it."[45] His director agreed, saying it was his best work to date.[46]

In sharp contrast to *Perfect*, most critics wrote admiringly of Bridges's work on *Bright Lights, Big City*, if not always the film itself, when it premiered on April 1, 1988. Rosenbaum praised "the spit and polish" provided by Bridges, Willis, and composer Donald Fagen, but asked, "[t]o what end?"[47] Roger Ebert, finally perceiving a thread through Bridges's films, wrote that "*Urban Cowboy* was in many ways an earlier version of the same story," which he considered to be one of "wasted days and misplaced nights."[48] Ebert also praised Fox, singling out his monologue in Megan's apartment as "the best thing he has ever done in a movie."[49]

The great champion of *September 30, 1955*, Janet Maslin, defended many aspects of the film, including the mood, the casting, and the *Gotham* scenes, but curiously had little to say about what Bridges brought to the table (despite the production's much-publicized switch in directors).[50] And while she rhapsodized about *Mike's Murder* only a few years earlier, Pauline Kael was characteristically indifferent about the new Bridges film: "The picture isn't terrible," she wrote, "just terribly dull."[51]

Kael singled out Houseman (as she had fifteen years earlier when reviewing *The Paper Chase*) as giving the film's "standout performance."[52] *Bright Lights, Big City* was not technically Houseman's last film; Woody Allen's *Another Woman* (in which he gave his finest performance since *The Paper*

Chase) was released several months later and the comedy *The Naked Gun* (in which he had a cameo as a driving school instructor) was released posthumously. But it is fitting that, near the end of his life, he was reunited with the director who gave him his career as a film actor.

* * *

The ending of *Bright Lights, Big City* is of a piece with the hopeful conclusions Bridges gave *Urban Cowboy* and *Perfect*. We are confident that Jamie, having reconciled himself to his mother's death and having disowned Tad and Amanda, will figure things out and "learn everything all over again," as he says in a voice-over.

This is not the finale to an old man's film. When *Bright Lights, Big City* was released, Bridges had only recently turned fifty-two and already had plans for his next film, which was to be his first set in Arkansas since *September 30, 1955*. He said it was "about someone who comes back to a small town to discover it very changed and attempts to set things back in their right place, to sort of turn the clock back, because he feels the town was much better before the arrival of the WalMarts, the McDonalds."[53] I don't know how far Bridges got with this script, but its protagonist sounds not unlike the mother of Peter Levi in Mary McCarthy's great novel *Birds of America*, who mourned the "changing" America. "Already it had been changing when she was a girl," McCarthy wrote. "It had only been in the summers, when she and her sisters went to their grandmother's farm, after their mother had died, that she had really seen the old America, which she connected with the speckled foxglove in her grandmother's yard."[54]

This unnamed project wasn't Bridges's only Arkansas-based screenplay after *September 30, 1955*. A 1977 Associated Press article mentioned *The Occupation of Paris*, which was about "what happens to a small Arkansas town surrounded by army camps in wartime."[55] (That's Paris, Arkansas, not Paris, France, that's referred to in the title.)

Cinematographer Reynaldo Villalobos remembered a screenplay called *Deer Season*, which also took place in Bridges's home state: "He had written this script and I read it and I thought it was great. It was a small film, but it was exciting. Deer hunting season would start and then prostitutes would come when they were hunting. They'd go into the woods. It was kind of strange."[56]

Another project planned during Bridges's last years was *The Desert Rose*, based on the novel by Larry McMurtry, whose novels *The Last Picture Show* and *Terms of Endearment* had been made into successful films. "The story is about a Las Vegas showgirl and her daughter," Kim Kurumada recalled. "We couldn't find an aging woman that could really pull that off that the studio would go for."[57]

"We had a greenlight from Tri-Star," Jack Larson said. "But they wanted one of two leading ladies, either Cher or Goldie Hawn. Jim didn't want either of them."[58] Kurumada added, "The thing that was sad about losing that project was that Jim had such a unique perspective on it.... It was amazing because he wanted to show the two sides of the Las Vegas showgirl, the day life and the night life. It really would have made a great film the way Jim wanted to do it. He was going to have all the people that work in the day and live at night, live like that. He said, 'Like a desert lizard, they sleep during the day and they only come out at night, so where they sleep during the day were these dark, aluminum trailers.'"[59]

His editor from *The China Syndrome* and *Urban Cowboy*, David Rawlins, was to rejoin Bridges on *The Desert Rose*. "He wanted me to do that film," Rawlins said. "And he was too darn sick to go to a meeting. Apparently, they gave him so much radiation that he said, 'Well, I can't sit down to do the meeting.' But we were going to do another film. The chemistry was there."[60]

When Clint Eastwood's *White Hunter Black Heart* was released in May 1990, Bridges received his final screen credit, as the film's co-writer (with Peter Viertel and Burt Kennedy). It was based upon Viertel's novel about the making of John Huston's *The African Queen*; Bridges had long hoped to make the film himself. But as with *The Desert Rose*, casting proved the sticking point. He couldn't agree with Columbia Pictures as to who should play the leading character, the director inspired by Huston. As Larson explained, "Jim wanted Sterling Hayden, and Columbia did not want him. Then they said Lee Marvin, and Jim went off to meet with Lee Marvin. He was in England and he thought, 'Yes, Lee Marvin could do it and he would be good.' He came back and in the meantime, Lee Marvin had a big flop and the studio didn't want him."[61] (Eastwood played the role in his film.) According to Larson, the screenplay Bridges worked on "basically survived" Eastwood's filming. "The only thing was, Jim felt it was absolutely necessary to kill an elephant. I don't know how he intended to do it."[62]

We were deprived of *The Desert Rose*—and *The Occupation of Paris* and *Deer Season* and his version of *White Hunter Black Heart*, too—because of the intestinal cancer that would ultimately claim James Bridges's life. "The tragedy of not having Jim around longer for all of us is that we don't get to experience more of his stories," Jack Bender observed. "When you go to a Jim Bridges film, there's a comfort zone. You're going to be on a comfortable sofa that's going to hold up and you may go places where you're not comfortable, but underneath you there is going to be this solid thing, which is called American storytelling that he definitely sprang from. It would have been really interesting to see where his filmography would have gone."[63] What would his last films have been like? Like Hitchcock's *Family Plot*? Like Mankiewicz's *The Honey Pot*? Like Kazan's *The Last Tycoon*? We will never know, and Bender chose the appropriate word — "tragedy" — to describe what we missed.

He could have made more films than he did. He was offered films all the time. Kurumada said, "I remember we were talking to a producer who wanted Jim to do *Working Girl*. They wanted Jim to do that. They wanted Meg Ryan, and Jim didn't want to do it with Meg Ryan. He wanted to do it more with somebody like Debra Winger. We had received advances, we had money to start working on that, and at one point Jim just got out his checkbook and wrote a check. He said, 'Well, how much have we spent so far?' They told him and he wrote out a check and handed it back over. He said, 'We're not doing it.'"[64] Perhaps this was stubbornness on Bridges's part; perhaps he would have left us more movies (even if they were not as personal as *The Occupation of Paris* might have been) had he been more flexible.

But Kurumada felt it was a matter of Bridges not wanting to have to explain his artistic decisions to those who didn't understand his vision: "You have to have confidence in that he knows what he's doing. To have to justify it, to have to go through reasons why he wanted to do certain things, was in the long run just draining on his energy and his resources that he wanted to devote to the project.... Usually when there was a problem, it came down to the studio thinking they knew what movie they wanted to make, which in Jim's eyes was not a good movie. It may have been a very commercial movie, but it was not based on substance and character. It was based on market surveys and analysis and things like that. For Jimmy, he worked best when he could surround himself with the people that he felt understood the way he worked."[65] Remarkably, he seemed to have attained this on each of his eight films, none of which was an unhappy experience for those who worked on them, a few of which (*September 30, 1955* and *Mike's Murder*) ended up being among the best American films.

James Bridges died on June 6, 1993, at the age of fifty-seven. "I was the only one of the old college crowd who attended Jim's funeral in Paris, Arkansas," Tom Bonner recalled. "The others were scattered and variously busy with their lives, some far away. It was a hot, mostly cloudy, humid Arkansas afternoon and after the service in the church we all went to the nearby graveyard for interment. After a few words were spoken and just after Jim's casket was lowered into the ground, we all began to disperse. Then, just as I got into my car and pulled out the gate of the graveyard, the most vicious thunderstorm I had seen in years broke loose. The lightning and torrents of rain were blinding, and the thunder was deafening! It was impossible to drive for a few minutes until it finally subsided. I couldn't resist a smile. I wrote Jack Larson, who had not been able to attend the Arkansas service, the next day and told him Jim had done it yet another time. His final exit was, of course, overly dramatic!"⁶⁶

Everybody who worked with Bridges, especially those who worked with him repeatedly, was bereaved. Debra Winger was abroad, filming *Shadowlands*. "It was pretty intense," she said. "The fact that I couldn't be with him at that time. I was with him a couple of weeks before [he died]. It was hard not to comfort Jack and be there for him."⁶⁷

Lisa Blount: "It just killed me when he died, and so quickly. It was really hard on a lot of people.... There were a lot of people who loved him. You couldn't not love him. He was funny. He always wore the jeans, cuffed up high with the white socks and the loafers. He could wear it better than anybody. It was goofy-looking and it was sexy at the same time. He was a really, really cool guy."⁶⁸

Mary Kai Clark: "Jim was Jim. And everybody loved him because of that. That's not the only reason they loved him, but that's one of the qualities about him that's so unique. He never changed. His goodness and genuineness probably spilled over to other people."⁶⁹

Jeff Gourson: "I terribly, terribly miss him. It was a great loss when he went, not only as a friend but as a filmmaker."⁷⁰

Barbara Hershey: "Still I can't believe Jim isn't with us. You don't say goodbye to those people."⁷¹

Marshall Schlom: "I wish we hadn't lost Jim so early. You'd want to be with him every day of your life."⁷²

* * *

In a way, Bridges still is with us, through the exemplary work of the Bridges/Larson Foundation, which was established after his death. "I knew about foundations because I had served for eleven years on the Rockefeller Foundation, on their funding for playwrights and theatre," recalled Jack Larson, himself the recipient of both Rockefeller Foundation and Ford Foundation grants as a playwright and librettist. "I was actually recommended for a Guggenheim [Fellowship] by John Ashbery! The foundation wrote me and said I'd been recommended and I would need four recommendations from people of some distinction in the field. So I got recommendations from Jerome Robbins — I had been a part of his American Laboratory Theatre; Virgil Thomson, of course; Lincoln Kirstein; and John Houseman. They gave me very strong recommendations to follow up on John's suggestion. And somehow I didn't get it!"⁷³

It was after Bridges had taken ill that the idea for what became the Bridges/Larson Foundation was first considered and the plans were made to set it up. "Then Jim took a turn for the worse," Larson said. "There was a film we were going to be doing and Jim was not well enough to do it, *Desert Rose*. And things got worse and then Jim passed away. And now there's this foundation. So it was up to me."[74]

Because Bridges had been a stage manager for John Houseman at the UCLA Theatre Group, Larson first contacted UCLA. "We had a meeting over at UCLA with what turned out to be a very wonderful development person, Rosalee Sass, and Gil Cates, who was the dean and who has produced the Academy Awards for many years, and Bob Rosen. We had a lunch and I described what I wanted to do. I wanted to begin a grant in their film department. It would be, how much would it cost [students] to make their Masters film at that point? They used to have to quit school and go to work and max out their credit cards to get their Masters degree in film. At that point, it cost $25,000. They could make it on that. So I wanted to set up that grant for $25,000, but they had to show excellence in theatre as well as film. And everybody was very excited about that."

There was a reason for Larson's insistence that students demonstrate "excellence in theatre." Before Bridges died, he discussed with Larson his aversion to the way most film schools were run. They remembered one incident in particular: "One night we were at a CAA dinner and Glenn Caron, who created a television series, *Moonlighting*, and had at that point moved into films, was sitting opposite Jim. Jim didn't know Glenn Caron. At some point around dessert, Glenn Caron said that he chalked up the success he'd had to Jim. Jim said, 'How so?'"[75] Caron reminded Bridges that he had visited the film department of the university Caron was attending. He sensed that Bridges was not "enthusiastic" about the film department.

"And so Glenn Caron said he went up to Jim and said that he had drawn this conclusion and could Jim give him any advice about how to have a career like Jim's, who he admired very much," Larson recalled. "And Jim said, 'Yes, get the hell out of film school and go join the theatre department and learn how to work with actors. You're all learning things here that, unless you're an idiot, you'll learn anyway on a soundstage — tracking shots, camera angles, all of these things. But when you put any of these film students in a room with three actors, they don't know what the hell to do.'"[76]

Since 1995, the James Bridges Award in Film Directing has been given at UCLA. "It instantly was very successful and instantly the students wanted to be able to compete for it," Larson said. "So basically the ones who would like the money enrolled in the theatre department.... Once I saw that it worked, I expanded that to USC, to the American Film Institute, and then to Columbia University."[77]

Several years later, the Melnitz Theater at UCLA was renovated thanks to a $500,000 donation from the Bridges/Larson Foundation.[78] "They talked to me about funding the theatre there," Larson said. "The theatre needed a lot of things. It's in Melnitz Hall, but it's their major motion picture theatre on the UCLA campus. They were going into a situation to give naming opportunities for a certain amount of money. There was an amount of money that I could commit to, to have it named the James Bridges Theater."[79]

And so it was. The Bridges/Larson Foundation also provides support to, among many others, the avant-garde performance space Highways, Project Angel Food, Aid for AIDS, LAMP Community, and amFAR, The Foundation for AIDS Research.[80]

James Bridges, Arkansan, "Everybody loved Jim," said Jack Larson. (Courtesy of the University of Central Arkansas Archives.)

And what would Bridges make of all of this? "I try not to think about it!" Larson said. "I believe he's around somewhere but I haven't felt a kick in the ass, let me put it that way!"[81]

* * *

In reflecting on Bridges's career, I think of the scene in Alan J. Pakula's film of *Sophie's Choice*, when Nathan toasts the aspirant writer Stingo on the Brooklyn Bridge. He says to him, in words absent from William Styron's novel, "On this bridge, where so many great American writers have stood and reached out for words to give America its voice, looking toward the land that gave us Whitman, who from its eastern edge dreamt his country's future and gave it words, from this span where Thomas Wolfe and Hart Crane wrote, we welcome Stingo into that pantheon of the gods." Here Nathan has honored Stingo, Pakula said, "in ways we all dream of being honored."[82] Did Bridges have such dreams? If he did, they were dreams fulfilled. His rightful admission to his own "pantheon of the gods"—comprised, presumably, of Tennessee Williams and of John Houseman, of James Dean and of Alfred Hitchcock—was long ago secured.

David Rawlins considered James Bridges to be "possibly the smartest, the most talented, the most sensitive man I ever met."[83] When you consider all that he accomplished in his fifty-seven years, how could he *not* have been?

Directorial Filmography

The Baby Maker (1970)

SCREENPLAY-DIRECTOR: James Bridges. PRODUCER: Richard Goldstone. CINEMATOGRAPHER: Charles Rosher, Jr. EDITOR: Walter Thompson. ART DIRECTOR: Morton Rabinowitz. MUSIC: Fred Karlin. CAST: Barbara Hershey (Tish), Collin Wilcox-Horne (Suzanne), Sam Groom (Jay), Scott Glenn (Tad), Jeannie Berlin (Charlotte), Lili Valenty (Mrs. Culnick), Helena Kallianiotes (Wanda), Jeff Siggins (Dexter), Phyllis Coates (Tish's Mother), Madge Kennedy (Tish's Grandmother), Ray Hemphill (Toy Store "Killer"), Sam Francis, Alan Keesling, Peter Mays, Jonathan Greene, Jonathan Lippinott, Jeffrey Perkins, Michael Scroggins (The Single Wing Turquoise Bird). TIME: 109 min. (Color). STUDIO: National General Pictures.

The Paper Chase (1973)

DIRECTOR: James Bridges. PRODUCERS: Rodrick Paul, Robert C. Thompson. Associate PRODUCER: Philip L. Parslow. SCREENPLAY: James Bridges, based on the novel by John Jay Osborn, Jr. CINEMATOGRAPHER: Gordon Willis. EDITOR: Walter Thompson. PRODUCTION DESIGNER: George Jenkins. MUSIC: John Williams. CAST: Timothy Bottoms (James T. Hart), Lindsay Wagner (Susan), Graham Beckel (Franklin Ford III), James Naughton (Kevin Brooks), Craig Richard Nelson (Willis Bell), Edward Herrmann (Thomas Craig Anderson), Robert Lydiard (O'Connor), Regina Baff (Asheley Brooks), Lenny Baker (William Moss, Tutor), David Clennon (Toombs), Irma Hurley (Mrs. Weasal), John Houseman (Charles W. Kingsfield, Jr.). TIME: 113 min. (Color). STUDIO: Twentieth Century–Fox Film Corporation.

September 30, 1955 (1978)

SCREENPLAY-DIRECTOR: James Bridges. PRODUCER: Jerry Weintraub. EXECUTIVE PRODUCER: Robert Larson. CINEMATOGRAPHER: Gordon Willis. EDITOR: Jeff Gourson. ART DIRECTOR: Robert Luthardt. MUSIC: Leonard Rosenman. CAST: Richard Thomas (Jimmy J.), Susan Tyrrell (Melba Lou), Deborah Benson (Charlotte), Lisa Blount (Billie Jean), Thomas Hulce (Hanley), Dennis Quaid (Frank), Mary Kai Clark (Pat),

Dennis Christopher (Eugene), Collin Wilcox (Jimmy J.'s Mother). TIME: 101 min. (Color). STUDIO: Universal Pictures.

The China Syndrome (1979)

DIRECTOR: James Bridges. PRODUCER: Michael Douglas. EXECUTIVE PRODUCER: Bruce Gilbert. SCREENPLAY: Mike Gray & T.S. Cook and James Bridges CINEMATOGRAPHER: James Crabe. EDITOR: David Rawlins. PRODUCTION DESIGNER: George Jenkins. CAST: Jane Fonda (Kimberly Wells), Jack Lemmon (Jack Godell), Michael Douglas (Richard Adams), Scott Brady (Herman De Young), James Hampton (Bill Gibson), Peter Donat (Don Jacovich). TIME: 122 min. (Color). STUDIO: Columbia Pictures.

Urban Cowboy (1980)

DIRECTOR: James Bridges. PRODUCERS: Robert Evans, Irving Azoff. EXECUTIVE PRODUCER: C.O. Erickson. SCREENPLAY: James Bridges and Aaron Latham, based on the story by Aaron Latham. CINEMATOGRAPHER: Reynaldo Villalobos. EDITOR: David Rawlins. PRODUCTION DESIGNER: Stephen Grimes. SCORE ADAPTED BY: Ralph Burns MUSIC COORDINATOR: Becky Shargo. CAST: John Travolta (Bud), Debra Winger (Sissy), Scott Glenn (Wes), Madolyn Smith (Pam), Barry Corbin (Uncle Bob), Brooke Alderson (Aunt Corene), Cooper Huckabee (Marshall), James Gammon (Steve Strange). TIME: 134 min. (Color). STUDIO: Paramount Pictures.

Mike's Murder (1984)

SCREENPLAY-DIRECTOR: James Bridges. EXECUTIVE PRODUCER: Kim Kurumada. ASSOCIATE PRODUCER: Jack Larson. CINEMATOGRAPHER: Reynaldo Villalobos. EDITORS: Jeff Gourson and Dede Allen. PRODUCTION DESIGNER: Peter Jamison. MUSIC: John Barry. ADDITIONAL MUSIC: Joe Jackson. MUSIC SUPERVISOR: Becky Shargo. CAST: Debra Winger (Betty), Mark Keyloun (Mike), Darrell Larson (Pete), Brooke Alderson (Patty), Paul Winfield (Philip), Daniel Shor (Richard), Robert Crosson (Sam), William Ostrander (Randy). TIME: 109 min. (Color). STUDIO: The Ladd Company thru Warner Bros.

Perfect (1985)

PRODUCER-DIRECTOR: James Bridges. EXECUTIVE PRODUCER: Kim Kurumada. CO-PRODUCER: Jack Larson. SCREENPLAY: Aaron Latham and James Bridges, based on articles in *Rolling Stone* by Aaron Latham. CINEMATOGRAPHER: Gordon Willis. EDITOR: Jeff Gourson. PRODUCTION DESIGNER: Michael Haller. MUSIC: Ralph Burns. MUSIC SUPERVISOR: Becky Mancuso. CAST: John Travolta (Adam Lawrence), Jamie Lee Curtis (Jessie Wilson), Anne De Salvo (Frankie), Marilu Henner (Sally), Laraine

Newman (Linda), Mathew Reed (Roger), Jann Wenner (Mark Roth), Stefan Gierasch (Charlie), Kenneth Welsh (Joe McKenzie), Ronnie Claire Edwards (Melody), Murphy Cross (Dita), Murphy Dunne (Peckerman), Paul Kent (Judge), Michael Laskin (Government Prosecutor). TIME: 120 min. (Color). STUDIO: Columbia Pictures.

Bright Lights, Big City (1988)

DIRECTOR: James Bridges. PRODUCERS: Mark Rosenberg and Sydney Pollack. EXECUTIVE PRODUCER: Gerald R. Molen. ASSOCIATE PRODUCER: Jack Larson. SCREENPLAY: Jay McInerney, based on the novel by Jay McInerney. CINEMATOGRAPHER: Gordon Willis. EDITORS: John Bloom and George Berndt. PRODUCTION DESIGNER: Santo Loquasto. MUSIC: Donald Fagen. ADDITIONAL MUSIC: Rob Mounsey. CAST: Michael J. Fox (Jamie), Kiefer Sutherland (Tad), Phoebe Cates (Amanda), Swoosie Kurtz (Megan), Frances Sternhagen (Clara), Tracy Pollan (Vicky), John Houseman (Mr. Vogel), Charlie Schlatter (Michael), David Warrilow (Rittenhouse), Dianne Wiest (Mother). TIME: 108 min. (Color). STUDIO: United Artists.

Chapter Notes

Preface

1. Tennessee Williams, *Memoirs* (New York: New Directions, 1975), p. 242.
2. Stephen Farber, "Blanche Wins the Battle," *The New York Times*, April 1, 1973.
3. Tom Buckley, "At the Movies: Fonda tilts forces of nuclear energy in *China Syndrome*," *The New York Times*, March 16, 1979.
4. Wayne Warga, "Recalling James Dean on 9/30/55," *Los Angeles Times*, September 25, 1977.
5. Frank Mulcahy, "*Days of the Dancing Entertaining, Offbeat*," *Los Angeles Times*, May 17, 1961.
6. Norman Lloyd, *Stages of Life in Theatre, Film, and Television* (New York: Limelight Editions, 1993), p. 175.
7. James Bridges, "Foreword," in Norman Lloyd, *Stages of Life in Theatre, Film and Television* (New York: Limelight Editions, 1993), p. ix.
8. Norman Lloyd, interview with the author, March 2, 2009.
9. *The Baby Maker* presskit (National General Pictures), p. 9.
10. Sergio Leemann, *Robert Wise on His Films: From Editing Room to Director's Chair* (Los Angeles: Silman-James Press, 1995), p. 223.
11. Norman Lloyd, interview with the author, March 2, 2009.
12. Debra Winger, email to the author, May 11, 2009.
13. Gordon Willis, email to the author, February 27, 2008.
14. Kim Kurumada, interview with the author, December 16, 2008.
15. Peter Tonguette, "Remembering Welles: A Conversation with Norman Lloyd," *The Film Journal*, July 2004, http://www.thefilmjournal.com/issue9/lloyd.html
16. Truman Capote, *Breakfast at Tiffany's: A Short Novel and Three Stories* (New York: Modern Library, 1994), p. 3.

Chapter One

1. Susan King, "Honoring James Bridges," *Los Angeles Times*, November 11, 1999.
2. Simon Callow, *Orson Welles: The Road to Xanadu* (London: Jonathan Cape, 1995), p. 15.
3. Jane Wilson, interview with the author, March 3, 2009.
4. Laurence Luckinbill, interview with the author, March 18, 2009.
5. Debra Winger, email to the author, May 11, 2009.
6. Jane Wilson, interview with the author, March 3, 2009.
7. Oral history by Martha Reid Scott, The James Bridges Collection — M99-14, University of Central Arkansas Archives.
8. *Ibid.*
9. Jane Wilson, interview with the author, March 3, 2009.
10. Mary Nell Taylor, "James Bridges: An Arkansas boy comes home," *The Echo*, April 1, 1976.
11. *Ibid.*
12. Tom Bonner, interview with the author, February 24, 2009.
13. *Ibid.*
14. *Ibid.*
15. Jay Carr, "*Bright Lights* Amid the Chaos," *The Boston Globe*, April 1, 1988.
16. Mary Nell Taylor, "James Bridges: An Arkansas boy comes home," *The Echo*, April 1, 1976.
17. Debbie Getlin, interview with the author, February 17, 2009.
18. Lee Grant, "Muddy Séance in Toad Suck Ferry," *Los Angeles Times*, October 21, 1976.

19. David Thompson, *Altman on Altman* (London: Faber and Faber, 2005), p. 17.
20. Tom Bonner, interview with the author, February 24, 2009.
21. *Ibid.*
22. Mary Nell Taylor, "James Bridges: An Arkansas boy comes home," *The Echo*, April 1, 1976.
23. *The Baby Maker* presskit (National General Pictures), p. 2.
24. Jay Carr, "*Bright Lights* Amid the Chaos," *The Boston Globe*, April 1, 1988.
25. Jack Larson, interview with the author, March 16, 2008.
26. Anthony Tommasini, *Virgil Thomson: Composer on the Aisle* (New York: W.W. Norton & Company, 1997), p. 478.
27. Barbara Hershey, interview with the author, June 28, 2009.
28. Tom Bonner, email to the author, February 26, 2009.
29. Dominique Paul Noth, "Bit actor is now starring, but behind the movie camera," *The Milwaukee Journal*, October 27, 1973.
30. *Ibid.*
31. Jack Larson, interview with the author, March 16, 2008.
32. *Ibid.*
33. John Houseman, *Final Dress* (New York: Simon & Schuster, 1983), p. 491.
34. Norman Lloyd, interview with the author, March 2, 2009.
35. *Ibid.*
36. Norman Lloyd, *Stages of Life in Theatre, Film, and Television* (New York: Limelight Editions, 1993), p. 175.
37. Norman Lloyd, interview with the author, March 2, 2009.
38. *Ibid.*
39. Ray Bradbury, "The Jar," in *The October Country* (New York: Ballantine Books, 1955), p. 94.
40. Norman Lloyd, interview with the author, March 2, 2009.
41. Ray Bradbury, "The Jar," in *The October Country* (New York: Ballantine Books, 1955), p. 95.
42. Norman Lloyd, interview with the author, March 2, 2009.
43. Collin Wilcox Paxton, interview with the author, March 4, 2008.
44. Jack Larson, interview with the author, July 15, 2008.
45. Norman Lloyd, interview with the author, March 2, 2009.
46. Collin Wilcox Paxton, interview with the author, March 4, 2008.
47. Ray Bradbury, "The Jar," in *The October Country* (New York: Ballantine Books, 1995), p. 91.
48. Collin Wilcox Paxton, interview with the author, April 20, 2008.
49. Norman Lloyd, interview with the author, March 2, 2009.
50. James Bridges, "Foreword," in Norman Lloyd, *Stages of Life in Theatre, Film and Television* (New York: Limelight Editions, 1993), p. x.
51. Dominique Paul Noth, "Bit actor is now starring, but behind the movie camera," *The Milwaukee Journal*, October 27, 1973.
52. Norman Lloyd, interview with the author, March 2, 2009.
53. *Ibid.*
54. Harry Gilroy, "Negro Detective Has Winning Way," *The New York Times*, April 23, 1966.
55. Jack Larson, interview with the author, March 15, 2009.

Chapter Two

1. Margaret Harford, "*Candied House*—Rhyme with Reason," *Los Angeles Times*, February 10, 1966.
2. Margaret Harford, "*Candied House* Delightful," *Los Angeles Times*, February 12, 1966.
3. Anthony Tommasini, "Golly, Jimmy Olsen Writes Librettos!," *The New York Times*, May 15, 1998.
4. Margaret Harford, "*Candied House* Delightful," *Los Angeles Times*, February 12, 1966.
5. Collin Wilcox Paxton, interview with the author, March 4, 2008.
6. *The Highlander*, "Playwright-actor Jim Bridges Much Pleased with Highlands," August 7, 1964.
7. Jack Larson, interview with the author, July 15, 2008.
8. Margaret Harford, "Actors Studio-West Offers Trio of Plays," *Los Angeles Times*, January 6, 1969.
9. Collin Wilcox Paxton, interview with the author, March 4, 2008.
10. Margaret Harford, "*Candied House*—Rhyme with Reason," *Los Angeles Times*, February 10, 1966.
11. Debbie Getlin, interview with the author, February 17, 2009.
12. Jack Larson, interview with the author, March 16, 2008.

13. *The Stage and Television Today*, "Happy homosexuals in a bedsitter," July 24, 1969.
14. Walter Reid, "Edinburgh Festival: *Cherry, Larry, Sandy, Doris, Jean, Paul* (Watson's Ladies' College)," *The Scotsman*, August 30, 1969.
15. Jack Bender, interview with the author, June 15, 2009.
16. *Ibid.*
17. *Ibid.*
18. Jack Larson, interview with the author, March 16, 2008.
19. Jack Bender, interview with the author, June 15, 2009.
20. Walter Reid, "Edinburgh Festival: *Cherry, Larry, Sandy, Doris, Jean, Paul* (Watson's Ladies' College)," *The Scotsman*, August 30, 1969.
21. Jack Larson, interview with the author, March 16, 2008.
22. Jack Bender, interview with the author, June 15, 2009.
23. Collin Wilcox Paxton, interview with the author, March 4, 2008.
24. Jack Larson, interview with the author, March 16, 2008.
25. Jack Bender, interview with the author, June 15, 2009.
26. *Ibid.*
27. *Ibid.*
28. John Jay Osborn, Jr., interview with the author, July 9, 2009.
29. Ephraim Katz, ed., *The Film Encyclopedia*, 2nd ed. (New York: HarperPerennial, 1994), p. 174.
30. Nathan Rabin, "*Bright Lights, Big City*," *The A.V. Club*, September 10, 2008, http://www.avclub.com/content/node/86245/print/
31. Jack Larson, interview with the author, March 16, 2008.
32. Barbara Hershey, interview with the author, June 28, 2009.
33. Michael Preece, interview with the author, May 28, 2009.
34. *Ibid.*
35. Eric Sherman, *Directing the Film: Film Directors on Their Art* (Los Angeles: Acrobat Books, 1976), p. 206.
36. Charles Rosher, Jr., interview with the author, May 3, 2009.
37. Kevin Brownlow, *The Parade's Gone By* ... (Berkeley: University of California Press, 1968), p. 235.
38. Charles Rosher, Jr., interview with the author, May 3, 2009.
39. Barbara Hershey, interview with the author, June 28, 2009.
40. Charles Rosher, Jr., interview with the author, May 3, 2009.
41. *The Baby Maker* presskit (National General Pictures), p. 16.
42. Barbara Hershey, interview with the author, June 28, 2009.
43. Charles Rosher, Jr., interview with the author, May 3, 2009.
44. Charles Rosher, Jr., interview with the author, May 3, 2009.
45. *The Baby Maker* presskit (National General Pictures), p. 12.
46. Collin Wilcox Paxton, interview with the author, March 4, 2008.
47. *The Hollywood Reporter*, October 1, 1970.
48. David Shipman, "Obituary: James Bridges," *The Independent*, June 8, 1993.
49. Barbara Hershey, interview with the author, June 28, 2009.
50. Dominique Paul Noth, "Bit actor is now starring, but behind the movie camera," *The Milwaukee Journal*, October 27, 1973.
51. Orson Welles and Peter Bogdanovich, *This Is Orson Welles*, rev. ed. (New York: Da Capo Press, 1998), p. 100.
52. Jack Larson, interview with the author, March 16, 2008.
53. *Ibid.*
54. *The Hollywood Reporter*, October 1, 1970.
55. Jack Larson, interview with the author, March 16, 2008.
56. Dominique Paul Noth, "Bit actor is now starring, but behind the movie camera," *The Milwaukee Journal*, October 27, 1973.
57. George Stevens, Jr., *Conversations with the Great Moviemakers of Hollywood's Golden Age at the American Film Institute* (New York: Vintage Books, 2006), p. 296.
58. Eric Sherman, *Directing the Film: Film Directors on Their Art* (Los Angeles: Acrobat Books, 1976), p. 250.
59. Jack Larson, interview with the author, March 16, 2008.
60. Michael Preece, interview with the author, May 28, 2009.
61. Barbara Hershey, interview with the author, June 28, 2009.
62. Mark Goodman, "Cinema: Rent-a-Womb," *Time*, October 19, 1970.
63. Roger Greenspun, "Barbara Hershey Stars in Bridges's *The Baby Maker*," *The New York Times*, October 2, 1970.
64. *Ibid.*
65. Roger Ebert, "*The Baby Maker*," *Chicago Sun-Times*, October 26, 1970.
66. Roger Greenspun, "Barbara Hershey Stars in Bridges's *The Baby Maker*," *The New York Times*, October 2, 1970.

67. Mark Goodman, "Cinema: Rent-a-Womb," *Time*, October 19, 1970.
68. A.D. Murphy, "*The Baby Maker*," *Variety*, September 30, 1970.
69. Armond White, "Lust-Caution Douses Woodstock," *New York Press*, August 26, 2009.
70. Barbara Hershey, interview with the author, June 28, 2009.
71. Charles Rosher, Jr., interview with the author, May 3, 2009.
72. Barbara Hershey, interview with the author, June 28, 2009.
73. Charles Rosher, Jr., interview with the author, May 3, 2009.
74. Barbara Hershey, interview with the author, June 28, 2009.
75. Collin Wilcox Paxton, interview with the author, March 4, 2008.
76. Barbara Hershey, interview with the author, June 28, 2009.
77. Michael Preece, interview with the author, May 28, 2009.
78. Charles Rosher, Jr., interview with the author, May 3, 2009.
79. *Ibid.*
80. Barbara Hershey, interview with the author, June 28, 2009.
81. Jack Larson, interview with the author, March 16, 2008.
82. Roger Ebert, "*The Baby Maker*," *Chicago Sun-Times*, October 26, 1970.
83. Mark Goodman, "Cinema: Rent-a-Womb," *Time*, October 19, 1970.
84. Barbara Hershey, interview with the author, June 28, 2009.

Chapter Three

1. Laurence Luckinbill, interview with the author, March 18, 2009.
2. W.I. Scobie, "The Art of Fiction No. 49: Christopher Isherwood," *The Paris Review*, Spring 1974.
3. Jack Larson, interview with the author, March 15, 2009.
4. Laurence Luckinbill, interview with the author, March 18, 2009.
5. Sam Waterston, interview with the author, April 13, 2009.
6. Laurence Luckinbill, interview with the author, March 18, 2009.
7. *Time*, "Books: Brothers & Others," April 21, 1967.
8. Sam Waterston, interview with the author, April 13, 2009.
9. Dan Sullivan, "*Meeting by the River* for NTN," *Los Angeles Times*, May 3, 1972.
10. Sam Waterston, interview with the author, April 13, 2009.
11. Jack Bender, interview with the author, June 15, 2009.
12. Sam Waterston, interview with the author, April 13, 2009.
13. Laurence Luckinbill, interview with the author, March 18, 2009.
14. Sam Waterston, interview with the author, April 13, 2009.
15. Laurence Luckinbill, interview with the author, March 18, 2009.
16. Jack Bender, interview with the author, June 15, 2009.
17. Jack Larson, interview with the author, March 15, 2009.
18. Laurence Luckinbill, interview with the author, March 18, 2009.
19. Sam Waterston, interview with the author, April 13, 2009.
20. Jack Larson, interview with the author, July 15, 2008.
21. John Jay Osborn, Jr., interview with the author, July 9, 2009.
22. *The New York Times*, "The Paper Chase," September 12, 1971.
23. Jack Larson, interview with the author, February 5, 2009.
24. John Jay Osborn, Jr., interview with the author, July 9, 2009.
25. John Houseman, *Final Dress* (New York: Simon & Schuster, 1983), p. 491.
26. John Jay Osborn, Jr., interview with the author, July 9, 2009.
27. John Houseman, *Final Dress* (New York: Simon & Schuster, 1983), p. 491.
28. *Ibid.*
29. John Jay Osborn, Jr., interview with the author, July 9, 2009.
30. John Houseman, *Final Dress* (New York: Simon & Schuster, 1983), pp. 493–94.
31. Michael Preece, interview with the author, May 28, 2009.
32. John Jay Osborn, Jr., interview with the author, July 9, 2009.
33. *Ibid.*
34. *Ibid.*
35. Edward Herrmann, interview with the author, February 20, 2009.
36. *Ibid.*
37. *Ibid.*
38. John Jay Osborn, Jr., interview with the author, July 9, 2009.
39. Graham Beckel, interview with the author, May 1, 2009.
40. John Jay Osborn, Jr., interview with the author, July 9, 2009.

41. *Ibid.*
42. *Ibid.*
43. *Ibid.*
44. Michael Preece, interview with the author, May 28, 2009.
45. Gordon Willis, email to the author, February 27, 2008.
46. *Ibid.*
47. Robert C. Thompson, commentary track, *The Paper Chase* DVD (Twentieth Century-Fox, 2003).
48. John Jay Osborn, Jr., interview with the author, July 9, 2009.
49. Vincent LoBrutto, *Principal Photography: Interviews with Feature Film Cinematographers* (Westport, CT: Praeger Publishers, 1999), p. 28.
50. Gordon Willis, email to the author, February 27, 2008.
51. Edward Herrmann, interview with the author, February 20, 2009.
52. *Ibid.*
53. Gordon Willis, email to the author, February 29, 2008.
54. John Jay Osborn, Jr., interview with the author, July 9, 2009.
55. Gordon Willis, email to the author, February 27, 2008.
56. Edward Herrmann, interview with the author, February 20, 2009.
57. *Ibid.*
58. Sam Waterston, interview with the author, April 13, 2009.
59. John Houseman, *Final Dress* (New York: Simon & Schuster, 1983), p. 494.
60. Edward Herrmann, interview with the author, February 20, 2009.
61. Graham Beckel, interview with the author, May 1, 2009.
62. Pauline Kael, "Un-People," in *Reeling* (New York: Warner Books, 1976), p. 263.
63. John Houseman, *Final Dress* (New York: Simon & Schuster, 1983), p. 529.
64. John Jay Osborn, Jr., interview with the author, July 9, 2009.
65. John Houseman, *Final Dress* (New York: Simon & Schuster, 1983), p. 510.
66. Peter Biskind, *Easy Riders, Raging Bulls* (New York: Simon & Schuster, 1998), p. 139.
67. John Jay Osborn, Jr., interview with the author, July 9, 2009.
68. John Jay Osborn, Jr., "Preface to Special Anniversary Edition," *The Paper Chase* anniversary ed. (Albany, NY: Whitston Publishing, 1993), p. x.
69. *Ibid.*, pp. ix-x.
70. Marilyn Berger, "John Houseman, Actor and Producer, 86, Dies," *The New York Times*, November 1, 1988.
71. Jay Cocks, "Cinema: Hells of Ivy," *Time*, October 29, 1973.
72. Andrew Sarris, "Critic's Choice," *The Village Voice*, January 10, 1974.
73. Jack Bender, interview with the author, June 15, 2009.
74. Clancy Sigal, "*The Paper Chase*," in *Time Out Film Guide* 12th ed., ed. John Pym (London: Penguin Books, 2003), p. 892.
75. Geoffrey Kabaservice, *The Guardians: Kingman Brewster, His Circle, and the Rise of the Liberal Establishment* (New York: Henry Holt and Company, 2004), p. 441.
76. Pauline Kael, "Un-People," in *Reeling* (New York: Warner Books, 1976), p. 265.
77. John Jay Osborn, Jr., interview with the author, July 9, 2009.
78. *Ibid.*
79. *Ibid.*
80. Edward Herrmann, interview with the author, February 20, 2009.
81. *Ibid.*
82. Graham Beckel, interview with the author, May 1, 2009.
83. John Jay Osborn, Jr., interview with the author, July 9, 2009.
84. Jack Larson, interview with the author, January 18, 2009.
85. John Jay Osborn, Jr., interview with the author, July 9, 2009.
86. *Ibid.*
87. Jack Bender, interview with the author, June 15, 2009.
88. *Ibid.*
89. *Ibid.*

Chapter Four

1. Janet Maslin, "Critic's Notebook: A Great Movie — If It Comes Out," *The New York Times*, January 23, 1978.
2. Norman Lloyd, interview with the author, March 2, 2009.
3. *Ibid.*
4. Jack Larson, interview with the author, July 15, 2008.
5. Norman Lloyd, interview with the author, March 2, 2009.
6. Jack Larson, interview with the author, July 15, 2008.
7. Sylvie Drake, "Bridges: *Streetcar* Conductor," *Los Angeles Times*, March 18, 1973.
8. *Ibid.*
9. Faye Dunaway, with Betsy Sharkey, *Look-*

ing for Gatsby: My Life (New York: Simon & Schuster, 1995), p. 238.
10. Sylvie Drake, "Bridges: *Streetcar* Conductor," *Los Angeles Times*, March 18, 1973.
11. Dan Sullivan, "*Streetcar* On, Off the Track," *Los Angeles Times*, March 21, 1973.
12. Stephen Farber, "Blanche Wins the Battle," *The New York Times*, April 1, 1973.
13. Faye Dunaway, with Betsy Sharkey, *Looking for Gatsby: My Life* (New York: Simon & Schuster, 1995), pp. 238–39.
14. Jack Bender, interview with the author, June 15, 2009.
15. Dan Sullivan, "*Streetcar* On, Off the Track," *Los Angeles Times*, March 21, 1973.
16. Stephen Farber, "Blanche Wins the Battle," *The New York Times*, April 1, 1973.
17. Tom Buckley, "At the Movies: Fonda tilts forces of nuclear energy in *China Syndrome*," *The New York Times*, March 16, 1979.
18. Tennessee Williams, "Where My Head Is Now and Other Questions," in *New Selected Essays: Where I Live* (New York: New Directions, 2009), p. 175.
19. Jack Larson, interview with the author, January 18, 2009.
20. Jack Larson, interview with the author, March 20, 2009.
21. Laurence Luckinbill, interview with the author, March 18, 2009.
22. Jack Larson, interview with the author, January 18, 2009.
23. Laurence Luckinbill, interview with the author, March 18, 2009.
24. Michiko Kakutani, "Joan Didion: Staking Out California," *The New York Times*, June 10, 1979.
25. Frederick Buechner, "The Longing for Home," in *Secrets in the Dark: A Life in Sermons* (New York: HarperSanFrancisco, 2006), p. 221.
26. Sonny Rhodes, "Movie director James Bridges: He hasn't forgotten his roots in Arkansas," *The Log Cabin Democrat*, October 11, 1977.
27. Janet Maslin, "He Was Obsessed With James Dean," *The New York Times*, April 5, 1976.
28. Lee Grant, "Muddy Séance at Toad Suck Ferry," *Los Angeles Times*, October 21, 1976.
29. Tom Bonner, interview with the author, February 24, 2009.
30. Jack Larson, interview with the author, July 15, 2008.
31. Wayne Warga, "Recalling James Dean on 9/30/55," *Los Angeles Times*, September 25, 1977.
32. Gordon Willis, email to the author, February 27, 2008.
33. Richard Thomas, interview with the author, March 26, 2009.
34. *Ibid.*
35. Mary Nell Taylor, "James Bridges: An Arkansas boy comes home," *The Echo*, April 1, 1976.
36. Lee Grant, "Muddy Séance at Toad Suck Ferry," *Los Angeles Times*, October 21, 1976.
37. Michael Preece, interview with the author, May 28, 2009.
38. Richard Thomas, interview with the author, March 26, 2009.
39. Michael Preece, interview with the author, May 28, 2009.
40. Richard Thomas, interview with the author, March 26, 2009.
41. Kim Kurumada, interview with the author, September 4, 2008.
42. *The Echo*, "Filming resumes—Bridges thinks 9/30/55 will be hit," September 16, 1976.
43. Richard Thomas, interview with the author, March 26, 2009.
44. Janet Maslin, "He Was Obsessed with James Dean," *The New York Times*, April 5, 1978.
45. Kim Kurumada, interview with the author, September 4, 2008.
46. Richard Thomas, interview with the author, March 26, 2009.
47. Kim Kurumada, interview with the author, September 4, 2008.
48. *Ibid.*
49. *Ibid.*
50. Jack Bender, interview with the author, June 15, 2009.
51. Molly Haskell, "The Nifty Fifties," *New York*, May 1, 1978.
52. Wayne Warga, "Recalling James Dean on 9/30/55," *Los Angeles Times*, September 25, 1977.
53. Richard Thomas, interview with the author, March 26, 2009.
54. Deborah Benson, interview with the author, February 28, 2009.
55. *Ibid.*
56. *Ibid.*
57. *Ibid.*
58. David Shipman, "Obituary: James Bridges," *The Independent*, June 8, 1993.
59. Richard Thomas, interview with the author, March 26, 2009.
60. Collin Wilcox Paxton, interview with the author, March 4, 2008.
61. Richard Thomas, interview with the author, March 26, 2009.
62. *Ibid.*
63. Collin Wilcox Paxton, interview with the author, March 4, 2008.
64. David Ansen, "*September 30, 1955*,"

Newsweek, April 17, 1978, in Michael Sragow, ed. *Produced and Abandoned: The Best Films You've Never Seen* (San Francisco: Mercury House, 1990), p. 95.

65. Janet Maslin, "Richard Thomas — Playing the Worshipper and Not the Hero," *The New York Times*, April 2, 1978.

66. David Ansen, "*September 30, 1955,*" *Newsweek*, April 17, 1978, in Michael, Sragow, ed. *Produced and Abandoned: The Best Films You've Never Seen* (San Francisco: Mercury House, 1990), p. 95.

67. Richard Thomas, interview with the author, March 26, 2009.

68. Vincent Canby, "Screen: *Sept. 30, 1955,* When James Dean Died: Admirer of Actor," *The New York Times*, March 31, 1978.

69. Vincent LoBrutto, *Stanley Kubrick: A Biography* (New York: Donald I. Fine Books, 1997), p. 19.

70. Janet Maslin, "Richard Thomas — Playing the Worshipper and Not the Hero," *The New York Times*, April 2, 1978.

71. Andrew Sarris, "Films in Focus: The Past Recaptured," *The Village Voice*, April 17, 1978.

72. Armond White, "Revolutionary Road," *New York Press*, December 23, 2008.

73. Samuel Fuller, *Hollywood Mavericks* documentary (American Film Institute, 1990).

74. Richard Thomas, interview with the author, March 26, 2009.

75. *Ibid.*

76. Lisa Blount, interview with the author, April 27, 2009.

77. Richard Thomas, interview with the author, March 26, 2009.

78. Lisa Blount, interview with the author, April 27, 2009.

79. *Ibid.*

80. *Ibid.*

81. Jane Wilson, interview with the author, March 3, 2009.

82. Mary Kai Clark, interview with the author, March 13, 2009.

83. *Ibid.*

84. Jane Wilson, interview with the author, March 3, 2009.

85. *Ibid.*

86. Mary Kai Clark, interview with the author, March 13, 2009.

87. Deborah Benson, interview with the author, February 28, 2009.

88. Lisa Blount, interview with the author, April 27, 2009.

89. Mary Kai Clark, interview with the author, March 13, 2009.

90. Kim Kurumada, interview with the author, September 4, 2008.

91. Richard Thomas, interview with the author, March 26, 2009.

92. *Ibid.*

93. Charles Champlin, "Critic at Large: James Dean: In Memoriam," *Los Angeles Times*, December 16, 1977.

94. Kim Kurumada, interview with the author, September 4, 2008.

95. Tom Bonner, interview with the author, February 24, 2009.

96. Wayne Warga, "Recalling James Dean on 9/30/55," *Los Angeles Times*, September 25, 1977.

97. Gordon Willis, email to the author, February 27, 2008.

98. Lisa Blount, interview with the author, April 27, 2009.

99. *Ibid.*

100. *Ibid.*

101. *Ibid.*

102. Roger Copeland, "The Habits of Consciousness," *Commonweal*, February 13, 1981, in Leland Poague, ed., *Conversations with Susan Sontag* (Jackson: University Press of Mississippi, 1995), p. 188.

103. Lisa Blount, interview with the author, April 27, 2009.

104. Kurt Vonnegut, *Slapstick, or: Lonesome No More!* (New York: Delacorte Press/Seymour Lawrence, 1976), p. 50.

105. Richard Thomas, interview with the author, March 26, 2009.

106. Chris Newman, interview with the author, June 4, 2009.

107. *Ibid.*

108. J. Hoberman and Jonathan Rosenbaum, *Midnight Movies* (New York: Da Capo Press, 1983), p. 19.

109. Lisa Blount, interview with the author, April 27, 2009.

110. Richard Thomas, interview with the author, March 26, 2009.

111. Lisa Blount, interview with the author, April 27, 2009.

112. Gordon Willis, email to the author, February 27, 2008.

113. Joe LeSueur, *Digressions on Some Poems by Frank O'Hara: A Memoir* (New York: Farrar, Straus and Giroux, 2003), p. 66.

114. Susan Sontag, interview by Susan Swain, *In Depth with Susan Sontag*, C-SPAN, March 2, 2003, http://www.c-spanvideo.org program/172991-1

115. Vincent Canby, "Screen: *Sept. 30, 1955,* When James Dean Died: Admirer of Actor," *The New York Times*, March 31, 1978.

116. *Ibid.*
117. Jeff Gourson, interview with the author, May 19, 2008.
118. *Ibid.*
119. Gordon Willis, email to the author, February 27, 2008.
120. Jeff Gourson, interview with the author, May 19, 2008.
121. *Ibid.*
122. Debbie Getlin, interview with the author, February 17, 2009.
123. *Ibid.*
124. Kim Kurumada, interview with the author, December 16, 2008.
125. Debbie Getlin, interview with the author, February 17, 2009.
126. Jeff Gourson, interview with the author, May 19, 2008.
127. Debbie Getlin, interview with the author, February 17, 2009.
128. Jeff Gourson, interview with the author, May 19, 2008.
129. Debbie Getlin, interview with the author, February 17, 2009.
130. Richard Thomas, interview with the author, March 26, 2009.
131. Gordon Willis, email to the author, February 27, 2008.
132. Janet Maslin, "Critic's Notebook: A Great Movie — If It Comes Out," *The New York Times*, January 23, 1978.
133. *Ibid.*
134. Richard Thomas, interview with the author, March 26, 2009.
135. Deborah Benson, interview with the author, February 28, 2009.
136. *Ibid.*
137. Lisa Blount, interview with the author, April 27, 2009.
138. *Ibid.*
139. *Ibid.*
140. *Ibid.*
141. *Ibid.*

Chapter Five

1. Dave Kehr, "*The China Syndrome*," *Chicago Reader*.
2. Peter Bogdanovich, "*Mogambo*," in *Peter Bogdanovich's Movie of the Week* (New York: Ballantine Books, 1999), p. 144.
3. Jack Larson, interview with the author, March 16, 2008.
4. Michael Douglas, *The China Syndrome: A Fusion of Talent* documentary, *The China Syndrome* DVD (Columbia, 2004).
5. Jane Fonda, *The China Syndrome: A Fusion of Talent* documentary, *The China Syndrome* DVD (Columbia, 2004).
6. *Ibid.*
7. Bruce Gilbert, *The China Syndrome: A Fusion of Talent* documentary, *The China Syndrome* DVD (Columbia, 2004).
8. Tom Buckley, "At the Movies: Fonda tilts forces of nuclear energy in *China Syndrome*," *The New York Times*, March 16, 1979.
9. Jack Larson, interview with the author, January 18, 2009.
10. Howard Zinn, *A People's History of the United States: 1942-Present* (New York: Harper Perennial Modern Classics, 2005), p. 613.
11. Jack Larson, interview with the author, January 18, 2009.
12. Kim Kurumada, interview with the author, September 4, 2008.
13. *Ibid.*
14. *Ibid.*
15. *Ibid.*
16. *Ibid.*
17. *Ibid.*
18. Jane Fonda, *The China Syndrome: A Fusion of Talent* documentary, *The China Syndrome* DVD (Columbia, 2004)
19. Kim Kurumada, interview with the author, September 4, 2008.
20. *Ibid.*
21. *Ibid.*
22. *Ibid.*
23. Marshall Schlom, interview with the author, March 17, 2009.
24. Debbie Getlin, interview with the author, February 17, 2009.
25. Richard T. Jameson, "China Is Near," *Film Comment*, May-June 1979.
26. *Ibid.*
27. Kim Kurumada, interview with the author, September 4, 2008.
28. Michael Douglas, *The China Syndrome: A Fusion of Talent* documentary, *The China Syndrome* DVD (Columbia, 2004).
29. Barbara Hershey, interview with the author, June 28, 2009.
30. Kim Kurumada, interview with the author, September 4, 2008.
31. Richard Thomas, interview with the author, March 26, 2009.
32. Debbie Getlin, interview with the author, February 17, 2009.
33. Jeff Gourson, interview with the author, May 19, 2008.
34. David Rawlins, interview with the author, May 4, 2009.
35. Francesca Emerson, interview with the author, May 23, 2009.

36. Jeff Gourson, interview with the author, May 19, 2008.
37. Francesca Emerson, interview with the author, May 23, 2009.
38. David Rawlins, interview with the author, May 4, 2009.
39. *Ibid.*
40. Francesca Emerson, interview with the author, May 23, 2009.
41. Marshall Schlom, interview with the author, March 17, 2009.
42. Gavin Smith, "Without Cutaways," *Film Comment*, May–June 1991.
43. Roger Ebert, "*The China Syndrome*," *Chicago Sun-Times*, January 1, 1979.
44. Vincent Canby, "Film: Nuclear Power Plant is Villain in *China Syndrome*: A Question of Ethics," *The New York Times*, March 16, 1979.
45. Janet Maslin, "He Was Obsessed with James Dean," *The New York Times*, April 5, 1978.
46. Debra Winger, email to the author, May 11, 2009.
47. David Rawlins, interview with the author, May 4, 2009.
48. Aaron Latham, "The Ballad of the Urban Cowboy," in *Perfect Pieces: Stardom, Scandals, and the New Saturday Night* (New York: Arbor House, 1987), p. 5.
49. *Ibid.*, p. 6.
50. Roderick Mann, "Travolta's Biggest Fan: His Director," *Los Angeles Times*, January 6, 1980.
51. Lawrence Van Gelder, "At The Movies: Production Prep," *The New York Times*, April 1, 1988.
52. Aaron Latham, "The Cowboy Chronicles," *New York*, September 25, 2000.
53. Lesley Stahl, *Reporting Live* (New York: Simon & Schuster, 1999), p. 97.
54. Kim Kurumada, interview with the author, October 7, 2008.
55. *Ibid.*
56. *Ibid.*
57. Roderick Mann, "Travolta's Biggest Fan: His Director," *Los Angeles Times*, January 6, 1980.
58. *Ibid.*
59. Kim Kurumada, interview with the author, October 7, 2008.
60. *Ibid.*
61. Lesley Stahl, *Reporting Live* (New York: Simon & Schuster, 1999), p. 97.
62. Kim Kurumada, interview with the author, October 7, 2008.
63. Debra Winger, *Undiscovered* (New York: Simon & Schuster, 2008), p. 31.
64. Debra Winger, email to the author, May 11, 2009.
65. Stephen Farber, "Where There's Smoke, There's a Fiery Actress Named Debra Winger," *The New York Times*, July 6, 1986.
66. Debra Winger, email to the author, May 11, 2009.
67. *Ibid.*
68. Kim Kurumada, interview with the author, October 7, 2008.
69. *Ibid.*
70. Brooke Alderson, interview with the author, February 2, 2010.
71. *Ibid.*
72. *Ibid.*
73. *Ibid.*
74. Kim Kurumada, interview with the author, September 4, 2008.
75. Reynaldo Villalobos, interview with the author, October 24, 2008.
76. Kim Kurumada, interview with the author, October 7, 2008.
77. Reynaldo Villalobos, interview with the author, October 24, 2008.
78. David Rawlins, interview with the author, May 4, 2009.
79. Reynaldo Villalobos, interview with the author, October 24, 2008.
80. Gordon Willis, email to the author, February 27, 2008.
81. Reynaldo Villalobos, interview with the author, October 24, 2008.
82. *Ibid.*
83. Kim Kurumada, interview with the author, October 7, 2008.
84. Peter Lester, "Two Sexy 'Urban Cowgirls'—One Called Debra Winger—Give Travolta a Run for His Movie," *People*, August 18, 1980.
85. Dave Kehr, "The Awful Truth," *Chicago Reader*.
86. Aaron Latham, "The Return of the Urban Cowboy," in *Perfect Pieces: Stardom, Scandals, and the New Saturday Night* (New York: Arbor House, 1987), p. 125.
87. Vincent Canby, "Film: *Mike's Murder*, with Debra Winger," *The New York Times*, March 9, 1984.
88. Fredric Jameson, *Late Marxism: Adorno; Or, The Persistence of the Dialectic* (London: Verso, 1990), p. 102.
89. Richard Thomas, interview with the author, March 26, 2009.
90. Vincent Canby, "Travolta, *Urban Cowboy*," *The New York Times*, June 11, 1980.
91. "Box office/business for *Urban Cowboy* (1980)," Internet Movie Database, http://www.imdb.com/title/tt0081696/business

Chapter Six

1. Michael Blowen, "*Mike's Murder* Rates as a Work of Art," *The Boston Globe*, April 20, 1984.
2. Pauline Kael, "*Mike's Murder*," in *For Keeps* (New York: Plume, 1994), p. 1108.
3. Donald Spoto, *The Art of Alfred Hitchcock: Fifty Years of His Motion Pictures* (New York: Anchor Books, 1992), p. 214.
4. David Ehrenstein, "Paul Winfield: The Gay Actor's Truest Role Was Seen By a Small Audience," *The Advocate*, April 13, 2004.
5. *Ibid.*
6. Jack Larson, interview with the author, October 4, 2008.
7. Kim Kurumada, interview with the author, October 7, 2008.
8. Jack Larson, interview with the author, October 4, 2008.
9. Vincent Canby, "Screen: *Sept. 30, 1955*, When James Dean Died: Admirer of Actor," *The New York Times*, March 31, 1978.
10. Wayne Warga, "Movies: Recalling James Dean on *9/30/55*," *Los Angeles Times*, September 25, 1977.
11. Leslie A. Fiedler, *Love and Death in the American Novel* (Dalkey Archive Press, 1960), p. 311.
12. Jack Larson, interview with the author, October 4, 2008.
13. Debra Winger, email to the author, May 11, 2009.
14. Michael Blowen, "Winger—Actress Is Hot in More Ways Than One," *The Boston Globe*, March 22, 1984.
15. Pauline Kael, "*Mike's Murder*," in *For Keeps* (New York: Plume, 1994), p. 1109.
16. François Truffaut, "*Bonjour Tristesse*," in *The Films in My Life* (New York: Da Capo Press, 1994), p. 140.
17. Dan Sallitt, "*Mike's Murder*," *L.A. Reader*, March 16, 1984.
18. Jack Larson, interview with the author, October 4, 2008.
19. *Ibid.*
20. David Thomson, "Telephones," *Film Comment*, August 1984.
21. Jeff Gourson, interview with the author, May 19, 2008.
22. Jack Larson, interview with the author, February 5, 2010.
23. *Ibid.*
24. Kevin Thomas, "*To Live and Die in L.A.*: Thriller Explores Loneliness in the City," *Los Angeles Times*, November 11, 1999.
25. Jack Larson, interview with the author, October 4, 2008.
26. Jack Larson, interview with the author, March 16, 2008.
27. Sheila Benson, "Hard World of *Mike's Murder*," *Los Angeles Times*, March 16, 1984.
28. Debra Winger, email to the author, May 11, 2009.
29. Vincent Canby, "Film: *Mike's Murder*, with Debra Winger," *The New York Times*, March 9, 1984.
30. Janet Maslin, "At the Movies," *The New York Times*, March 9, 1984.
31. David Denby, "The Lost Week," *New York*, April 11, 1988.
32. Michael Blowen, "The L.A. Dream Turned Nightmare," *The Boston Globe*, May 9, 1985.
33. Pauline Kael, "*Mike's Murder*," in *For Keeps* (New York: Plume, 1994), p. 1108.
34. Janet Maslin, "At the Movies," *The New York Times*, March 9, 1984.
35. Michael Blowen, "Winger—Actress Is Hot in More Ways Than One," *The Boston Globe*, March 22, 1984.
36. Kim Kurumada, interview with the author, October 7, 2008.
37. Reynaldo Villalobos, interview with the author, October 24, 2008.
38. Michael Blowen, "*Mike's Murder* Rates as a Work of Art," *The Boston Globe*, April 20, 1984.
39. Ronald Bergan, *Jean Renoir: Projections of Paradise* (Woodstock, NY: The Overlook Press, 1992), p. 338.
40. Cornel West, *The Cornel West Reader* (New York: Basic Books, 1999), pp. xv-xvi.
41. Marty P. Ewing, interview with the author, May 8, 2009.
42. Marshall Schlom, interview with the author, March 17, 2009.
43. Jack Larson, interview with the author, October 4, 2008.
44. *Ibid.*
45. Mark Litwak, *Reel Power: The Struggle for Influence and Success in the New Hollywood* (Los Angeles: Silman-James Press, 1986), p. 108.
46. Kim Kurumada, interview with the author, October 7, 2008.
47. Jack Larson, interview with the author, October 4, 2008.
48. Jeff Gourson, interview with the author, May 19, 2008.
49. *Ibid.*
50. *Ibid.*
51. Marty P. Ewing, interview with the author, May 8, 2009.
52. Jack Larson, interview with the author, October 4, 2008.

53. Jeffrey Wells, "Again, *Mike's Murder*," *Hollywood Elsewhere*, http://www.hollywoodelsewhere.com/2009/04/again_mikes_mur.php
54. Janet Maslin, "At the Movies," *The New York Times*, March 9, 1984.
55. Pauline Kael, "*Mike's Murder*," in *For Keeps* (New York: Plume, 1994), p. 1108.
56. Kim Kurumada, interview with the author, October 7, 2008.
57. Debbie Getlin, interview with the author, February 17, 2009.
58. *Ibid.*
59. *Ibid.*
60. Reynaldo Villalobos, interview with the author, October 24, 2008.
61. Kim Kurumada, interview with the author, December 16, 2008.
62. Jack Larson, interview with the author, March 16, 2008.
63. On *Perfect*, Larson received a co-producer credit; on *Bright Lights, Big City*, he received an associate producer credit.
64. Debra Winger, email to the author, May 11, 2009.
65. Mary McCarty, "Holding On To The Air," *Cincinnati Magazine*, April 1992.
66. Debra Winger, email to the author, May 11, 2009.

Chapter Seven

1. Aaron Latham, "Perfect!," in *Perfect Pieces: Stardom, Scandals, and the New Saturday Night* (New York: Arbor House, 1987), p. 38.
2. Kim Kurumada, interview with the author, December 16, 2008.
3. *Ibid.*
4. *Ibid.*
5. Aaron Latham, "Perfect!," in *Perfect Pieces: Stardom, Scandals, and the New Saturday Night* (New York: Arbor House, 1987), p. 39.
6. Michael Blowen, "The Making of a Movie: The Unanticipated Is All You Can Anticipate," *The Boston Globe*, July 8, 1984.
7. Kim Kurumada, interview with the author, December 16, 2008.
8. *Ibid.*
9. Michael Blowen, "The Making of a Movie: The Unanticipated Is All You Can Anticipate," *The Boston Globe*, July 8, 1984.
10. *Ibid.*
11. Kim Kurumada, interview with the author, December 16, 2008.
12. Aaron Latham, "Perfect!," in *Perfect Pieces: Stardom, Scandals, and the New Saturday Night* (New York: Arbor House, 1987), p. 39.
13. Jack Larson, interview with the author, July 15, 2008.
14. Michael Blowen, "Shooting the Middle Scenes Last," *The Boston Globe*, November 25, 1984.
15. Kim Kurumada, interview with the author, December 16, 2008.
16. *Ibid.*
17. Gordon Willis, email to the author, February 27, 2008.
18. *Ibid.*
19. Marty P. Ewing, interview with the author, May 8, 2009.
20. Mike Nichols, commentary track, *The Graduate* 40th anniversary edition DVD (MGM Home Entertainment, 2007).
21. Michelle Green, "While She May Not Be Perfect, Laraine Newman Braces Herself for Another Shot at Stardom," *People*, July 8, 1985.
22. Aaron Latham, *Perfect* diary, April 14, 1984 entry, unpublished.
23. Kim Kurumada, interview with the author, December 16, 2008.
24. Aaron Latham, *Perfect* diary, April 14, 1984 entry, unpublished.
25. Jay Carr, "Travolta Can't Save *Perfect*," *The Boston Globe*, June 7, 1985.
26. Michael Blowen, "He Listens to His Movie," *The Boston Globe*, April 21, 1985.
27. Jack Larson, letter to the editor, *The New York Times*, October 8, 1995.
28. Dave Kehr, "*Perfect*," *Chicago Reader*.
29. Jane Gross, "Movies and the Press Are An Enduring Romance," *The New York Times*, June 2, 1985.
30. Jeff Gourson, interview with the author, May 19, 2008.
31. Jack Larson, interview with the author, July 15, 2008.
32. *Ibid.*
33. Dave Kehr, "*Perfect*," *Chicago Reader*.
34. Jay Carr, "Travolta Can't Save *Perfect*," *The Boston Globe*, June 7, 1985.
35. Vincent Canby, "Film: *Perfect*: Gym and Journalism," *The New York Times*, June 7, 1985.
36. *Ibid.*
37. Kim Kurumada, interview with the author, December 16, 2008.
38. Marty P. Ewing, interview with the author, May 8, 2009.
39. Chris Fujiwara, *Jerry Lewis* (Urbana and Chicago: University of Illinois Press, 2009), p. 75.
40. Vincent Canby, "Robert Altman's Satire 'Health,'" *The New York Times*, April 7, 1982.

Chapter Eight

1. Zoltan Abadi-Nagy, "Serenity, Courage, Wisdom: A Talk with Kurt Vonnegut" in Peter J. Reed and Marc Leeds, ed. *The Vonnegut Chronicles: Interviews and Essays* (Westport, CT: Greenwood Press, 1996), p. 33.
2. Michiko Kakutani, "Books of the Times: Alienated Young and Their Solipsistic Pleasures," *The New York Times*, May 7, 1988.
3. Jay McInerney, *Jay McInerney's The Light Within* documentary, *Bright Lights, Big City* DVD (MGM Home Entertainment, 2008).
4. John Bloom, interview with the author, May 28, 2009.
5. Jack Larson, interview with the author, March 15, 2009.
6. Debra Goldman, "Bright Lights, Camera, Action," *American Film*, January-February 1988.
7. Caryn James, "*Bright Lights, Big City*— Big Trouble," *The New York Times*, January 10, 1988.
8. Jay Carr, "*Bright Lights* Amid the Chaos," *The Boston Globe*, April 1, 1988.
9. Gordon Willis, email to the author, February 27, 2008.
10. Swoosie Kurtz, interview with the author, January 6, 2010.
11. Gordon Willis, email to the author, February 27, 2008.
12. Lawrence Van Gelder, "At the Movies," *The New York Times*, April 1, 1988.
13. John Bloom, interview with the author, May 28, 2009.
14. Swoosie Kurtz, interview with the author, January 6, 2010.
15. Lawrence Van Gelder, "At the Movies," *The New York Times*, April 1, 1988.
16. John Bloom, interview with the author, May 28, 2009.
17. Jay Carr, "*Bright Lights* Amid the Chaos," *The Boston Globe*, April 1, 1988.
18. *Ibid.*
19. Caryn James, "*Bright Lights, Big City*— Big Trouble," *The New York Times*, January 10, 1988.
20. Gordon Willis, email to the author, February 27, 2008.
21. Jay McInerney, *Jay McInerney's The Light Within* documentary, *Bright Lights, Big City* DVD (MGM Home Entertainment, 2008).
22. Jay McInerney, *Bright Lights, Big City* (New York: Vintage Contemporaries, 1984), p. 179.
23. Jay McInerney, *Jay McInerney's The Light Within* documentary, *Bright Lights, Big City* DVD (MGM Home Entertainment, 2008).
24. Janet Maslin, "A Tale of the Dark Side: *Bright Lights, Big City*," *The New York Times*, April 1, 1988.
25. Gordon Willis, email to the author, February 27, 2008.
26. Norman Lloyd, interview with the author, March 2, 2009.
27. *Ibid.*
28. Caryn James, "*Bright Lights, Big City*— Big Trouble," *The New York Times*, January 10, 1988.
29. Swoosie Kurtz, interview with the author, January 6, 2010.
30. *Ibid.*
31. *Ibid.*
32. Jonathan Rosenbaum, "Dim Wits, Small Potatoes," *Chicago Reader*, April 1, 1988.
33. Swoosie Kurtz, interview with the author, January 6, 2010.
34. Gordon Willis, email to the author, February 27, 2008.
35. Jonathan Rosenbaum, "Dim Wits, Small Potatoes," *Chicago Reader*, April 1, 1988.
36. Swoosie Kurtz, interview with the author, January 6, 2010.
37. Elizabeth Wurtzel, "Coke Adds Life," *The Harvard Crimson*, April 22, 1988.
38. Jay McInerney, commentary track, *Bright Lights, Big City* DVD (MGM Home Entertainment, 2008).
39. Swoosie Kurtz, interview with the author, January 6, 2010.
40. *Ibid.*
41. *Ibid.*
42. *Ibid.*
43. Kim Kurumada, interview with the author, September 4, 2008.
44. John Bloom, interview with the author, May 28, 2009.
45. Swoosie Kurtz, interview with the author, January 6, 2010.
46. Lawrence Van Gelder, "At the Movies," *The New York Times*, April 1, 1988.
47. Jonathan Rosenbaum, "Dim Wits, Small Potatoes," *Chicago Reader*, April 1, 1988.
48. Roger Ebert, "*Bright Lights, Big City*," *Chicago Sun-Times*, April 1, 1988.
49. *Ibid.*
50. Janet Maslin, "A Tale of the Dark Side: *Bright Lights, Big City*," *The New York Times*, April 1, 1988.
51. Pauline Kael, *Bright Lights, Big City*, in *5001 Nights at the Movies* (New York: Henry Holt and Company, 1991), p. 103.
52. *Ibid.*
53. Lawrence Van Gelder, "At the Movies," *The New York Times*, April 1, 1988.

54. Mary McCarthy, *Birds of America* (New York: Harcourt Brace Jovanovich, 1971), pp. 34–35.
55. Associated Press, "Film's Birth: James Dean's Death," *The Palm Beach Post*, September 23, 1977.
56. Reynaldo Villalobos, interview with the author, October 24, 2008.
57. Kim Kurumada, interview with the author, December 16, 2008.
58. Jack Larson, interview with the author, February 5, 2010.
59. Kim Kurumada, interview with the author, December 16, 2008.
60. David Rawlins, interview with the author, May 4, 2009.
61. Jack Larson, interview with the author, July 15, 2008.
62. Jack Larson, interview with the author, January 18, 2009.
63. Jack Bender, interview with the author, June 15, 2009.
64. Kim Kurumada, interview with the author, December 16, 2008.
65. *Ibid.*
66. Tom Bonner, email to the author, February 25, 2009.
67. Susan King, "Honoring James Bridges," *Los Angeles Times*, November 11, 1999.
68. Lisa Blount, interview with the author, April 27, 2009.
69. Mary Kai Clark, interview with the author, March 13, 2009.
70. Jeff Gourson, interview with the author, May 19, 2008.
71. Barbara Hershey, interview with the author, June 28, 2009.
72. Marshall Schlom, interview with the author, March 17, 2009.
73. Jack Larson, interview with the author, February 13, 2010.
74. *Ibid.*
75. *Ibid.*
76. *Ibid.*
77. *Ibid.*
78. Susan King, "Honoring James Bridges," *Los Angeles Times*, November 11, 1999.
79. Jack Larson, interview with the author, February 13, 2010.
80. *Ibid.*
81. *Ibid.*
82. Alan J. Pakula, commentary track, *Sophie's Choice* DVD (Live Entertainment, 1998).
83. David Rawlins, interview with the author, May 4, 2009.

Bibliography

Books and Articles

The Baby Maker presskit. National General Pictures.

Benson, Sheila. "Hard World of 'Mike's Murder.'" *Los Angeles Times*, March 16, 1984.

Bergan, Ronald. *Jean Renoir: Projections of Paradise*. Woodstock, NY: Overlook Press, 1992.

Berger, Marilyn. "John Houseman, Actor and Producer, 86, Dies." *The New York Times*, November 1, 1988.

Biskind, Peter. *Easy Riders, Raging Bulls*. New York: Simon & Schuster, 1998.

Blowen, Michael. "He Listens to His Movie." *The Boston Globe*, April 21, 1985.

_____. "The L.A. Dream Turned Nightmare." *The Boston Globe*, May 9, 1985.

_____. "The Making of a Movie: The Unanticipated Is All You Can Anticipate." *The Boston Globe*, July 8, 1984.

_____. "'Mike's Murder' Rates as a Work of Art." *The Boston Globe*, April 20, 1984.

_____. "Shooting the Middle Scenes Last." *The Boston Globe*, November 25, 1984.

_____. "Winger—Actress Is Hot in More Ways Than One." *The Boston Globe*, March 22, 1984.

Bogdanovich, Peter. *Peter Bogdanovich's Movie of the Week*. New York: Ballantine Books, 1999.

"Books: Brothers & Others." *Time*, April 21, 1967.

"Box office / business for *Urban Cowboy* (1980)." Internet Movie Database. http://www.imdb.com/title/tt0081696/business

Bradbury, Ray. *The October Country*. New York: Ballantine Books, 1955.

Brownlow, Kevin. *The Parade's Gone By ...* Berkeley: University of California Press, 1968.

Buckley, Tom. "At the Movies: Fonda tilts forces of nuclear energy in 'China Syndrome.'" *The New York Times*, March 16, 1979.

Buechner, Frederick. *Secrets in the Dark: A Life in Sermons*. New York: Harper San Francisco, 2006.

Callow, Simon. *Orson Welles: The Road to Xanadu*. London: Jonathan Cape, 1995.

Canby, Vincent. "Film: 'Mike's Murder,' with Debra Winger." *The New York Times*, March 9, 1984.

_____. "Film: Nuclear Power Plant Is Villain in 'China Syndrome': A Question of Ethics." *The New York Times*, March 16, 1979.

_____. "Film: 'Perfect': Gym and Journalism." *The New York Times*, June 7, 1985.

_____. "Robert Altman's Satire 'Health.'" *The New York Times*, April 7, 1982.

_____. "Screen: 'Sept. 30, 1955,' When James Dean Died: Admirer of Actor." *The New York Times*, March 31, 1978.

_____. "Travolta, 'Urban Cowboy.'" *The New York Times*, June 11, 1980.

Capote, Truman. *Breakfast at Tiffany's: A Short Novel and Three Stories*. New York: Modern Library, 1994.

Carr, Jay. "'Bright Lights' Amid the Chaos." *The Boston Globe*, April 1, 1988.

_____. "Travolta Can't Save *Perfect*." *The Boston Globe*, June 7, 1985.

Champlin, Charles. "Critic at Large: James Dean: In Memoriam." *Los Angeles Times*, December 16, 1977.

Cocks, Jay. "Cinema: Hells of Ivy." *Time*, October 29, 1973.

Denby, David. "The Lost Week." *New York*, April 11, 1988.

Drake, Sylvie. "Bridges: 'Streetcar' Conductor." *Los Angeles Times*, March 18, 1973.

Dunaway, Faye, with Betsy Sharkey. *Looking for Gatsby: My Life*. New York: Simon & Schuster, 1995.

Ebert, Roger. "The Baby Maker." *Chicago Sun-Times*, October 26, 1970.

_____. "Bright Lights, Big City." *Chicago Sun-Times*, April 1, 1988.

_____. "The China Syndrome." *Chicago Sun-Times*, January 1, 1979.

Ehrenstein, David. "Paul Winfield: The Gay Actor's Truest Role Was Seen by a Small Audience." *The Advocate*, April 13, 2004.

Farber, Stephen. "Blanche Wins the Battle." *The New York Times*, April 1, 1973.

_____. "Where There's Smoke, There's a Fiery Actress Named Debra Winger." *The New York Times*, July 6, 1986.

Fiedler, Leslie A. *Love and Death in the American Novel*. Champaign, IL: Dalkey Archive Press, 1960.

"Filming Resumes — Bridges Thinks '9/30/55' Will Be Hit." *The Echo*, September 16, 1976.

"Film's Birth: James Dean's Death." *The Palm Beach Post*, Associated Press, September 23, 1977.

Fujiwara, Chris. *Jerry Lewis*. Urbana and Chicago: University of Illinois Press, 2009.

Gilroy, Harry. "Negro Detective Has Winning Way." *The New York Times*, April 23, 1966.

Goldman, Debra. "Bright Lights, Camera, Action." *American Film*, January/February 1988.

Goodman, Mark. "Cinema: Rent-a-Womb." *Time*, October 19, 1970.

Grant, Lee. "Muddy Séance in Toad Suck Ferry." *Los Angeles Times*, October 21, 1976.

Green, Michelle. "While She May Not Be Perfect, Laraine Newman Braces Herself for Another Shot at Stardom." *People*, July 8, 1985.

Greenspun, Roger. "Barbara Hershey Stars in Bridges's 'The Baby Maker.'" *The New York Times*, October 2, 1970.

Gross, Jane. "Movies and the Press Are an Enduring Romance." *The New York Times*, June 2, 1985.

"Happy Homosexuals in a Bedsitter." *The Stage and Television Today*, July 24, 1969.

Harford, Margaret. "Actors Studio-West Offers Trio of Plays." *Los Angeles Times*, January 6, 1969.

_____. "'Candied House' Delightful." *Los Angeles Times*, February 12, 1966.

_____. "'Candied House' — Rhyme with Reason." *Los Angeles Times*, February 10, 1966.

Haskell, Molly. "The Nifty Fifties." *New York*, May 1, 1978.

Hoberman, J., and Jonathan Rosenbaum. *Midnight Movies*. New York: Da Capo Press, 1983.

The Hollywood Reporter, October 1, 1970.

Houseman, John. *Final Dress*. New York: Simon & Schuster, 1983.

James, Caryn. "'Bright Lights, Big City' — Big Trouble." *The New York Times*, January 10, 1988.

Jameson, Fredric. *Late Marxism: Adorno; Or, The Persistence of the Dialectic*. London: Verso, 1990.

Jameson, Richard T. "China Is Near." *Film Comment*, May/June 1979.

Kabaservice, Geoffrey. *The Guardians: Kingman Brewster, His Circle, and the Rise of the Liberal Establishment*. New York: Henry Holt and Company, 2004.

Kael, Pauline. *5001 Nights at the Movies*. New York: Henry Holt and Company, 1991.

_____. *For Keeps*. New York: Plume, 1994.

_____. *Reeling*. New York: Warner Books, 1976.

Kakutani, Michiko. "Books of the Times: Alienated Young and Their Solipsistic Pleasures." *The New York Times*, May 7, 1988.

_____. "Joan Didion: Staking Out California." *The New York Times*, June 10, 1979.

Katz, Ephraim, ed. *The Film Encyclopedia*.

2nd ed. New York: Harper Perennial, 1994.
Kehr, Dave. "The Awful Truth." *Chicago Reader*.
_____. "The China Syndrome." *Chicago Reader*.
_____. "Perfect." *Chicago Reader*.
King, Susan. "Honoring James Bridges." *Los Angeles Times*, November 11, 1999.
Larson, Jack. Letter to the Editor. *The New York Times*, October 8, 1995.
Latham, Aaron. "The Cowboy Chronicles." *New York*, September 25, 2000.
_____. *Perfect Pieces: Stardom, Scandals, and the New Saturday Night*. New York: Arbor House, 1987.
Leemann, Sergio. *Robert Wise on His Films: From Editing Room to Director's Chair*. Los Angeles: Silman-James Press, 1995.
Lester, Peter. "Two Sexy 'Urban Cowgirls'— One Called Debra Winger — Give Travolta a Run for His Movie." *People*, August 18, 1980.
LeSueur, Joe. *Digressions on Some Poems by Frank O'Hara: A Memoir*. New York: Farrar, Straus and Giroux, 2003.
Litwak, Mark. *Reel Power: The Struggle for Influence and Success in the New Hollywood*. Los Angeles: Silman-James Press, 1986.
Lloyd, Norman. *Stages of Life in Theatre, Film and Television*. New York: Limelight Editions, 1993.
LoBrutto, Vincent. *Principal Photography: Interviews with Feature Film Cinematographers*. Westport, CT: Praeger Publishers, 1999.
_____. *Stanley Kubrick: A Biography*. New York: Donald I. Fine Books, 1997.
Mann, Roderick. "Travolta's Biggest Fan: His Director." *Los Angeles Times*, January 6, 1980.
Maslin, Janet. "At the Movies." *The New York Times*, March 9, 1984.
_____. "Critic's Notebook: A Great Movie — If It Comes Out." *The New York Times*, January 23, 1978.
_____. "He Was Obsessed with James Dean." *The New York Times*, April 5, 1976.
_____. "Richard Thomas — Playing the Worshipper and Not the Hero." *The New York Times*, April 2, 1978.
_____. "A Tale of the Dark Side: 'Bright Lights, Big City.'" *The New York Times*, April 1, 1988.
McCarthy, Mary. *Birds of America*. New York: Harcourt Brace Jovanovich, 1971.
McCarty, John, and Brian Kelleher. *Alfred Hitchcock Presents: An Illustrated Guide to the Ten-Year Television Career of the Master of Suspense*. New York: St. Martin's Press, 1985.
McCarty, Mary. "Holding On to the Air." *Cincinnati Magazine*, April 1992.
McInerney, Jay. *Bright Lights, Big City*. New York: Vintage Books, 1984.
Mulcahy, Frank. "'Days of the Dancing' Entertaining, Offbeat." *Los Angeles Times*, May 17, 1961.
Murphy, A.D. "The Baby Maker." *Variety*, September 30, 1970.
Nichols, Peter M., ed. *The New York Times Guide to the Best 1,000 Movies Ever Made*. New York: Times Books, 1999.
Noth, Dominique Paul. "Bit Actor Is Now Starring, but Behind the Movie Camera." *The Milwaukee Journal*, October 27, 1973.
Osborn, John Jay, Jr. *The Paper Chase*. anniv. ed. Albany, NY: Whitston Publishing Company, 1993.
"The Paper Chase." *The New York Times*, September 12, 1971.
"Playwright-actor Jim Bridges Much Pleased with Highlands." *The Highlander*, August 7, 1964.
Poague, Leland, ed. *Conversations with Susan Sontag*. Jackson: University Press of Mississippi, 1995.
Pym, John, ed. *Time Out Film Guide*. 12th ed., London: Penguin Books, 2003.
Rabin, Nathan. "Bright Lights, Big City." *The A.V. Club*, September 10, 2008, http://www.avclub.com/content/node/86245/print/
Reed, Peter J., and Marc Leeds, ed. *The Vonnegut Chronicles: Interviews and Essays*. Westport, CT: Greenwood Press, 1996.
Reid, Walter. "Edinburgh Festival: 'Cherry, Larry, Sandy, Doris, Jean, Paul' (Watson's Ladies' College)." *The Scotsman*, August 30, 1969.
Rhodes, Sonny. "Movie director James Bridges: He hasn't forgotten his roots in

Arkansas." *The Log Cabin Democrat*, October 11, 1977.

Rosenbaum, Jonathan. "Dim Wits, Small Potatoes." *Chicago Reader*, April 1, 1988.

Sallitt, Dan. "Mike's Murder." *L.A. Reader*, March 16, 1984.

Sarris, Andrew. "Critic's Choice." *The Village Voice*, January 10, 1974.

_____. "Films in Focus: The Past Recaptured." *The Village Voice*, April 17, 1978.

Scobie, W.I. "The Art of Fiction No. 49: Christopher Isherwood." *The Paris Review*, Spring 1974.

Sherman, Eric. *Directing the Film: Film Directors on Their Art*. Los Angeles: Acrobat Books, 1976.

Shipman, David. "Obituary: James Bridges." *The Independent*, June 8, 1993.

Smith, Gavin. "Without Cutaways." *Film Comment*, May/June 1991.

Spoto, Donald. *The Art of Alfred Hitchcock: Fifty Years of His Motion Pictures*. New York: Anchor Books, 1992.

Sragow, Michael, ed. *Produced and Abandoned: The Best Films You've Never Seen*. San Francisco: Mercury House, 1990.

Stahl, Lesley. *Reporting Live*. New York: Simon & Schuster, 1999.

Stevens, George, Jr. *Conversations with the Great Moviemakers of Hollywood's Golden Age at the American Film Institute*. New York: Vintage Books, 2006.

Sullivan, Dan. "'Meeting by the River' for NTN." *Los Angeles Times*, May 3, 1972.

_____. "'Streetcar' on, Off the Track." *Los Angeles Times*, March 21, 1973.

Taylor, Mary Nell. "James Bridges: An Arkansas Boy Comes Home." *The Echo*, April 1, 1976.

Thomas, Kevin. "To Live and Die in L.A.: Thriller Explores Loneliness in the City." *Los Angeles Times*, November 11, 1999.

Thompson, David. *Altman on Altman*. London: Faber and Faber, 2005.

Thomson, David. "Telephones." *Film Comment*, August 1984.

Tommasini, Anthony. "Golly, Jimmy Olsen Writes Librettos!" *The New York Times*, May 15, 1998.

_____. *Virgil Thomson: Composer on the Aisle*. New York: W.W. Norton & Company, 1997.

Tonguette, Peter. "Remembering Welles: A Conversation with Norman Lloyd." *The Film Journal*, July 2004, http://www.thefilmjournal.com/issue9/lloyd.html

Truffaut, François. *The Films in My Life*. New York: Da Capo Press, 1994.

Van Gelder, Lawrence. "At the Movies: Production Prep." *The New York Times*, April 1, 1988.

Vonnegut, Kurt. *Slapstick, or: Lonesome No More!* New York: Delacorte Press/Seymour Lawrence, 1976.

Warga, Wayne. "Recalling James Dean on '9/30/55.'" *Los Angeles Times*, September 25, 1977.

Welles, Orson, and Peter Bogdanovich. *This Is Orson Welles*, rev. ed. New York: Da Capo Press, 1998.

Wells, Jeffrey. "Again, *Mike's Murder*." *Hollywood Elsewhere*, http://www.hollywood-elsewhere.com/2009/04/again_mikes_mur.php

West, Cornel. *The Cornel West Reader*. New York: Basic Books, 1999.

White, Armond. "Lust-Caution Douses Woodstock." *New York Press*, August 26, 2009.

_____. "Revolutionary Road." *New York Press*, December 23, 2008.

Williams, Tennessee. *Memoirs*. New York: New Directions, 1975.

_____. *New Selected Essays: Where I Live*. New York: New Directions, 2009.

Winger, Debra. *Undiscovered*. New York: Simon & Schuster, 2008.

Wurtzel, Elizabeth. "Coke Adds Life." *The Harvard Crimson*, April 22, 1988.

Zinn, Howard. *A People's History of the United States: 1942—Present*. New York: Harper Perennial Modern Classics, 2005.

DVDs and Videos

The China Syndrome: A Fusion of Talent documentary. *The China Syndrome* DVD. Columbia, 2004.

The Graduate 40th anniversary edition DVD. commentary track. MGM Home Entertainment, 2007.

Hollywood Mavericks documentary. American Film Institute, 1990.

Jay McInerney's The Light Within documentary. *Bright Lights, Big City* DVD. MGM Home Entertainment, 2008.
The Paper Chase DVD. commentary track. Twentieth Century–Fox, 2003.
Sontag, Susan. interview by Susan Swain. *In Depth with Susan Sontag*. C-SPAN, March 2, 2003, http://www.c-spanvideo.org/program/172991-1
Sophie's Choice DVD. commentary track. Live Entertainment, 1998.

Unpublished Materials

Latham, Aaron. *Perfect* diary.

Oral History

Oral history by Martha Reid Scott, The James Bridges Collection — M99-14, University of Central Arkansas Archives.

Author Interviews

Brooke Alderson, February 2010
Graham Beckel, May 2009
Jack Bender, June 2009
Deborah Benson, February 2009
John Bloom, May 2009
Lisa Blount, April 2009
Tom Bonner, February 2009
Mary Kai Clark, March 2009
Francesca Emerson, May 2009
Marty Ewing, May 2009
Debbie Getlin, February 2008
Jeff Gourson, May and June 2008
Edward Herrmann, February 2009
Barbara Hershey, June 2009
Swoosie Kurtz, January 2010
Kim Kurumada, September, October, and December 2008
Jack Larson, March, July, and October 2008; January, February, and March 2009; February 2010
Norman Lloyd, March 2009
Laurence Luckinbill, March 2009
Chris Newman, June 2009
John Jay Osborn, Jr., July 2009
Collin Wilcox Paxton, March and April 2008
Michael Preece, May 2009
David Rawlins, May 2009
Charles Rosher, Jr., May 2009
Marshall Schlom, March 2009
Richard Thomas, March 2009
Reynaldo Villalobos, October 2008
Sam Waterston, April 2009
Gordon Willis, February 2008
Jane Wilson, March 2009
Debra Winger, May 2009

Index

The Adventures of Superman 11, 132
The African Queen (Huston) 167
The Age of Innocence (Scorsese) 12
Albee, Edward 17, 18, 87
Alderson, Brooke 118, 120, 136
The Alfred Hitchcock Hour 1, 3, 12–13, 14, 15, 17, 136
Alfred Hitchcock Presents 12
Alice's Restaurant (Penn) 35
All the President's Men (Pakula) 69, 71, 111, 154
Allen, Dede 99, 131, 139–140
Allen, Woody 50, 165
Altman, Robert 9, 26, 68, 124, 155
Amadeus (Forman) 102
An American in Paris (Minnelli) 63
Annie Hall (Allen) 148
Another Woman (Allen) 165
Ansen, David 79
The Appaloosa (Furie) 19
Ashbery, John 87, 169
Ashley, Elizabeth 131
Attenborough, Richard 129, 157
Avanti! (Wilder) 115
Avildsen, John G. 110
The Awful Truth (McCarey) 124
Azoff, Irving 119

The Baby Maker (Bridges) 4, 10, 11, 13, 18, 19, 22, 24–38, 40, 47, 48, 57, 62, 74, 78, 97, 110, 111, 120, 138
Bachardy, Don 22, 39, 40
Bachelor Furnished (Bridges) 13, 17–18, 152
Badham, John 114
Balanchine, George 143
"The Ballad of the Urban Cowboy: America's Search for True Grit" (Latham) 115, 116
Banks, Barbara 6, 8, 10
Barry, John 129, 141
Barrymore, Ethel 2, 11
Basinger, Kim 118
Beatty, Warren 139
Beckel, Graham 46–47, 53–54, 58–59
Before Sunrise (Linklater) 130

Before Sunset (Linklater) 130
Behrens, Ralph 6, 7
Bellamy, Ralph 124
Bender, Jack 2, 20–21, 22–23, 40, 42, 56, 60–61, 65, 74, 167
Benson, Deborah 69, 76, 77–78, 83, 85–86, 102, 103
Benson, Sheila 133
Benton, Robert 37
Bergman, Ingrid 63
Berlin, Jeannie 30
The Berlin Stories (Isherwood) 22
Bernaleck, Mark 127, 133
Birds of America (McCarthy) 166
The Birthday Party (Pinter) 18
Bishop, Stephen 114
Biskind, Peter 4, 54–55
Blame It on Rio (Donen) 136
Blankenchip, John 20
Bloom, John 157, 158
Blount, Lisa 2, 69, 83–84, 86, 89–91, 94–95, 96, 102, 103, 169
Blow Out (De Palma) 145
Blowen, Michael 126
Bogdanovich, Peter 44, 54–55, 59, 62, 97, 104, 126
Bonjour Tristesse (Preminger) 18, 129
Bonner, Tom 7–8, 10, 11, 68, 76, 88, 168–169
Bonnie and Clyde (Penn) 55, 139
Bottoms, Timothy 44, 49, 50, 53, 58
Bowles, Paul 152
The Boys in the Band (Crowley) 40
Bradbury, Ray 13, 14, 47, 67
Brady, Scott 113
Brando, Marlon 19
Breakfast at Tiffany's (Capote) 3
The Breakfast Club (Hughes) 140
Breaking Away (Yates) 76
Brent, George 52
Brickman, Paul 136
The Bridge on the River Kwai (Lean) 18
Bridges, Doy (father) 5
Bridges/Larson Foundation 169–171

Bright Lights, Big City (Bridges) 4, 24, 36, 51, 59, 126, 127, 134, 149, 156–166
Bright Lights, Big City (McInerney) 156, 158, 163
Brimley, Wilford 113
Brokeback Mountain (Lee) 59
Brooks, James L. 129
Brown, Blair 55
Brownlow, Kevin 25
Buechner, Frederick 67
Burckhardt, Rudy 120
Burnett, Charles 62
Buttram, Pat 13

Cabaret (Fosse) 22
Cagney, James 53
Callow, Simon 5
Canby, Vincent 80, 97, 115, 124, 125, 128, 133, 154, 155
The Candied House (Larson) 17, 18–19, 20
Cantor, Jay 127–128
Capote, Truman 3
Carnal Knowledge (Nichols) 81
Carola (Renoir) 62–63
Caron, Glenn Gordon 170
Caron, Leslie 22, 63
Carpenter, John 54
Carr, Jay 151, 154
Cassavetes, John 2, 15–16, 126
Cates, Phoebe 158, 160
Champlin, Charles 88
Chekhov, Anton 138
Chelsea Girls (Warhol) 23
Cher 167
Cherry, Larry, Sandy, Doris, Jean, Paul (Larson) 19–20, 23, 41, 132
The China Syndrome (Bridges) 8, 24, 52, 62, 74, 104–115, 116, 120–121, 125, 126, 127, 131, 133–134, 136, 139, 167
Chopra, Joyce 156–157
Christopher, Dennis 76
Chuck (Larson) 30
Clark, Mary Kai 69, 76, 83, 84, 85, 86–87, 169
Clayton, Jack 40
Clift, Montgomery 2, 11, 15, 22, 23
Cocks, Jay 56
Colossus—The Forbin Project (Sargent) 19
Coming Home (Ashby) 106, 147
Cook, Fielder 67
Cook, T.S. 108, 115
Copeland, Roger 90
Coppola, Francis Ford 49
Corbin, Barry 118
Costner, Kevin 130
Cox, Archibald 56
Crabe, James 110, 111, 116
Crosson, Robert 131, 132–133
Crowley, Mart 40
Cukor, George 31, 60, 81, 143
Curtis, Jamie Lee 145, 149, 150, 151, 153, 154

Daisy Miller (Bogdanovich) 62
Dangerous Liaisons (Frears) 162
Davis, Bette 52, 67
The Day of the Dolphin (Nichols) 58
Day-Lewis, C. 12, 13
Day-Lewis, Daniel 12
The Days of the Dancing (Bridges) 1–2, 12
Dean, James 8, 68, 69, 74, 76–77, 82, 127, 159, 171
Deegan, Denis 12
Deer Season (Bridges project) 166
Denby, David 134
De Palma, Brian 145
The Desert Rose (Bridges project) 166–167, 170
Didion, Joan 67
Digressions on Some Poems by Frank O'Hara (LeSueur) 96–97
Dingilian, Bob 153
Dog Day Afternoon (Lumet) 139
Donat, Peter 113
Donen, Stanley 136
Douglas, Melvyn 53
Douglas, Michael 104–105, 106, 107, 108, 111, 112, 113, 121
Dunaway, Faye 1, 64, 65
Dunne, Irene 124

East of Eden (Kazan) 8, 9, 74–75, 82, 96
Eastwood, Clint 167
Easy Rider (Hopper) 55
Easy Riders, Raging Bulls (Biskind) 4, 54–55
Ebert, Roger 34, 115, 165
Edwards, Blake 126
Ehrenstein, David 127
Elmslie, Kenward 87
Emerson, Francesca 114, 116
Emerson, Ralph Waldo 97, 147
Erickson, C.O. 122
Evans, Robert 117, 119, 121, 122, 123
Ewing, Marty 139, 140–141, 148–149, 154, 157

Faces (Cassavetes) 15–16, 24
Fagen, Donald 165
Family Plot (Hitchcock) 168
Family Ties 165
Farber, Stephen 1, 65
Farrell, Suzanne 143
Farris, John 131
Fast Times at Ridgemont High (Heckerling) 160
Fat City (Huston) 89
Faulkner, William 67
Feiffer, Jules 81
Felker, Clay 116
Fiedler, Leslie A. 128
Fields, Verna 97–98
The Film Encyclopedia (Katz) 24
Five Easy Pieces (Rafelson) 30
Flesh (Morrissey) 130
The Fog (Carpenter) 54
Fonda, Henry 57

Fonda, Jane 24, 103, 104, 105, 106, 108, 110, 113, 115
Force of Evil (Polonsky) 31
Ford, John 57, 97, 104
Forman, Milos 102
The Formula (Avildsen) 110
Forty Deuce (Morrissey) 130
Fox, Michael J. 156, 163, 165
Fujiwara, Chris 154
Fuller, Samuel 81
Furie, Sidney J. 19

Gallo, Fred 106
Gandhi (Attenborough) 157
Gere, Richard 102, 128
Getlin, Debbie 8–9, 19, 99, 100, 101, 109–110, 113, 141–142
Gielgud, John 41
Gigi (Minnelli) 63
Gilbert, Bruce 105
Glenn, Scott 26, 30, 120, 121
The Godfather (Coppola) 49, 93
Gourson, Jeff 97–99, 100–101, 113–114, 131, 135, 140, 153, 157, 169
The Graduate (Nichols) 149
Grant, Cary 124
Gray, Billy 30
Gray, Mike 104, 108, 115
The Great Gatsby (Clayton) 40
The Great Waldo Pepper (Hill) 58
Greenspun, Roger 34
Grimes, Stephen B. 31, 122
Groom, Sam 24, 30
Grubb, Davis 13
Guare, John 162

Hammett, Dashiell 13
Hampton, James 110
Hanson, Curtis 59
Hardly Working (Lewis) 154
Harford, Margaret 17, 18
Harris, Julie 74
Haskell, Molly 75
The Haunting (Wise) 37
Hawn, Goldie 167
Hayden, Sterling 167
Hayden, Tom 106
HealtH (Altman) 155
The Heartbreak Kid (May) 30
Heat (Morrissey) 130
Heaven Knows, Mr. Allison (Huston) 31
Hellman, Jerome 147
Hemingway, Ernest 67
Henner, Marilu 149
Hepburn, Katharine 5, 66–67, 143
Herrmann, Edward 46, 50–51, 52, 53–54, 58
Hershey, Barbara 11, 24–25, 26, 27, 28, 29, 36, 37, 38, 111, 169
Hill, George Roy 58, 139
Hitchcock, Alfred 14, 15, 126, 135, 163, 168, 171

Hoberman, J. 94
Hockney, David 143
Holliman, Earl 65
The Honey Pot (Mankiewicz) 168
Horne, Geoffrey 18, 78
The House of Blue Leaves (Guare) 162
Houseman, Joan 12
Houseman, John 2, 12, 19, 21, 22, 39, 44–45, 49, 50, 51, 53–54, 55–56, 57, 58, 59, 60–61, 157, 160–161, 165–166, 169, 170, 171
How Many Times Have You Seen East of Eden? (Bridges) 68
Hulce, Tom 79, 102
Huston, John 31, 89, 167
Hutton, Lauren 153

I Want to Live! (Wise) 37
Irving, John 13
Isherwood, Christopher 2, 22, 39, 40, 42
Ivory, James 29

Jackson, Joe 141
James, Caryn 159, 161
James, Henry 128
The James Dean Story (Altman) 9
Jameson, Fredric 124
Jameson, Richard T. 110, 115
Jane Eyre (Stevenson) 31
"The Jar" (Bradbury) 13, 14, 47
Jaws (Spielberg) 97
Jenkins, George 51–52, 111, 115
Johnny Trouble (Auer) 2, 11
Jones, James 29, 67
Jones, T.C. 15
Jost, Larry 57
Joyce, Stephen 12
Julius Caesar (Shakespeare) 12

Kabaservice, Geoffrey 56
Kael, Pauline 3, 4, 54, 56, 126, 129, 135, 141, 165
Kakutani, Michiko 67, 156
Kallianiotes, Helena 30
Kalp, Gayla 20, 21
Karen, James 108, 113
Katz, Ephraim 24
Kaufman, Philip 59, 127
Kazan, Elia 8, 74, 168
Kehr, Dave 104, 124, 152, 154
Kellaway, Cecil 11
Kerr, John 15
Keyloun, Mark 74, 128, 130, 139
Kibbee, Roland 19
Killer of Sheep (Burnett) 62
The King of Marvin Gardens (Rafelson) 62
Kirstein, Lincoln 169
Kjellin, Alf 12
Klute (Pakula) 49, 93
Koch, Howard, Jr. 49
Kubrick, Stanley 80

Kurtz, Swoosie 149, 157–158, 161–162, 163–164, 165
Kurumada, Kim 3, 70–71, 72–74, 87, 88, 99–100, 105–108, 109, 111, 112, 116–118, 119, 120–121, 123, 136, 140, 141, 142–143, 144–145, 146, 147–148, 150–151, 157, 164–165, 166, 167, 168

L.A. Confidential (Hanson) 59
Ladd, Alan, Jr. 127, 141
Lambert, Gavin 22
Lampert, Zohra 12
Landis, John 150
Larson, Darrell 129, 132, 140
Larson, Jack 11–12, 14, 15–16, 17, 18, 19, 20, 21, 22, 24, 29–30, 38, 39, 42–44, 58, 59, 63, 99, 104, 105, 106, 111, 120, 127–128, 130, 132–133, 139, 140, 141, 143, 146, 152, 153, 157, 167, 168, 169–171
The Last Picture Show (Bogdanovich) 44, 55, 81
Last Summer (Perry) 24
The Last Tycoon (Kazan) 168
The Late Show (Benton) 37
Latham, Aaron 2, 4, 115, 116, 118, 124, 144, 145, 147, 149, 152
Lean, David 18, 31
Lee, Ang 59
Lemmon, Jack 105, 106, 108, 109, 113, 115
LeMond, Bob 143
LeSueur, Joe 66, 96
Lewis, Jerry 154
Limelight (Chaplin) 12
Linklater, Richard 130
Little Murders (Arkin) 93
Lloyd, Norman 2, 3, 6, 12, 13, 14–15, 62–63, 161
LoBrutto, Vincent 50, 80
"Looking for Mr. Goodbody: Perfect!" (Latham) 144
Loquasto, Santo 158, 163
Love Streams (Cassavetes) 126
Luckinbill, Laurence 5, 39, 40, 42, 43, 66, 67
Lumet, Sidney 139, 142

Magnani, Anna 8
The Magnificent Ambersons (Welles) 111
Maidstone (Mailer) 96
Mailer, Norman 34, 96
The Manchurian Candidate (Frankenheimer) 107
Mankiewicz, Joseph L. 168
Marlowe, Christopher 21
Marnie (Hitchcock) 135
The Marrying Kind (Cukor) 81
Marvin, Lee 167
*M*A*S*H* (Altman) 55
Maslin, Janet 62, 71, 101, 133, 160, 165
May, Elaine 30
McCarey, Leo 124
McCarthy, Mary 166

McElwaine, Guy 100, 147, 150–151
McInerney, Jay 4, 13, 67, 156, 159, 160
McKeen, Celestine (mother) 5
McMurtry, Larry 166
McNally, Terrence 87
A Meeting by the River (Isherwood and Bachardy) 23, 39–43, 52, 66
Metropolitan (Stillman) 160
Midnight Cowboy (Schlesinger) 23
Mike's Murder (Bridges) 3, 4, 8, 15, 29, 36, 74, 99, 124, 126–143, 144, 146, 152, 159, 160, 165, 168
Millar, Margaret 13
Minnelli, Vincente 81
The Misfits (Huston) 31
Mitchell, Donald O. 57
Monroe, Marilyn 80
Morrissey, Paul 130
Muhl, Edward 99
Mulcahy, Frank 1
Mulligan, Robert 13
Murnau, F.W. 25

Nashville (Altman) 68
Naughton, James 46, 54, 59
Nelson, Craig Richard 46
The New Biographical Dictionary of Film (Thomson) 4
Newman, Chris 92–94
Newman, Joseph 15
Newman, Laraine 149
Nichols, Mike 53, 58, 81, 114, 149
The Night of the Iguana (Huston) 31
Nine to Five (Higgins) 135–136
Nixon, Richard 56
Nolte, Eugene 6, 7
The Nun's Story (Zinnemann) 31

Oates, Joyce Carol 156–157
The Object of My Affection (Wasserstein) 143
The Occupation of Paris (Bridges project) 166
Odds Against Tomorrow (Wise) 37
Of the Farm (Updike) 13, 66–65
An Officer and a Gentleman (Hackford) 102, 103, 128, 140
Old Boyfriends (Tewkesbury) 54
O'Neill, Eugene 78
Orson Welles Remembered (Tonguette) 2, 4
Osborn, John Jay, Jr. 13, 24, 43, 44–45, 46, 47–48, 51, 54, 55, 57–58, 59, 60, 61, 67, 116
Ostrander, William 133
O'Toole, Annette 118

Page, Geraldine 78
Pakula, Alan J. 49, 69, 171
The Paper Chase (Bridges) 2, 3, 24, 36, 43–61, 62, 63, 65, 74, 97, 104, 108, 111, 112, 116, 122, 148, 160, 161, 165–166
The Paper Chase (series) 59–61
Paper Moon (Bogdanovich) 97

The Parallax View (Pakula) 69
Parone, Ed 19–20
Penn, Arthur 35
A People's History of the United States (Zinn) 105
Perfect (Bridges) 3, 4, 24, 36, 74, 112, 126, 142, 144–156, 158, 161, 165, 166
Perry, Frank 24
Le Petit Théâtre de Jean Renoir (Renoir) 138
Pfeiffer, Michelle 118
Pinter, Harold 17
Pollack, Sydney 23, 31, 54, 157
Polonsky, Abraham 31
Popeye (Altman) 124
Preece, Michael 25, 31–32, 38, 45, 48, 69–70, 97
Preminger, Otto 18, 40, 92, 129
Price, Frank 107
Principal Photography (LoBrutto) 50
The Purple Rose of Cairo (Allen) 50

Quaid, Dennis 76, 85, 102
Quintero, Jose 78

Rabin, Nathan 24
Rafelson, Bob 30, 62
Rawlins, David 114, 115–116, 122, 167, 171
Rear Window (Hitchcock) 126
Rebel Without a Cause (Ray) 70, 84, 94
Red Harvest (Hammett) 13
Redford, Robert 12, 142, 146
Reed, Mathew 149
Reid Scott, Martha 6
Renoir, Jean 31, 62–63, 138
Richardson, Elliot 56
Risky Business (Brickman) 136
Ritter, John 20, 21, 22, 23, 41
Robards, Jason 160
Robbins, Jerome 169
Robinson, Edward G. 44
Rocky (Avildsen) 110
Roosevelt, Franklin Delano 80
Rope (Hitchcock) 163
The Rose Tattoo (Mann) 8
Rosemary's Baby (Polanski) 79
Rosenbaum, Jonathan 94, 162–163, 165
Rosenman, Leonard 75
Rosher, Charles, Jr. 25, 26–27, 32, 36–37, 38
Ross, Herbert 164
Rue, Vickie 21
Ryan's Daughter (Lean) 31

Saboteur (Hitchcock) 12
Saint Joan (Preminger) 129
Sargent, Joseph 19
Sarris, Andrew 56, 80–81
Satterfield, Bush 5
Satterfield, Katherine 5
Saturday Night Fever (Badham) 114, 123
Scales, Gussie 6
Schindler's List (Spielberg) 114

Schjeldahl, Peter 120
Schlatter, Charlie 159
Schlom, Marshall 109, 114, 139, 169
Schrager, Sheldon 147
Seberg, Jean 18, 129, 160
Seldes, Marian 66
Seldes, Tim 66
Self-Reliance (Emerson) 147
September 30, 1955 (Bridges) 1, 3, 4, 5, 6, 8, 9–10, 13, 36, 47, 62–103, 104, 106, 108, 109, 111, 112, 115, 116, 123, 125, 126, 127, 128, 131, 134, 147, 148, 154, 159, 166, 168
The Set-Up (Wise) 37
Shadowlands (Attenborough) 129, 169
Shadows (Cassavetes) 15
Shaw, George Bernard 34
The Sheltering Sky (Bowles) 152
Silkwood (Nichols) 114
Simon, Carly 146, 153
Six Degrees of Separation (Guare) 162
Slapstick (Vonnegut) 91
Slaughterhouse-Five (Hill) 139
Smith, Madolyn 123–124
Smooth Talk (Chopra) 156–157
A Soldier's Daughter Never Cries (Ivory) 29
Some Came Running (Minnelli) 81
Sontag, Susan 90, 97
Sophie's Choice (Pakula) 171
The Sound of Music (Wise) 2, 37
Spencer, Dorothy 97
Spielberg, Steven 97, 139
Sragow, Michael 155
Stagecoach (Ford) 97
Stahl, Lesley 116, 118
Stein, Gertrude 22
Sterling, Jan 12
Sternhagen, Frances 160
Stevenson, Robert 31
Stillman, Whit 160
Strange Interlude (O'Neill) 78
A Streetcar Named Desire (Williams) 1, 43, 63–65, 103
Styron, William 171
Such Good Friends (Preminger) 40
Sullivan, Dan 41, 65
Sunrise (Murnau) 25
Sutherland, Kiefer 160

Tarzan and Jane Regained ... Sort Of (Warhol) 2, 24
Tell Me That You Love Me, Junie Moon (Preminger) 92
Terms of Endearment (Brooks) 129
Tewkesbury, Joan 54
Texasville (Bogdanovich) 59
They All Laughed (Bogdanovich) 126
This Property Is Condemned (Pollack) 31
Thomas, Kevin 133
Thomas, Richard 8, 68, 69, 70, 71, 72, 77, 78–79, 80, 81, 87, 88, 92, 95, 101, 102, 106, 113, 125, 134

Thompson, David 9
Thompson, Robert C. 49–50
Thompson, Walter 31–32, 33, 57, 97
Thomson, David 4, 131
Thomson, Virgil 2, 11, 22, 169
Three Days of the Condor (Pollack) 54
3 Women (Altman) 26
To Kill a Mockingbird (Mulligan) 13, 14
Tommasini, Anthony 11, 17
Too Far to Go (Cook) 67
Torn, Rip 96
Trading Places (Landis) 150
Traffic (Soderbergh) 71
Trash (Morrissey) 130
Travolta, John 117, 118, 122, 123, 143, 145, 146, 151, 154, 161
Tree, Romney 12
Tyrrell, Susan 89–90

Undiscovered (Winger) 118
Updike, John 13, 66
Urban Cowboy (Bridges) 2, 5, 8, 24, 31, 36, 45, 62, 74, 104, 112, 113, 115–125, 126, 128, 129, 130, 131, 136, 139, 143, 144, 145, 152, 154, 166, 167

Valdez, Daniel 110
Valenty, Lili 27
Veitch, John 107–108
Victor/Victoria (Edwards) 126
Viertel, Peter 67, 167
Viertel, Salka 2, 11–12, 15, 67
Villalobos, Reynaldo 31, 120–123, 135–136, 142, 166
Voight, Jon 1, 64, 65
Vonnegut, Kurt 91, 156

Wagner, Lindsay 45, 47, 59
The Waltons 70, 113
Warhol, Andy 2, 23
Wasserstein, Wendy 143
Waterston, Sam 5, 40, 41–42, 43, 52–53
A Wedding (Altman) 26

Wee Willie Winkie (Ford) 31
Weintraub, Jerry 68, 78, 100
Welles, Orson 2, 5, 12, 28, 111, 161
Wells, Jeffrey 141
Wenner, Jann 146
West, Cornel 138
West Side Story (Wise and Robbins) 2, 37
When Michael Calls (Leacock) 105, 131
"Where Are You Going? Where Have You Been?" (Oates) 156–157
White, Armond 35, 81
The White Album (Didion) 67
The White Dawn (Kaufman) 59
White Hunter Black Heart (Eastwood) 167
Whitman, Stuart 11
Who's Afraid of Virginia Woolf? (Albee) 18
Wiest, Dianne 159
Wiggins, Melvin (stepfather) 6
Wilcox, Collin 13–14, 17, 18, 22, 24, 28, 30, 37, 69, 78–79
Wilder, Billy 115
Williams, Ralph 18
Williams, Tennessee 1, 2, 12, 43, 63, 103, 171
Willis, Gordon 2, 3, 49–52, 54, 68–69, 71, 72, 73, 74, 88–89, 93–94, 96, 98, 106, 110, 122, 142, 147–148, 155, 157–158, 159, 161, 162, 163
Wilson, Jane 5, 6, 84, 85
Winfield, Paul 127, 128, 133, 134, 135
Winger, Debra 2–3, 5, 45, 74, 102, 115, 117, 118–119, 121, 128–129, 131, 133, 139, 140, 143, 146, 168, 169
Wise, Robert 2, 19, 20, 21, 23, 37–38, 66
The World According to Garp (Irving) 13
Wurtzel, Elizabeth 163
Wynter, Dana 15

Young, B.A. 21
Young Mr. Lincoln (Ford) 31

Zinn, Howard 105
Zinnemann, Fred 31

www.ingramcontent.com/pod-product-compliance
Lightning Source LLC
Chambersburg PA
CBHW032058300426
44116CB00007B/798